RADICAL
HISTORY *Review*

03

D0783308

Reconceptualizations of the African Diaspora

Editors' Introduction

In contemporary scholarship, discussions of diaspora often begin and end with the topics of migration, dispersal, and mobility.[1] Efforts to think about the meaning of diasporas in more material and political terms tend to focus either on the concept as signifying movements that transcend the nation or on very specific cases in which ethnonationalist movements engage a politics concerned with both the original homeland and the place of the migrant's settlement abroad. African diaspora political movements such as pan-Africanism fit very uncomfortably into both of these definitions, given that the "homeland" under discussion is, centuries after the Middle Passage, more often a landscape of the imaginary than a specific, original nation-state. Such a politics also often seems incommensurable with the contemporary experiences of those new, mobile black populations from the Caribbean, Latin America, Africa, Europe, and even Asia who move in response to the forces shaping a global political economy without necessarily challenging or engaging the politics of the nation or nationalism as a whole.

These gaps between how we understand the African diaspora itself and the scholarship on global diasporas more broadly raise one of the generative questions for this issue of the *Radical History Review* titled "Reconceptualizations of the African Diaspora." Can we think of the notion of diaspora as a concept flexible enough to capture not only historical migrations and movements but also the political consciousnesses generated from such movements, especially when they produce populations who fit uncomfortably into the racial boundaries and gendered norms of particular receiving societies and states? In African diaspora studies, we think of diaspora in political terms precisely because centuries of mobilization around racial identity and consciousness are an inescapable part of the histories of slavery and colonialism as forms of state-sponsored structural violence. The series of African migrations into the New World, the explicit labor dimensions of these movements,

Radical History Review
Issue 103 (Winter 2009)   DOI 10.1215/01636545-2008-028
© 2009 by MARHO: The Radical Historians' Organization, Inc.

and the rise of racialist thought placed discussions about race and racism at the center of how states both functioned and defined themselves across the region. These discussions then created transnational intellectual exchanges and forms of political mobilization that existed long before the term *diaspora* was coined as relevant for the histories of African Atlantic subjects in the mid-twentieth century.

The coeditors of this issue firmly believe that the essays included here demonstrate how the notion of an African diaspora moves beyond the question of Africa as homeland to encompass centuries of black political work and consciousness raising that are much broader and less bounded. The very irony of black diasporic *political* consciousnesses is precisely that these only transcend national boundaries *as they engage* in intimate conflicts and dialogues with specific nation-states. As a result, despite multiple calls for forms of black globality throughout the nineteenth and twentieth centuries, some in the realm of real politics, others in the worlds of literary and cultural imagination, African diasporic politics have rarely been invoked for the express purpose of creating a transnational black state. Rather, the language and discourse of a racial diaspora has often been most effectively wielded against specific national politics in particular contexts and times, used by certain diasporic populations in an effort to fight local fights, even as they are aware of other transnational and international movements. In many of the issue's feature pieces, the national becomes the very space in which the intersecting vectors of transnational gender and class formations become visible.

In the three feature essays, the authors demonstrate compellingly how much African diaspora politics have been, historically, simultaneously global and local, and how such politics cannot be accurately assessed without attention to gender, sexuality, the role of the state, and nationalisms. For Anne-Marie Angelo, a local-global-local diasporic consciousness fueled a wave of activism in Britain as African-descended Londoners organized in the 1970s against British state violence and police brutality using symbolisms that originated with the U.S.-based Black Panther Party. Moving backward in time to the 1950s and the period leading up to national independence in the Anglophone Caribbean, Rochelle Rowe argues that Jamaican nationalists used a gendered and racial lens to insist on Jamaican political modernity. The theater of Jamaican hybridity, enacted by a harmonious rainbow of young beauty queens—ten racial "types" from dark to light—was hailed by national leaders as indisputable proof of Jamaican postcolonial modernity, but also as a model of racial advancement by race activists in the United States. For Theresa Runstedtler, popular culture served as an important vehicle for early-twentieth-century black internationalism, and she argues that black boxers migrating to France in the 1900s and 1910s engaged the period's transnational discourses of race and offered a working-class form of masculine, black cultural politics.

The question of violence and its relation to certain gendered and sexual discourses in the formation of black identities and politics is the subject of Deborah

A. Thomas's interdisciplinary intervention, "The Violence of Diaspora." Thomas addresses most directly the state in the diaspora, a theme long omitted in scholarship but especially important as the postcolonial states in the Caribbean and its U.S. neighbor have routed ideas of black violence through gendered discourses on black poverty, sexuality, and "culture." Thomas examines comparative discourses from the mid-twentieth century and the early twenty-first on the black family in a transnational frame, such as the Moyne Commission Report in Jamaica and the Moynihan Report in the United States. These mid-century discourses, which circulated between North America and the English-speaking Caribbean, constituted a highly gendered and sexualized archive of ideas about blackness, heteronormativity, and their relationship to the state.

The violence of both discursive erasure and state policy continues to resonate in the forum on blackness in Latin America, where three essays on Afro-Bolivian, Afro-Venezuelan, and Afro-Mexican populations take on the question of the place of the African-descended in a Latin American imaginary. Sara Busdiecker, Cristóbal Valencia Ramírez and Anita González speak to important debates in the field concerning the study of the African-descended in Latin America and the place of racial consciousness and activism within and beyond Latin American national identities.[2] They do so, however, in very different ways, using the different conceptual lenses of the geography of memory, political science and the study of organizing and social movements, as well as cultural and performance studies. All three discuss how African identities have been subsumed within or relegated to the margins of conceptions of a specific Latin American nationality even as evidence of everyday awareness and political consciousness of blackness has been imprinted regionally and geographically in the nation to such a degree that the African-descended seem to be both everywhere and nowhere. These forum contributors also suggest that the burden shouldered by black populations in Latin America is centered on the conundrum of having to choose between race and nation, even though definitions of nation may be broadly constructed as radical, anti-imperialist, populist (and highly inclusive), or pro-labor.

If, as cultural and ideological formations, the national and the diasporic appear to have countervailing and irresolvable tensions, what happens when the states under discussion, whether in Africa, Latin America, or the Caribbean, are also by the mid- to late twentieth century "black" as often as they are "white?" Lisa Brock, Anthony Bogues, Christopher J. Lee, Patrick Bond, Ashwin Desai, and Molefi Mafereka ka Ndlovu all comment on the trajectory and utility of the diaspora concept in the context of contemporary postcolonial, global politics. Together they offer frameworks for thinking about the African diaspora as a contemporary *intellectual* formation and as a lens for viewing the history of the present—a post–Cold War, postcolonial, postapartheid, and, to use Lee's provocative phrasing, "post-diasporic" world.

The "(Re)Views" section of this issue extends this conversation about the transnational forces shaping black populations within local contexts by covering recent works on the place of the African-descended in France, Britain, and Germany; African Americans' relationships to specific state projects in Ghana and Liberia; and recent revisionist accounts of the central figure of Claude McKay that complicate the lenses of race and ethnicity with insights afforded by postcolonial, gendered, and sexual analyses of his formation as a black diasporic political subject.

Many of the pieces already mentioned wrestle with and respond in their own, case-specific ways to the question: "If nationally based movements understand their relationship to the nation and the nation-state as critical, does this mean these are *not* African diaspora movements?" Prudence D. Cumberbatch's contribution to "Teaching Radical History" explores how one might use the history of transnational conversations about shared black political interests and struggles to create an intra-racial conversation between contemporary multiethnic black students across the U.S. academy. From a different angle, Kevin Mumford's contribution to "Teaching Radical History," "Black Global Metropolis: Sexual History," is singular for the author's timely discussion of both some of the challenges prompted by and some of the reconfigurations of history and periodization required for thinking and teaching race and sexuality together in our stories of African diasporic sites and populations.

In "Curated Spaces," diaspora is reimagined as a curated space that still exhibits the black body and the work of diaspora artists in both gendered and provincial terms. For Jacqueline Francis, true diasporic innovation requires a move away from older, gendered, and racialized figurations of blackness to the newer and more conceptual modes of artists such as Kojo Griffin and Laylah Ali. For Leon Wainwright, a turn away from the hegemony of a United States–based cultural politics of black representation requires looking at the other landscapes and ways of seeing blackness that constitute a diasporic world imaginary.

As evident in "Curated Spaces" and many of the pieces throughout, *RHR* 103 foregrounds alongside the role of the state the biopolitics of diaspora; that is, it looks at how we figure the blackness of diaspora in terms of questions of gender and sexuality, race and color. In the minds of the editors, this issue aims to continue the important black feminist project of using intersectional approaches to create greater attention to multiple categories of identity. Yet in the context of African diaspora studies, this approach may explicate as much as blur, complicate, and confuse some of the field's already long-held wisdoms. Perhaps this critically important confusion is best represented by the issue's cover, a photo taken by Agustín Victor Casasola in 1915, at the height of the Mexican Revolution. Titled "La soldadera" ("The Woman Soldier"), the photo makes visible the place that women cleared for themselves — whether they mended clothes or fought and even led battles — in the midst of a civil war that is often recounted in historical records as an almost exclusively male endeavor. "La soldadera" disturbs epistemologies of revolution, radicalism, and leadership that permeate what is broadly construed as "political" throughout the diaspora. As Carmelo Esterrich insists,

The way she defiantly looks straight at the camera erases immediately the image of her as simply a caretaker or a follower. Her medals possibly document a brilliant, recognized strategist. Her body language literally pushes *through* masculinity to render it open, usable, and ultimately malleable. Her gaze stops the penetrating look of the camera. She is not about erasing femininity, but about redefining it. She could be an indigenous woman, but she could also very possibly be part of the community of Afro-Mexicans, perhaps from the region of Veracruz by the Gulf of Mexico. This makes the image even more pertinent: we are before a subaltern woman resisting the photographic record and bringing the racial impressions of Mexico's visual culture to a screeching halt. She makes prescient the complex transformations in the Americas of gender, class and race.[3]

In the same way that one cannot really tell from the photo if this woman is "black" or "Mexican" (as if these were mutually exclusive, or as if this were the most useful question), one cannot unravel the relationship between the cultural space from which such a question may arise—that old bugaboo of so-called identity politics in which race, gender, and sexuality are often subsumed by the lenses of nation and class—and the specific political conditions shaping her uniquely quiet yet physically powerful stance and armed revolutionary image. "La soldadera" serves both as a useful bookend to these introductory comments and as a great point of departure for the different vectors of reconceptualizing radical histories of diaspora that the issue's contributors offer. By joining national discourses of blackness and of color in a transnational arena of geohistory, African diaspora studies as a field can expose some of the blurring of the lines between state borders and national discourses that underlie discussions of black populations and histories.

—Erica Ball, Melina Pappademos, and Michelle Stephens

Notes

1. See such recent collections as Jana Evans Braziel, *Diaspora: An Introduction* (Hoboken, NJ: Wiley-Blackwell, 2008); and Stephane Dufoix, *Diasporas* (Berkeley: University of California Press, 2008).

2. See, for example, the debate between Pierre Bourdieu and Loïc Wacquant and Michael Hanchard in *Theory, Culture, and Society* (Bourdieu and Wacquant, "On the Cunning of Imperialist Reason," *Theory, Culture, and Society* 16 [1999]: 41–58; Hanchard, "Acts of Misrecognition: Transnational Black Politics, Anti-imperialism, and the Ethnocentricisms of Pierre Bourdieau and Loïc Wacquant," *Theory, Culture, and Society* 20 [2003]: 5–29).

3. Provided with the kind permission of Carmelo Esterrich at the request of the coeditors. Esterrich is a professor of Spanish and cultural studies in the Department of Liberal Education at Columbia College, Chicago, and is working on a book about the arts produced, distributed, sponsored, and consumed in Puerto Rico during the 1950s.

Nation and the Cold War: Reflections on the Circuitous Routes of African Diaspora Studies

Lisa Brock

Two Steps Back

In 1996, in an attempt (neither the first nor the most vigorous) to jog the African Studies Association (ASA) out of its nearly forty-year Cold War slumber on the question of the African diaspora, I coordinated an issue of the ASA's polemical journal, *Issue: A Journal of Opinion*, titled "African [Diaspora] Studies." I asked scholars, activists, and graduate and undergraduate students to write short pieces from their vantage point about the ways they were and were not engaging African studies with the African diaspora. An editor of this issue of *Radical History Review*, Melina Pappademos, then a graduate student interested in work on blacks in Latin America and the Caribbean, wrote about her frustration at not finding support at the graduate level to study the African diaspora. Similarly, for those of us trained in African history, the signal was clear: the study of Africa was an enterprise completely separate from the study of people of African descent in the Americas, Europe, or Asia.

Moreover, we were trained to focus on discrete ethnic and/or national groups or regions because, it was argued, Africa is huge and each people and language too distinct to make possible broad assumptions or establish theses across societal or national divides. This local-versus-global distinction gave those of us who studied

Radical History Review
Issue 103 (Winter 2009)   DOI 10.1215/01636545-2008-029
© 2009 by MARHO: The Radical Historians' Organization, Inc.

Africa a much needed research posture, for it discouraged the use of stereotypes to examine Africa's historical processes. However, for radical historians like myself, finding a "usable past" that could make visible common interests toward struggle proved very difficult under these conditions. While microwork was important and valuable to a radical project, especially work looking at gender, class, colonialism, political economy, race, nation, sexuality, and so on, there was also a need for a body of work that asked big questions across ethnicities, regions, language groups, nations, and continents.[1]

Interestingly, however, before the formal organization of the U.S.-based ASA in 1957 or the inclusion of the study of the African Americas in mainstream academic organizations, most literature on Africa and the African (not of the social Darwinist kind) actually focused on more diasporic questions. While some probed, explained, and revealed the black/African condition, others mined histories, sociologies, and political ideas for hopeful solutions to racial oppression. Few had access to publishing houses or academic audiences; instead, they struggled to self-publish in newspapers, magazines, pamphlets, and black journals or by "making known" in speeches and through word of mouth.[2] Most also evidenced an African-rooted/race-based sensibility that crossed peoples, lands, colonies, islands, and continents. These earlier works (by archivists, collectors, researchers, griots, and scholars) showed a double agenda, as both the bearers of black histories, artifacts, and culture—lest they be lost—*and* as the tools of witness-agitators against the hardship and struggle of black peoples of the day. As Michael Gomez notes and others have echoed, engagement with the African diaspora has always been both an "academic project and [a] social agenda."[3]

Much of this written and oral literature extends all the way back to the slave trade and to the beginnings of an African presence in Europe and the Americas. Just a few examples include the race consciousness and extraterritorial pull of Boukman's Prayer (1790s) during the early part of the Haitian Revolution; Eugenio María de Hostos's Pan-Caribbeanism in the League of the Antilles newspaper, *Antillanos* (1875); the antigenocidal plea of Sol Plaatje's *Native Life in South Africa* (1914), which he took on tour in the United States and Canada in 1921; the "black subjective voice" of João dos Santos Albasini's *O brado africano* (*The African Outcry*) (Mozambique, 1919); the transcolonial call to African women of Fumilayo Ramsome-Kuti (Nigeria, 1950s); and the powerful pan-African acuity of Nnamdi Azikiwe, C. L. R. James, Aimé Césaire, and other West Indians and Africans organizing in Europe between the 1930s and the 1950s.[4] Because these authors and agitators—and the hundreds, possibly thousands of others like them—lacked citizenship rights in the lands in which they were born (either as slaves, second-class free persons, or as colonial or neocolonial subjects), they lived a kind of "cosmopolitanism" or "global citizenry" that focused on their common struggles against racism, imperialism, and injustice. This is not to say that every person of African descent had intimate knowledge of "a black world"—that would have been impossible—but that there was a *desire* to connect and to know. And in most cases, there was some level of knowledge of other black areas beyond one's own—even if only from south to north, country-side to town, one colony to the next.

Nation Time

Over time, two largely twentieth-century pressures complicated these earlier forms of "knowing" in the black world, namely, the development of the nation form as the central model for a modern black politics across the diaspora and the exten-sion of Cold War liberal ideologies into the academy. In the twentieth century, a greater proportion of Africans and their descendents focused their attention on the relationships they had as noncitizens or second-class citizens with their nation, colony, or neocolony. The nation-state took center stage in the struggles for equality and human rights among Africans, people of African descent, and other people of color. The civil rights movement, African independence movements, and the Cuban and Mozambican revolutions, for instance, argued for equal rights and citizenship within nations and as nations within a world of dominant northern/Western, white-dominated states. This fight was crucial to the betterment of the everyday lives of the masses of oppressed black peoples.[5]

Some intellectuals also took the nationalistic politics of this century to argue for a black modernity that would distance them from Africa and allow their inclu-sion into the world of "white civilized" nation-states. This was the case in instances as varied as the uplift movements among missionaries in the United States, the whit-ening schemes of Latin America and the Caribbean, the role of Afro-Cuban politi-cians in the suppressing of the uprising of 1912, and even the negritude writers' con-struction of an oppositional black consciousness within a fairly elitist French context. All of these activities illustrated unique forms of Du Boisian double consciousness, made visible by a highly problematic and contradictory politics of national inclusion. Many peoples of African descent grew to feel (and still do) a tension between loyal-ties to nation and a broader swath of African and African-descended peoples.

Even so, within these two developments, there still was a progressive modernity to which anticolonial, black, and revolutionary struggles could strive. Vijay Prashad has called the middle decades of the twentieth century the most promising for international solidarity among peoples of color. In the hearts and minds of Ghana's Kwame Nkrumah, India's Jawajarlal Nehru, Egypt's Gamal Abdel Nasser, Indone-sia's Ahmed Sukarno, Algeria's Ben Bella, Cuba's Fidel Castro, and Vietnam's Ho Chi Minh, the "Third World was not a place . . . but . . . a project."[6] The historic sum-mits in Bandung in 1955, in Belgrade in 1961, and in Havana in 1966 all focused on the possibility of new pathways for people of color to work together toward eco-nomic and social leveling. In fact, the United Nations became a site of contestation between emerging nations and those of Europe and the United States. Resolutions were passed against apartheid South Africa and for agencies like UNESCO and the United Nations Development Programme.

More specifically, a good number of African-descended peoples continued to draw on the black diasporic tradition and to engage in solidarity and movement building across the Atlantic and Pacific Oceans and the Mediterranean and Caribbean seas.[7] Some African Americans felt so inspired by the African freedom movements that they relocated to the continent in the 1950s, 1960s, and 1970s, while others, such as Sidney Poitier and Thurgood Marshall, made it their business to attend independence celebrations in Africa. Both Malcolm X's international pilgrimage and Martin Luther King Jr.'s anti–Vietnam War stance were as much connected to these progressive impulses in the world as they were to their own religious and moral compasses.

Cold War Liberalism

The Cold War (1945–90) was the second twentieth-century force to have a significant impact on the study of Africa and the African diaspora. In an effort to stop the progressive nationalisms mentioned above, as well as their emerging relations with each other and the Soviet Union, the United States for the first time shaped an African foreign policy in the 1950s. It fashioned new posts such as the assistant secretary of state for Africa and new African divisions in USAID, the U.S. Information Agency, the American Federation of Labor, and the Central Intelligence Agency (CIA). Similarly, in Britain and France there was a rush to "Africanize" colonial institutions after World War II.[8] As David Robinson notes, "colonial Africa might require study commissions and training programs for civil servants, [but] independent Africa required a whole new structure."[9] Key to these new structures was the role of clandestine organizations like the CIA and the Federal Bureau of Investigation (FBI). In Africa, the CIA—along with its allies—instigated coups, assassinations, and destabilization efforts, while in the United States, the leaders of the largest and most effective African solidarity organization to date—the Council on African Affairs—were banned and jailed as communist sympathizers.

For an increasing number of African Americans, the only way to connect with Africa (or with the African diaspora, for that matter) was through State Department tours or by joining one of the United States' highly problematic government agencies. The United States was actively concerned with its so-called race-relations image abroad; for, after all, how could it win the hearts and minds of newly independent Africans if it was seen to have a "race" problem? So it offered African American artists and spokespersons state-sponsored work and travel opportunities. For some African Americans, working with the U.S. government represented an inclusion they had longed for, and a small number thought of their participation as helpful to Africa. Those, however, who refused to be a part of the new African foreign policy initiatives and traveled independently often found themselves targeted and under surveillance.[10]

It was during this time that the United States Departments of State and Education and philanthropic agencies such as Rockefeller, Ford, and Carnegie Foundations decided to fund emerging African studies programs at major U.S. universities. While the largely white and male scholars who founded the ASA in 1958 were rarely direct operatives of U.S. foreign policy, they did suffer from two misconceptions. One was that they believed they could influence through persusasion the U.S. government to do good work in Africa—a proposition that few African Americans believed (even those artists who went on U.S. State Department tours). Second, they reflected in their scholarly agendas an amnesia or complete denial of the intellectual and political history of and in the African diaspora.

The result was a largely white and male ASA in a liberal fog, constructing paradigms and agendas while beginning to work with emerging African universities in isolation from any acknowledgment of the history mentioned above. It is quite astonishing that from 1958 to 1970, in the minutes of business meetings and conference proceedings, one discovers near total silence on African-descended people dispersed throughout the globe and on the historical, political, and intellectual linkages they had with Africa.

A similar U.S. Cold War thrust catapulted a series of fledgling Latin American studies groups into the Latin American Studies Association (LASA) in May 1966. According to Howard Cline, there was no official interest in the United States for Latin America studies until progressive movements in the region began to gain traction. In fact, it was the United States' inability to derail the Cuban Revolution that pushed the government to fund Latin American studies programs. Cline goes on to posit that LASA "might well erect a monument to Fidel Castro, [its] remote godfather. His actions . . . jarred complacency in official and university circles, dramatically revealing that all was not well in Latin America and that something must be done about it."[11]

What was "done about it" was the founding of university-based programs to train PhDs in Latin American studies with the hope that their work might be useful to U.S. political, military, and business interests in the region. Latin American studies shared the National Defense Education acts titles IV and VI funds with African and Asian studies known collectively as language and area studies programs and began to receive funds from Ford, the Social Science Research Council (SSRC), the Brookings Institution, and the Fulbright Program. Again, while they were rarely actual agents of the CIA, largely white and male scholars within LASA marginalized the study of black peoples in the Americas and their connections to Africa.

It is important to note, however, that the marginalization of the study of peoples of African descent had its own particular trajectory in Latin America and the Caribbean. In fact, it was in the ideologies of nationalism — especially in those areas colonized by Spain, Portugal, and France — that black and indigenous peoples' histories and conditions tended to be ignored.[12] Throughout the region, national myths of racial democracies were created to serve as bulwarks against imperialism and internal racial strife. However, because these national narratives unfolded in a context of slave-based, conquest-based whiteness, they tended to silence African-descended and indigenous voices and studies while normalizing and empowering European-centered ones.

The U.S. State Department apparatus used this narrative as best it could to influence and prop up racist and military elites in the region in much the same way it did African elites on the continent. And as in its African policy, it used African Americans as part of state-sponsored initiatives, especially in countries with large black populations such as Brazil and Cuba. Those who chose to connect with these countries on their own were, like those who independently went to Africa, targeted. For instance, Josephine Baker, known at the time for speaking out on U.S. racism, traveled on her French passport through Latin America and the Caribbean. Shortly before she was due to arrive in Cuba in 1953, her Cuban agents were pressured to cancel her tour and newspaper editorials slammed her. Yet she arrived anyway. Once there, she was denied access to the premises where she was supposed to perform and was picked up by military police. The police questioned her for three hours and said that "the questioning was in response to a suggestion by the U.S. Federal Bureau of Investigation . . . that Miss Baker might be an active Communist."[13] Interestingly, though, the American embassy report issued sometime after this interrogation seemed only concerned with Baker's potential contact with and influence on "Cuban Negroes."[14]

Tangled Webs

Overall, the Cold War and the politics of the nation served to block large-scale, independent ties that might bind among Africans and people of African descent. In Africa and the black Americas these pressures were felt in various ways. In Cuba, for instance, the life chances of Cubans of African descent were immensely enhanced by the revolution, with universal health care, education, and employment open to all yet their voices and cultural initiatives were severely constrained and marginalized early in the revolution by the combined forces of the national myth of racial democracy, a vitriolic U.S. embargo, and the Marxist belief that class leveling would end racism. In the United States, it was black student activism in the North and civil rights struggles in the South that catapulted black studies into the curriculums of many colleges and schools. Yet with the white Right attacking black studies in general and the black Left severely excised from it, the result was a twofold compromise. Afrocentrism and heritage studies jostled for centrality in African diaspora studies, while a liberal and sanitized "national inclusion" of the black experience in the United States was slowly and unevenly added to curriculums. The result was a less politicized and a more cultural engagement with the diaspora.

The situation in Africa during the same period also deserves further commentary. African universities sprang up in every country as the result of national independence, and since most African universities were public institutions, the euphoria of nation building forged strong partnerships between academics and the state. However, as economic and political problems became intractable, tension grew between these two sectors. The political class became less interested in funding universities, and scholars became more critical of corruption and the state's coercive control of universities. In turn, more funding came from foreign donors, and while many African scholars found this income crucial, many also found themselves serving as "consultants" to outside agencies and their agendas. Paul Zeleza summed up the problem beautifully in a lecture he delivered at the University of Malawi in June 2000, stating: "In most African countries, the development of the universities and research has been firmly tied to the vagaries of the state policies, the shifting missions and mandates of international donor agencies, and the unpredictable demands and dislocations of civil society." African universities, therefore, are suffering, and many African academics work abroad. Yet they, too, often find themselves "caught in the bind of addressing African realities in borrowed languages and paradigms [and] conversing with each other through publications and media controlled by foreign academic communities."[15]

What Time Is It?

Interestingly, Zeleza's words bring us full circle as new cohorts of African-descended researchers are now pushing the African diaspora onto the research agendas of major academic organizations. Zeleza himself ended his important speech by arguing that the way forward for African scholars was to focus less on support from international agencies and to reengage a pan-Africanist agenda as a guide. The emergence of new regional, as opposed to national, African institutes is one area where outside funding has proven most useful and is also illustrative of a resurgence of pan-Africanism on the continent. Zeleza's focus, though, is transcontinental as well as transnational, for it is in a reframing of Africa with African diaspora studies that he sees hope.

The ASA's *African Studies Review* issued a special edition on the African diaspora in 2000, and its 2001 annual theme also centered around the African diaspora. Similarly, LASA now has a section on ethnicity, race, and indigenous peoples, founded in 2005, and there continues to be healthy discussion and debate about its direction. LASA has also taken key positions against imperialism in the region. Alongside the founding of ASWAD, the Association for the Study of the Worldwide African Diaspora, in 2000, important older organizations and institutions have also gained new life. The Association for the Study of African-American Life and History, founded by Carter G. Woodson in 1915, once again boasts record numbers of conference attendees. Harlem's Schomburg Library, dedicated to scholarship on the African diaspora, bustles with local, national, and international research activity. Finally, in Cuba, amid national discussions on race that began in 2000, Gloria Rolando's 2007 film on the 1912 uprising and massacre of thousands of black and poor people in Oriente province, *Roots of My Heart*, aired on Cuban television. This episode in Cuban history, long ignored and denied, now has a national commission to make public its memory.

Given the hundreds of millions of people of African descent throughout the world whose histories and conditions are in need of research and study, the bearers of African diaspora studies (archivists, collectors, researchers, scholars, griots) will continue to have work to do. The challenge is to make it possible again for the witness-agitators to have a voice and place in this field. As Russell Adams wrote in the *Journal of Negro Education* in 1977, "Black Studies has two major traditions: an off-campus tradition and an on-campus tradition. The location of Black Studies at any given point in time is crucial to the way the studies have been pursued, the ends to which the information has been put and the kinds of focus blacks take on matters that have to do with liberation."[16] What time is it now?

Notes

1. Interestingly, it was these types of works—such as Walter Rodney's *How Europe Underdeveloped Africa* (London: Bogle-L'Ouverture, 1972); Basil Davidson's *The Lost Cities of Africa* (Boston: Little, Brown, 1959) and *Black Mother: The Years of the African Slave Trade* (Boston: Little, Brown, 1961); Frantz Fanon's *The Wretched of the Earth*, trans. Constance Farrington (New York: Grove, 1963); and Edward Said's *Orientalism* (London: Routledge and Kegan Paul, 1978)—that would then become known outside the academy and important to broader epistemologies concerned with Africa and with people of color in the world.

2. Some examples of these journals are *Journal of Negro History*, *Phylon*, *Présence africaine*, *O brado africano*, and black U.S. newspapers such as the *Chicago Defender*, the *New York Amsterdam News*, and the *West African Pilot*. According to the Merriam-Webster online dictionary (*www.merriam-webster.com*) "to publish" is "to make known," whether in print or through word of mouth.

3. Michael A. Gomez, "Of Du Bois and Diaspora: The Challenge of African American Studies," *Journal of Black Studies* 35 (2004): 177.

4. This prayer, from the ceremony at *Bwa Kayiman*, has traditionally been ascribed to Boukman Dutty. It is translated somewhat differently in various publications, but the general theme of liberation from the white man's gods is the same. See Carolyn Fick, *The Making of Haiti: The Saint Domingue Revolution from Below* (Knoxville: University of Tennessee Press, 1990), 93; Donna Marie Wolf, "The Caribbean People of Color and the Cuban Independence Movement" (PhD diss., University of Pittsburgh, 1973), 220; Solomon Plaatje, *Native Life in South Africa, before and since the European War and the Boer Rebellion* (1916; New York: Negro Universities Press, 1969); and Brian Willan, *Sol Plaatje, South African Nationalist, 1876–1932* (Berkeley: University of California Press, 1984); Jeanne Marie Penvenne, "João dos Santos Albasini (1876–1922), *Journal of African History* 37 (1996): 419–64.

5.   Tyler Stovall has argued, in fact, that the role of the nation-state has been neglected in more recent diasporic and transnational studies. See Tyler Stovall, "Race and the Making of the Nation, Blacks in Modern France," in *Diasporic Africa: A Reader*, ed. Michael Gómez (New York: New York University Press, 2006), 200–18.

6.   Vijay Prashad, *The Darker Nations: A Peoples History of the Third World* (New York: Norton, 2007), xv.

7.   Kwame Nkrumah, Julius Nyerere, and R. N. Duchein are just a few of the leaders and intellectuals for whom pan-Africanism remained a strong pull at the beginning of the independence era, even as they worked to build strong nation-states.

8.   Hakim Ali, *West Africans in Britain, 1900–1960: Nationalism, Pan Africanism, and Communisim* (London: Lawrence and Wishart, 1998), 161.

9.   David Robinson, "The African Studies Association at Age Thirty-Five: Presidential Address to the 1993 African Studies Association Annual Meeting," *African Studies Review* 37 (1994): 3.

10. Daniel Aldridge III calls this the beginnings of black powerlessness in international affairs. See Daniel Aldrige III, "Black Powerlessness in a Liberal Era: The NAACP, Anti-colonialism, and the United Nations Organization, 1942–1945," in *Imperialism on Trial: International Oversight and Colonial Rule in Historical Perspective*, ed. R. M. Douglas, Michael D. Callahan, and Elizabeth Bishop (Oxford: Lexington, 2006).

11. Howard Cline, "The Latin American Studies Association: A Summary Survey with Appendix," *Latin American Research Review* 2 (1966): 64.

12. Jean Muteba Rahier, "The Study of Latin American 'Racial Formations': Different Approaches and Different Contexts," *Latin American Research Review* 39 (2004): 282.

13. Mary L. Dudziak, "Josephine Baker, Racial Protest, and the Cold War," *Journal of American History* 81 (1994): 561–63.

14. Ibid., 563.

15. Paul Tiyambe Zeleza, "The Politics of Historical and Social Science Research," *Africa: Journal of Southern African Studies*, special issue on Malawi, 21 (2002): 9–23.

16. Russell Adams, "Black Studies Perspectives," *Journal of Negro Education* 46 (1977): 100.

The Black Panthers in London, 1967–1972:

A Diasporic Struggle Navigates

the Black Atlantic

Anne-Marie Angelo

The history of Black Power in Britain is the history of the shit class trying to organize themselves.
—Obi Egbuna, *Destroy This Temple*

On March 2, 1970, roughly one hundred people protested outside the U.S. embassy in Grosvenor Square, London, in support of the U.S. Black Panther founder Bobby Seale, who was on trial for murder in New Haven, Connecticut. They chanted "Free Bobby!" and carried posters proclaiming "Free, Free Bobby Seale" and "You Can Kill a Revolutionary but Not a Revolution." Demonstrator Tony Thomas waved a large red and yellow flag emblazoned with a Black Panther symbol. Claiming that "their joint actions amounted to a general threat to passers by," London police arrested sixteen of the protestors that day. Police charged these three women and thirteen men with threatening and assaulting police officers, distributing a flier entitled "The Definition of Black Power," intending to incite a breach of the peace, and willful damage to a police raincoat. At trial, the judge dropped the raincoat charge and found five of the accused, named as "Black Panther Defendants," guilty of the remaining charges.[1]

Radical History Review
Issue 103 (Winter 2009)   DOI 10.1215/01636545-2008-030
© 2009 by MARHO: The Radical Historians' Organization, Inc.

Here, the symbols, chants, and demands of the U.S. Black Panther Party (USBPP) crossed the Atlantic, stimulating shared racial and class identifications across national borders and intersecting with these Afro-Britons who identified themselves as the British Black Power Movement from 1967 to 1968 and as the British Black Panther Movement (BBPM) from 1968 to 1972. As the first Black Panther Movement to form independently outside the United States, the British Panthers took their ideological inspiration from the U.S. Panthers. The U.K. Panthers appropriated the U.S. Panthers' revolutionary aesthetic as a model for protest, necessary violence, and for engaging with the state. The "Definition of Black Power" flier that protestors had distributed revealed that its authors thought their plight was part of an international anticapitalist struggle, asserting that

The history of the oppressed peoples of Africa, Asia, the Caribbean, and the Americas over the last four hundred years has demonstrated that the world has been divided into two irreconcilable camps. A handful of western capitalist imperialist nations have mercilessly oppressed and exploited the broad toiling masses and ravaged the material wealth of the three continents. That the well-being of the imperialist nations rests on the hundreds of millions of broken backs in Asia, Africa, the Caribbean and the Americas is the reality.

Black Power, the authors maintained, provided "the political slogan which gives expression to the pent up fury that rages in the oppressed peoples of the world." The authors claimed that a long history of oppression had forced them to take up Black Power as a matter of necessity.[2] The flier and concomitant protest would be the first in a series of altercations between the BBPM and the City of London Metropolitan Police in 1970.

The literature on internationalism and the USBPP has centered on the party's influence on pan-Africanist movements, revolutionary movements, and anticolonial struggles.[3] Kathleen Cleaver charts the development of the first international wing of the Black Panther Party in Algeria in 1969. John McCartney demonstrates the direct influence of the USBPP on the Vanguard Nationalists and the Socialist Party in the Bahamas. Ruth Reitan traces the relationship between Panther leader Eldridge Cleaver and the Castro regime, paying particular attention to Cuba as a haven for revolutionary black exiles from the United States. Most recently, Jeffrey O. G. Ogbar shows how the party influenced the Young Lords, a Puerto Rican nationalist group that was active in the United States from 1966 to 1972.[4]

In this article, I am less concerned with the U.S. party's official activities abroad than with spontaneous Black Panther party formations. Michael Clemons and Charles Jones lay the groundwork for this examination in their identification of several global emulators of the USBPP. Although the USBPP set up few formal international party affiliates, it catalyzed grassroots formations of small, cell-style insurgent groups in Bermuda, Israel, Australia, India, and the United Kingdom between 1967 and 1987. These groups adopted the party's name and symbol, benefiting from the Panthers' rhetorical power and role "in the global network of the New Left."[5] In varied local settings, these emulators enacted goals, community programs, and confrontational styles based on the model of U.S. Panther activism, but each international Panther party also developed its own ideologies and political critiques, which will be reflected here in the case of the U.K. Panthers.

An examination of spontaneous Panther group formations opens up several questions. By looking at inflections of racial and political tropes we can learn how transnational, national, and local identifications merged in the U.K. Panthers' constructions of blackness. Although the British definition of "black" differed broadly from the American context (Indians, Pakistanis, West Indians, and continental Africans were all considered "coloured" or black by the government and in political culture), the British Black Power movement grew out of specific racial and class tensions experienced by London's Afro-Caribbean community.[6] A study of police files allows us to situate the Panthers in the relationship between London's Afro-Caribbean community and city police more generally in the early 1970s. A consideration of the ways that U.K. Panthers identified themselves reveals salient aspects of the global cultural and political influence of the American Panthers—of the "penumbra" of the USBPP.[7]

I argue that the U.K. Panthers represented an initial step in the U.S. Panthers' goal of inculcating a global anti-imperialist struggle that would give race equal attention with class. The hegemony of American capitalism served as the driving force behind this larger network of consciousness. As the historian Davarian Baldwin maintains, "The [U.S.] Panthers' engagement with the U.S. empire of transnational capital took place precisely through their manipulation and production of mass cultural products and ideas at that particular moment. In their hands, blackness became the conduit for a cultural politics of decolonization, connecting black ghettos to the Third World."[8] The British Panthers adopted the strains of Black Power made accessible through the style and communication strategies of the U.S. Panthers, indicating their class and racial solidarity and their recognition that blackness and diaspora were ultimately modern concepts.[9]

This article also belongs to literatures on the long legacy of black internationalism and its more recent development of Black Power. Historian Peniel E. Joseph defines Black Power as a politics that "trumpeted a militant new race consciousness that placed black identity as the soul of a new radicalism."[10] Black Power activists argued for a fundamental alteration of society, rather than reform. In the United States, the politics of Black Power appealed to a broad range of people and organizations including black nationalists, Marxists, pan-Africanists, trade unionists, feminists, and liberals, as well as to a limited number of conservatives invested in its call for black entrepreneurship. From its beginning as a progressive call for black consciousness in 1966, Black Power evolved into a revolutionary ideology that the

Panthers articulated in 1968. Black Power, not just the Panthers, appeared in varying forms in many international contexts, such as in Trinidad, where several journalists and scholars have focused on the 1970 Black Power Revolution.[11]

The U.S. Panthers offered the most transnationally appropriable formation
of Black Power. This visibility during a moment of global cultural upheaval afforded
the Panthers what Baldwin has called "representational legitimacy," which catalyzed
the emergence of Black Panther parties outside the U.S. context.[12] The earliest U.S.
Panther ideology consisted of arguments for racial solidarity and black nationalism
with elements of Marxism, which evolved by 1968 to a more explicit fusion of Marxism with revolutionary nationalism. After 1970, the USBPP espoused global socialism through Huey Newton's idea of revolutionary intercommunalism.[13] The sources
to be examined here demonstrate that although British Panthers may not have used
the term *intercommunalism*, they supported a global socialist revolution that would
expose the nation-state as irrelevant.

The British Panthers acted within a spectrum of organizations, known as
the British Black Power Movement, that promoted pan-Africanism, black nationalism, and communism. Taking these organizations into account, I am specifically
interested in why and how the British Panthers formed when other options for radical activism associated with Black Power were already available.[14] Utilizing Paul
Gilroy's "suggestion that cultural historians could take the Atlantic as one single,
complex unit of analysis in their discussions of the modern world and use it to produce an explicitly transnational and intercultural perspective," I will show how the
U.K. Panthers adapted American Black Power to suit a transnational yet also local
struggle.[15] I argue that the U.S. Panthers provided an appropriable ideology through
visible cultural markers that melded with the legacy of West Indian radicalism to
create a fluid, albeit short-lived, U.K. Black Panther Movement and that the well-
traveled "routes" of the Black Atlantic allowed Britain to be the first site at which an
international Panther group emerged.[16]

The findings in this article are based on an examination of London police files
and a collection of essays by the Biafran novelist, playwright, lawyer, and imprisoned
Black Power leader Obi Egbuna. In 1971, Egbuna published *Destroy This Temple:
The Voice of Black Power in Britain*, in which he reflected on the accomplishments
and strategies of Black Power in the United Kingdom. Between 1970 and 1972, the
British Director of Public Prosecutions compiled files involving the Panthers and
the City of London Metropolitan Police for archiving as "Black Panther cases" at the
U.K. Public Record Office. By interweaving Egbuna's personal narrative with police
records from the state archives, I will analyze the ways in which the British Black
Panthers engaged in a struggle with the Metropolitan Police over issues of immigration, blackness, violence, anti-imperialism, and social space.

"It Was Not Meant for Us": Immigration Politics and Black Power in London

Between 1961 and 1964, Britain's black population tripled from about 300,000 to 1 million.[17] Between 1955 and June 1962, 259,540 people migrated from the Caribbean to the United Kingdom. These immigrants brought with them a tradition of activism that laid the groundwork for the emergence of Black Power.[18] Their notion of Black Power was elastic, drawing on the writings of Marcus Garvey, C. L. R. James, George Padmore, and Frantz Fanon and incorporating cultural consciousness, the politics of decolonialization, and calls for an antiracist, anticapitalist revolution.[19] Some adopted classical leftist formations, represented, for example, by the work of Trinidadian-born journalist-activist Claudia Jones. Younger, second-generation immigrants embraced radical confrontational styles and disapproved of the antiracist politics of the established Left. Another Trinidadian intellectual and activist, James, served as a mentor to these young radicals and to the British Marxist-internationalist journal *Race Today*.[20]

Despite the popularity of black radical political discourse, figures in the media, politicians, and cultural leaders denied the existence of Black Power in the United Kingdom. These writers and leaders claimed that although race was an international problem, Black Power was an inherently American phenomenon. For example, in 1969, the *Times* critic Irving Wardle characterized the African American playwright Ed Bullins's *The Gentlemen Caller* and *How Do You Do?* as "two Black Power plays . . . written for the black American community," saying "there is something absurd in seeing them performed to white British spectators, let alone in treating them as reviewing fodder . . . it seems pretty crude stuff but then, it was not meant for us."[21] Wardle separated white Britons from "crude" black arts and portrayed Black Power as alterity, as a phenomenon meant for black Americans but not for "us."

Afro-British activists, however, believed they had much in common with their African American counterparts. In between the U.K. visits of Malcolm X in 1964–65 and of Stokely Carmichael in 1967, Egbuna flew to America in 1966 where he "tramped the Black ghettos of the United States and delved into the soul of the grass roots."[22] Inspired by this visit as well as by several ideas he found in the media and in black radical literature, Egbuna returned to the United Kingdom ready to develop a Black Power organization.[23] He attended meetings of black organizations at which other activists asked him to explain the significance of the new Panther badge that he wore.[24] Gaining support from these interactions, Egbuna and a group known as the Universal Coloured People's Association (UCPA) launched Black Power from a Brixton flat in September 1967.[25] They wrote a fourteen-page credo with a black panther emblazoned on the cover to "explain to the British people what Black Power in [Britain] really [was] . . . [the] totality of the economic, cultural, political, and if necessary, military power which the black peoples of the world must acquire in order to get the white oppressor off their backs." These Black Power advocates claimed that they were "no initiators of violence. But if a white man lays his hand on one of us we will regard it as an open declaration of war against all of us."[26] Egbuna, the president of the UCPA, told the *Times* that the movement had recruited 778 members in seven weeks.

Seven months later, Egbuna did an about-face in his vision for Black Power. He called the UCPA annual general meeting six months earlier than planned in April 1968, resigned as chairman, and founded the BBPM, which advertised itself as a revolutionary socialist group.[27] Struck by a lack of consensus about the meaning of Black Power within the UCPA, Egbuna struck out on his own, borrowing the term *Black Power* and related symbols from the U.S. Panthers. He insisted that the movement had to be ideologically coherent and masculine because "the secret of the Panthers' success to date, even if limited, lies in this insistence . . . that the movement must be a fraternity of brothers of strictly identical ideological orientation."[28] This ideology combined a Marxist-Leninist class revolution with an analysis of racial discrimination. Egbuna derived his racial analysis from Karl Marx: "I cannot see how any man who called on workers to unite because they are oppressed as workers could deny men of colour the right to unite when they are victimized as men of colour."[29]

The ideological orientation of the British Panthers differed in some ways from that of their U.S. counterparts in terms of relationships with the white Left and of the embrace of cultural nationalism. Egbuna insisted that "the White 'Marxists,' with their usual presumption that only they have read Marx, persist in deriding Black Power as narrow, nationalistic, and un-Marxian." He believed that British Panthers should remain independent from sympathetic whites and claimed that white liberals "enjoy[ed] a certain degree of security from the system of society." This contrasted with the U.S. Panthers' view that coalitions with whites formed an essential part of the revolution. As the British Panthers gained notoriety, however, they began to accept the support of some whites. While the U.S. Panthers rejected the central Black Power tenet of cultural nationalism as romantic and inefficacious, the U.K. Panthers aimed to spread what they termed "black consciousness" through meetings that showcased poetry, music, and film from the West Indies and West Africa. Although the black consciousness espoused by the U.K. Panthers did not constitute a full-scale adoption of cultural nationalism in the style of Maulana Karenga and the US Organization, the British Panthers' interest in the arts mirrored the black arts movement in the United States, showcased an emerging black British identity, and fit well with the founding of the Notting Hill Carnival, an annual two-day street festival celebrating Britain's West Indian community, in 1966.[30]

The British Panther movement also formed outside the official auspices of the U.S. Panthers because the latter had not yet internationalized its organizing scope in 1967. The USBPP had certainly expressed support for international activities and had sent members to parts of Africa, Asia, Cuba, Germany, and Scandinavia. But it lacked the institutional infrastructure necessary to establish an anti-imperialist front or overseas chapters. It was not until 1969, after solidifying its organizational structure and discussing the possibilities offered by Marxism-Leninism, that the U.S. party helped form the Algerian Black Panther Party, its first affiliate abroad. By this time, it had already inspired the formation of the U.K. Panthers, although possibly without knowing it.[31]

The British Black Panther Cases

In the government's eyes, West Indians were the most problematic of Britain's "coloured" immigrant groups. A 1963 Home Office report complained that "the West Indians, while making little effort to accommodate themselves to a different way of life, are demanding equal opportunities and equal treatment generally."[32] Furthermore, as James Whitfield has noted, the police believed that West Indians corrupted "traditional" British social values through sexual relationships with white women, participation in the illicit drug trade, and patronage of illegal drinking and gambling clubs. Permanent surveillance in black neighborhoods, particularly in Brixton, the center of the London West Indian community, and a lack of adequate race-relations training led police to see any crime in those neighborhoods as a crime of the entire community. Police then responded with "uncompromising firmness in which the end was not frequently seen to justify the means."[33] Unsurprisingly, the West Indian community and the London police simply did not trust each other.

Three London court cases from 1970 expose the conflicts between police and British Panthers by revealing moments in which police concerns about Black Power and the Panthers' aspirations are laid bare. In the aforementioned embassy protest of March 1970, a Black Panther solidarity demonstration for Seale turned violent when police and protestors clashed, leading to the arrest of sixteen Panthers. In August, police accused the Panthers of distributing a leaflet designed to defame the judge during a high-profile court case known as the Mangrove Nine. Later that same month, a stolen watch allegation led police to a social hall where Black Panthers were holding a dance. The police investigation provoked the Panthers, who attacked the police as they left the building. In two of the court cases, the state criminalized the Panthers for the size of their events, which numbered one hundred reported protestors at the embassy and as many as four hundred dancers at the Oval House social event.[34] The judge in the Oval House brawl defined "riotous assembly" as at least three persons assembled together, using his definition to find three of the defendants guilty.[35] Most of those arrested in the three cases were West Indian, male, and young. Of the twenty-six named defendants in these cases, twenty-three were male and fourteen of West Indian origin.[36] Whitfield identifies black youth and immigrants as two of the London police's late 1960s "errant scapegoat groups," which suggests that these young West Indian men may have been profiled by the police.[37] All of the Panthers arrested in the embassy protest and the Oval House brawl cases were between the ages of seventeen and thirty-five.[38]

On August 9, 1970, a Black Panther group protested "the white racist system's use of their police force to invade . . . the places where black people frequent." In this case, the Panthers were opposed to the aggressive policing of the Mangrove restaurant in Notting Hill, a popular meeting place for black radicals.[39] A group of 150 protestors marched through the community toward Notting Hill, Notting Dale, and Harrow Road police stations to "expose the racist brutality that black people experience[d] at the hands of the police." Police and protestors clashed during the march, and police arrested nineteen black protestors, charging them with assault, possession of an offensive weapon, and incitement to riot.[40] Ten defendants' charges were soon dropped, but support swelled for the other nine accused, who became known as the Mangrove Nine. C. L. R. James summoned the remaining protestors the day after the arrest and urged them to continue their fight, emphasizing the seriousness of the charges against their comrades.[41] The Mangrove Nine trial began in October 1971 and captured media attention. During the trial, Black Panthers and their allies demonstrated outside the central criminal court, the Old Bailey.[42]

On the last day of trial testimony, police turned over a leaflet called "Battle for Freedom at Old Bailey" to Judge Edward Clarke, who believed the leaflet might be in contempt of the court.[43] Constable Roger Buckley had apprehended the leaflet while on duty in the Notting Dale neighborhood on December 11, 1971. The leaflet charged that a biased judge and jury had colluded to skew the proceedings of the case against the Mangrove Nine, claiming that "the case has been a systematic exposure of police lies, the way in which the prosecution, having no evidence, tries to play on the prejudices of the jury, of the way in which the judge plays the part of chief prosecutor, attacking and obstructing the defence."[44] After a four-month investigation, the officer P. J. Palmes concluded that the police lacked sufficient evidence to identify the authors of the leaflet, "which in any event might be ill-advised at this stage as likely to exacerbate racial feelings."[45] This led Judge Clarke to drop the contempt of court charge, and later that year, he acquitted the Mangrove Nine.

The Afro-British community was further empowered by the case of the Oval House brawl, which began at approximately 10 p.m. on August 31, 1970, just three weeks after the Mangrove march. That evening, Peter Pace and David Proberts, two white schoolboys, were leaving Oval Underground station as two black boys approached them.[46] One of these boys said a girl wanted to speak to Pace and Proberts just around the corner. Pace and Proberts followed around the corner, and one of the black boys allegedly stole Pace's watch. The white boys claimed that the assailants ran into Oval House, a social hall rented out for a Black Panther–sponsored reggae dance that evening. The boys ran home and told Pace's mother, who returned with them to Oval House.

When Mrs. Pace approached, a Black Panther at the door told her that the event was a wedding and that only private guests could enter. Reportedly, another Panther pushed Mrs. Pace back from the doorway, after which she sent her son to get the police and waited outside. Shortly thereafter, two plainclothes detectives arrived at the hall and showed a warrant card to two men sitting by the door. The two men refused the detectives entry beyond the lobby as they did not have a pass to join the alleged wedding party. Police quarreled with a growing crowd of Panthers and solicited reinforcement before entering the hall. Accompanied by Pace and Proberts, the police stopped the dance music, circulated among the dancing couples, and searched for the stolen watch, but they were unable to find it.[47]

As the officers exited, Panther Keith Spencer (who emigrated from Jamaica in 1957) jumped onstage and chanted through the microphone, "Out with the pigs, fascist pigs, throw them out" and "Kill the pigs, kill the whities." After another song ended, Spencer continued his chant, allegedly to the beat of drums. The police suspected that this was the signal that led dance attendees to hurl objects at them. During the altercation, bottles, cans, and chairs struck seven police officers. Most injuries were not serious, but two officers were knocked unconscious.[48] As the attack continued, Spencer spat at the police officer Sheppard and shouted, "Don't touch me, white shit." Other attendees shouted, "Get out, fascist fuzz!" Seemingly threatened, the police refused to reenter the dance and elected not to arrest Spencer and his fellow organizer Edmund Lecointe (who emigrated from Dominica in 1960), on the scene. But they did ultimately arrest four Panther members, accusing them of assault on police, possession of a weapon, incitement to murder, and aiding and abetting in assault. On June 28, 1971, Judge Gillis found Spencer, Lecointe, and Leonard Anderson guilty but elected to give them suspended sentences. The judge told the Panther defendants that they had been shown "a measure of mercy" by the court.[49]

"Acts of Bravery in a Racist State:" Building a Panther Cadre

The Black Panthers channeled their community's resentment of the police into a critique of police violence. In the "Battle for Freedom" leaflet, Mangrove Nine supporters insisted: "The police of that area in London had for years harassed and brutalised the people of Notting Hill. The Mangrove Restaurant, one of the nerve centres of the community, had been raided without reason several times. Evidence in the trial showed how high the resentment of the brothers and sisters, both defendants and witnesses, against this constant unchecked brutality was."[50] Police also found a flier titled "Organised Action in Self Defence" in Leonard Anderson's pocket after his arrest at the reggae dance that identified two recent cases in which police had used attack dogs against black people. The flier also claimed that over six hundred police had been present at the Mangrove march and that there, too, they had released dogs on black protestors. In the words of the flier's author, "when over one hundred black youths in the Islington area marched to Caledonian Road police station to inquire about four brothers and sisters who had been brutalized and arrested, fear hit the racist pig police and they let loose dogs on black people."[51]

In response to these and other violent incidents, the Panthers emphasized their own preparedness and willingness to confront police when necessary.[52] They claimed weapons as central to their definition of Black Power: "Only when the most oppressed sections of the world are totally liberated will it be possible for the oppressed peoples to lay down their arms."[53] This rhetoric did not essentialize black violence, as the Panthers believed that Black Power allowed all oppressed people to express their extant anger. Like their U.S. counterparts, the British Panthers in some cases also carried weapons. Given stricter gun laws in the United Kingdom and the relative inaccessibility of guns compared to the U.S. context, in the court record Panthers appear to have only carried knives—Spencer carried a knife at the reggae dance, and Lecointe had previously been fined for possessing an "offensive weapon."[54] Through physical training, Black Panthers also prepared for encounters with the state. Peter Oliver explained in his court testimony how he had lent Oval House to the Black Panthers for karate lessons and other forms of physical training.[55]

The Panthers counterbalanced their preparation for violence by fostering community among London's West Indians. They established community programs as the U.S. Panthers had done, such as organized activities for teenage West Indians held at the Oval House. Oliver stated in court that he was "impressed by the [Black Panthers'] work. The relationship between the 'panthers' and the club has been deepened and strengthened over the last three months." The reggae dance was the third in a series of such dances, and Oliver believed that it was a part of the Panthers' outreach to local youth.[56] These initiatives mirrored U.S. Panther efforts to draw in the "brothers on the block." U.K. Panther programs sent a message to fellow immigrants that they were concerned about West Indians' social spaces, educational opportunities, and their overall quality of life.

Urban space proved a contested terrain, as the Panthers identified and labeled centers of oppression within the city. The Panthers saw officers outside their events, believed they were under police surveillance, and responded by claiming social spaces rhetorically and physically. In their promotional literature, the Mangrove Nine demonstrators sought to "expos[e] the racist brutality . . . at the three main centres of fascist repression in the area—Notting Hill, Notting Dale, and Harrow Road Police Stations."[57] The Panthers saw urban space as a battle zone, claiming that protestors committed "act[s] of bravery in a racist state."[58]

The Panthers sought to control this battle zone, as when they confronted the police in the Oval House brawl. After forcing the police out of Oval House, the Panthers used the building as a fortress: they waited inside the doors, swung them open just long enough to throw cans and bottles at the police, and then quickly pulled them shut.[59] The superintendent of police barred his officers from returning to the building out of concern for further violence. More important, Panthers believed that their sense of community trumped battles over physical spaces. When Judge Clarke did not allow the Mangrove Nine supporters to enter the courtroom, the Panthers responded that "the courtroom and the dock have not been able to isolate these nine brothers and sisters from the community of struggle of which they are a part."[60]

"With Iron Hands in Velvet Gloves":
Confronting American and British Imperialisms

Despite establishment attempts to posit Black Power as an American-only idea, in the three cases discussed here, British Black Power advocates saw the concept as potent and applied it to their activism; they used "Black America" as a rhetorical and stylistic benchmark for oppression and resistance. They compared their social treatment to that of African Americans, demonstrated connections between the two groups, and appropriated aspects of the U.S. Panthers' resistance. At the embassy protest, Seale supporters claimed that through an interstate conspiracy, the U.S. government was officially plotting to wipe out the BPP and to continue the repression of black and progressive white Americans. The Panthers' flier stated:

America plots state execution and cold blooded murder of Black Freedom
Fighter, Bobby Seale, Chairman, Black Panther Party. . . . Now he is to be
handed over to the blood-sucking mad dogs and murdering pig-hangmen in
Connecticut to be butchered. . . . Black People and All Progressive People
in Britain!! This American Murder Plot, this policy of widespread ruthless
suppression against the Panthers is also directly against all of us here in Britain.
Therefore all of us must resist it here and now.[61]

The leaflet authors called for resistance because they saw themselves not merely as allies of Seale but as the direct victims of American oppression. They saw this oppression taking official state form and believed that the American government was against them as well.

While the Panthers' flier maintained that American policies oppressed Americans and Britons, Egbuna felt that white Britons exploited the racial situation in the United States to obscure their own race prejudices. Egbuna contended that racial biases in the United Kingdom were more insidious because they were less public than in the United States. He saw the white Englishman's subtlety as sinister:

In Mississippi, the White man tells you straight that he does not want you in his
neighbourhood and you know where you stand with him. In Wimbledon, the
Englishman will apologise most profusely when he refuses you accommodation
on racial grounds: "Room to let, sorry no coloureds, Irish or dogs." When you
confront him personally, it is never his fault, he of course never has racial

prejudice, it is always the neighbour who is the villain. The American will lynch you and doesn't give a damn who knows it. But the Englishman always has enough residue of subtlety to lynch you with iron hands in velvet gloves.[62]

Egbuna believed British racism was a silent demon clothed in white middle-class propriety. Using metaphorical bastions of white supremacy (Mississippi and Wimbledon), he delineated what he saw as divergent systems of overt and covert prejudice. Some white Britons' refusal to admit to racist attitudes angered Egbuna the most, further fueling his desire for Black Power in the United Kingdom.

Despite these perceived differences in the ways that racism was expressed in the two nations, the BBPM stressed a shared black identity with the American Panthers. When Spencer was asked why he supported Seale, he responded, "I am always angry as far as black people are concerned."[63] British Panthers recognized a shifting transatlantic relationship between the growing American empire and contracting British colonialism. This relationship, characterized by Gilroy as part of the "Black Atlantic," made black American concerns also black British concerns in the minds of the Panthers. Panthers insisted that the imprisonment of Seale formed part of a policy of suppression targeted at blacks everywhere. One of their fliers stated: "Remember: America dominates and so controls Britain economically and even politically! America controls our homelands in Africa, Asia, and the Caribbean. Therefore American suppressive policies, fascism, and international murder plots concern all of us."[64] From a postcolonial critique of American dominance the U.K. Panthers derived a shared diasporic black identity, asserting that the imperialist United States oppressed black people globally.

The British Black Panthers exposed local audiences to these global networks by promoting a transnational black working-class revolution. Panthers pointed out that the police formed part of a larger framework of oppression. When asked why the embassy protest was directed at the police, Spencer responded that he "[didn't] see why the police in this country should interpret this as being directed to them."[65] He explained that the demonstration was only against the police in the sense that they were part of the British establishment. By emphasizing the notion of the establishment, Spencer suggested that the need for a revolution was more palpable and urgent than what could be accomplished by a narrow critique of the local police.

The Panthers made clear that "the revolution" must articulate the mutually reinforcing nature of race and class. In their reasoning, all people who worked in an imperialist/capitalist system, including the white working class, and refused to participate in a revolution, were complicit in the oppression of the black working class. The authors of the Mangrove Nine leaflet adapted a white working-class axiom that stated, "One law for the rich, another for the poor," changing it based on the trial to say, "One law for blacks, another for whites."[66] Despite these racial distinctions, however, the Panthers encouraged white support at other times, indicating a lack of internal resolution about this issue.

One such group of supporters were middle-class whites, classic participants in the New Left, who marched in the embassy protest, broadening the Panthers' collective base and reinforcing their role as a vanguard party. Protestors included white men and women, such as the American Jane Grant, a film editor living in Regent's Park, a predominantly white middle-class neighborhood. She noted the privileging of her race, gender, and perhaps her nationality when she claimed that Spencer "was probably shouting as I was 'Free Bobby,' [but] I was not arrested."[67] Additionally, the fliers distributed there called to "all Progressive People in Britain," referring to urban middle-class leftist, and perhaps communist, supporters rather than a majority working-class group.[68]

From the U.S. Panthers to the U.K. Panthers and Back Again

The six emulatory Panther parties identified by Clemons and Jones reveal that the U.S. Black Panthers appealed across ethnic and geographic boundaries to a global network of African-descended people, seeking their solidarity and provoking them to seek power through blackness. The Panthers developed a transatlantic reach due to the dynamic relationship among visual culture, mass production, and politics during this period. The stylistic, iconographic, and rhetorical formations of the Panthers affected those outside the United States in variegated ways and called on specific historical narratives including slavery, class conflict, and state oppression. The historian William VanDeburg maintains that Black Power was an essentially cultural form that captured and inspired people, that "in the words of Lerone Bennett, Jr., it 'made everything political and everything cultural.'"[69] More than simply making "everything political and everything cultural," Black Power interpolated Black Britons by evoking connections to their experiences of government oppression and to the popularity of African American style during this period. As Jacqueline Nassy Brown has argued with regards to Liverpool, "a nascent American hegemony actually facilitated the development of radical blackness."[70] But although American cultural and political dominance on the world stage made available the symbols and ideas of Black Power, West Africans and West Indians in London appropriated these concepts for their own purposes and with local constructions of race in mind.

In several ways, the interactions between U.K. Panthers and the City of London Metropolitan Police are familiar to those who know the narrative of the Panthers in the United States. Police watched the Panthers, Panthers defended themselves when attacked, and Panthers invoked particular tropes and icons from the USBPP, symbols that activated powerful connections to radical ideologies already present in London's black community. Ambalavaner Sivanandan, a librarian and later the director of London's Institute for Race Relations, explained, "Black Power, in particular, spoke to me very directly because it was about race and class both at once. More than that, it was about the politics of existence."[71]

Throughout their existence, the U.K. Panthers insisted on a transnational framework for their struggle. Egbuna claimed, "We do not dream for one moment that the Black people in Britain can organise themselves as a unit totally separate from other Black forces in the world. Black Power is an international concept."[72] There were several geographic sites at which Black Power as "an international concept" might have taken hold when it first did in the United Kingdom in 1967. Scholars could use these multiple possibilities and eventual Black Power movements to solidify current historiographical frameworks establishing a transnational black civil rights movement. This potential "Wide Civil Rights Movement" reached places with racial formations as diverse as India, Israel, New Zealand, and the United Kingdom.[73] Although the local subjectivities of its emulators always varied along the crossing lines of race, class, and gender, the Black Panther Party provided a desired, selectively appropriated, and malleable group identity in a quest for black global transformation.

Notes

This research was first presented to the Triangle Area Labor and Civil Rights History Working Group in Durham, North Carolina. I am grateful for the useful critiques received from this group, as well as from Tina Campt, William Chafe, Sarah Deutsch, Emily Newhouse Dillingham, Claudia Koonz, Adriane Lentz-Smith, Orion Teal, and the *RHR*'s two anonymous reviewers.

1.   "Persons Charged Following the Black Panther Demonstration on the 2nd March 1970," London, Public Record Office, Director of Public Prosecutions (DPP) 2/4827, 1970.

2.   Black Panther Movement, "The Definition of Black Power," DPP 2/4827 and 2/4889, 1970.

3.   One exception to this is Jennifer Smith's work, which narrates U.S. Panther visits to Halifax and Nova Scotia, Canada. As Smith's work focuses on the visits of Panther leaders to Canada and not the founding of an indigenous Panther party, I have chosen not to focus on it here. Kathy Lothian presents the first careful study of one of the six parties identified by Clemons and Jones. She finds that from 1968 onward, newspapers, theoretical works, and the state-run Australian Broadcasting Corporation television network exposed Aborigines to African American activism. She concludes that the Australian Panthers "owed their genesis to the Black Panther community survival projects in America" and argues that unlike the U.S. Panthers, the Aboriginal Panthers did not forge alliances with working-class whites. See Jennifer Smith, *An International History of the Black Panther Party* (New York: Garland, 1999); Kathy Lothian, "Seizing the Time: Australian Aborigines and the Influence of the Black Panther Party, 1969–1972," *Journal of Black Studies* 35 (2005): 179–200.

4.   Kathleen Neal Cleaver, "Back to Africa: The Evolution of the International Section of the Black Panther Party (1969–1972)," in *The Black Panther Party (Reconsidered)*, ed. Charles E. Jones (Baltimore: Black Classic Press, 1998), 211–54; John T. McCartney, "The Influences of the Black Panther Party (USA) on the Vanguard Party of the Bahamas, 1972–1987," in *Liberation, Imagination, and the Black Panther Party: A New Look at the Panthers and Their Legacy*, ed. Kathleen Cleaver and George Katsiaficas (New York: Routledge, 2001), 156–63; Ruth Reitan, "Cuba, the Black Panther Party, and the U.S.

Black Movement in the 1960s: Issues of Security," in Cleaver and Katsiaficas, *Liberation, Imagination, and the Black Panther Party*, 164–74; Jeffrey O. G. Ogbar, "Puerto Rico en Mi Corazón: The Young Lords, Black Power, and Puerto Rican Nationalism in the U.S., 1966–1972," *Centro Journal* 18 (2006): 148–69.

5. Michael L. Clemons and Charles E. Jones, "Global Solidarity: The Black Panther Party in the International Arena" in Cleaver and Katsiaficas, *Liberation, Imagination, and the Black Panther Party*, 20–39, 26. See also George Katsiaficas, *The Imagination of the New Left: A Global Analysis of 1968* (Boston: South End, 1987).

6. Dilip Hiro, *Black British, White British* (New York: Monthly Review Press, 1973), 253; Ron Ramdin, *Reimaging Britain: Five Hundred Years of Black and Asian History* (Sterling, VA: Pluto, 1999), 269.

7. The Oxford English Dictionary defines *penumbra* as "a peripheral region of uncertain extent; a group of things only partially belonging to some central thing." I see the U.K. Panthers' self-identification and activities as partially belonging to the U.S. Panthers, but the uncertain extent of that overlap suggests that the U.S. Panthers' influence may be more dynamic and culturally based than analyses of official international Panther activities allow. See "penumbra, *n*." *OED Online*, dictionary.oed.com/ cgi/entry/50174882 (accessed September 6, 2005).

8. Davarian L. Baldwin, "'Culture Is a Weapon in Our Struggle for Liberation': The Black Panther Party and the Cultural Politics of Decolonization," in *In Search of the Black Panther Party: New Perspectives on a Revolutionary Movement*, ed. Jama Lazerow and Yohuru Williams (Durham, NC: Duke University Press, 2006), 295.

9. On the cultural strategies of the Panthers, see Simon Wendt, "The Roots of Black Power? Armed Resistance and the Radicalization of the Civil Rights Movement," in *The Black Power Movement: Re-thinking the Civil Rights–Black Power Era*, ed. Peniel E. Joseph (New York: Routlege, 2006), 145–65, 332n67; Jama Lazerow and Yohuru Williams, introduction to *In Search of the Black Panther Party*, 2. I am influenced by Robin Kelley's argument that ideology resides within representations of style and by Dick Hebdige's claim that deviation from social norms in the form of style constitutes a subversive refusal of the dominant order. Robin D. G. Kelley, *Race Rebels: Culture, Politics, and the Black Working Class* (New York: Free Press, 1996); Dick Hebdige, *Subculture: The Meaning of Style* (New York: Routledge, 1981), 2–3.

10. Peniel E. Joseph, introduction to *The Black Power Movement*, 3.

11. Ibid., 279n3; Wendt, "The Roots of Black Power?" 332n67; Mahin Gosine, *East Indians and Black Power in the Caribbean: The Case of Trinidad* (New York: Africana Research Publications, 1986); William R. Lux, "Black Power in the Caribbean," *Journal of Black Studies* 3 (1972): 207–25; Brian Meeks, *Radical Caribbean: From Black Power to Abu Bakr* (Kingston, Jamaica: University of the West Indies Press, 1996); Ivar Oxaal, *Race and Revolutionary Consciousness: A Documentary Interpretation of the 1970 Black Power Revolt in Trinidad* (Cambridge, MA: Schenkman, 1971); Raoul Pantin, *Black Power Day: The 1970 February Revolution, A Reporter's Story* (Santa Cruz, Trinidad: Hatuey, 1990).

12. Baldwin, "'Culture Is a Weapon in Our Struggle for Liberation,'" 290.

13. Wendt, "The Roots of Black Power?" 332n67.

14. Hakim Adi, *West Africans in Britain, 1900–1960: Nationalism, Pan-Africanism, and Communism* (London: Lawrence and Wishart, 1990).

15. Paul Gilroy, *The Black Atlantic: Modernity and Double Consciousness* (Cambridge, MA: Harvard University Press, 1993), 15.

16. For more on the history of West Indian radicalism in the United Kingdom, see Trevor Carter, *Shattering Illusions: West Indians in British Politics* (London: Lawrence and Wishart, 1986); Carol Boyce Davies, *Left of Karl Marx: The Political Life of Black Communist Claudia Jones* (Durham, NC: Duke University Press, 2007); Winston James and Clive Harris, eds., *Inside Babylon: The Caribbean Diaspora in Britain* (London: Verso, 1993); Marika Sherwood, *Claudia Jones: A Life in Exile* (London: Lawrence and Wishart, 2000).

17. James Whitfield, *Unhappy Dialogue: The Metropolitan Police and Black Londoners in Post-war Britain* (Portland, OR: Willan, 2004), 22. These statistics were government estimates since accurate counting for new immigrants only began in 1955.

18. Cedric J. Robinson, *Black Marxism: The Making of the Black Radical Tradition* (London: Zed, 1983).

19. E. Patrick Johnson's conception of blackness as a performative yet nonetheless material construct informs this claim. He argues that "'Blackness' does not belong to any one individual or group. Rather, individuals or groups *appropriate* this complex and nuanced racial signifier in order to circumscribe its boundaries or to elude other individuals or groups." E. Patrick Johnson, *Appropriating Blackness: Performance and the Politics of Authenticity* (Durham, NC: Duke University Press, 2003), 2–3.

20. Brian W. Alleyne, *Radicals against Race: Black Activism and Cultural Politics* (New York: Berg, 2002), 29.

21. Irving Wardle, "Black Power Pep Plays," *Times*, March 24, 1969. For U.K. Foreign Office coverage of Black Power in the United States, see London, Public Record Office, Foreign Office (FO) 371, Americas–United States (AU) 1821/6.

22. Egbuna, *Destroy This Temple: The Voice of Black Power in England* (London: MacGibbon and Kee, 1971), 79. Following Carmichael's speech at the "Dialectics of Liberation" conference held at the Institute of Phenomenological Studies in London, Home Secretary Roy Jenkins proposed a successful ban that prevented Carmichael from returning to the United Kingdom. For more on these visits, see "British Ban on Stokely Carmichael," *Times*, July 28, 1967; David Cooper, ed., *The Dialectics of Liberation* (Baltimore: Penguin, 1968), back cover, 7; Norman Fowler, "Stokely Carmichael Recordings for Sale," *Times*, August 5, 1967; "Malcolm X Off to Smethwick," *Times*, February 12, 1965.

23. Cape Publishers in London released Carmichael and Charles Hamilton's *Black Power: The Politics of Liberation in America* in the United Kingdom in 1967; it is considered to be the ideological treatise of the U.S. movement.

24. See "British Ban on Stokely Carmichael"; and Egbuna, *Destroy This Temple*, 17.

25. The more militant UCPA was among a range of leftist groups organizing for racial change in Britain during this period, including the Campaign against Racial Discrimination (CARD), founded in 1965, and the Racial Adjustment Action Society (RAAS), founded in 1964. As Dilip Hiro argues, CARD and RAAS, respectively, reflected the differences between the styles of Martin Luther King Jr. and Malcolm X in the United States. Also in existence by 1968 were the Black Peoples Alliance (BPA), the Black Unity and Freedom Party (BUFP), and the Black Workers' Movement (BWM). For more on these groups, see Alleyne, *Radicals against Race*; Peter Fryer, *Staying Power: The History of Black People in Britain* (London: Pluto, 1984); Hiro, *Black British, White British*, 51–53; Ramdin, *Reimaging Britain*; Edward Scobie, *Black Britannia: A History of Blacks in Britain* (Chicago: Johnson, 1972).

26. Rita Marshall, "Black Power Men Launch Credo," *Times*, September 11, 1967.

27. Egbuna, *Destroy This Temple*, 21–22.

28. Marshall, "Black Power Men Launch Credo," 3.

29. Egbuna, *Destroy This Temple*, 148.

30. Egbuna, *Destroy This Temple*, 146, 145–46; Lazerow and Williams, introduction, 2; Hiro, *Black British, White British*, 91. For more on the U.S. Panthers' rejection of cultural nationalism, see Scot Brown, *Fighting for US: Maulana Karenga, the US Organization, and Black Cultural Nationalism* (New York: New York University Press, 2003), 113–20; Jeffrey O. G. Ogbar, *Black Power: Radical Politics and African-American Identity* (Baltimore: Johns Hopkins University Press, 2004), 94–95, 195–96. The Notting Hill Carnival is an annual two-day street festival in its eponymous neighborhood that celebrates the West Indian community in Britain. Cecily Jones, "Notting Hill Carnival," and Erin Somerville, "Notting Hill Riots," in *The Oxford Companion to Black British History*, ed. David Dabydeen, John Gilmore, and Cecily Jones (New York: Oxford University Press, 2007), 344–46, 346–48.

31. Smith, *An International History of the Black Panther Party*, 78; Cleaver, "Back to Africa," 211, 215, 225.

32. London, Public Record Office, Home Office 376/128; Commonwealth Immigration 63412/612/1, undated, but compiled on or before September 26, 1963, qtd in Whifield, *Unhappy Dialogue*, 23.

33. Ibid., 144, 158.

34. Metropolitan Police Report, "Queen vs. 'Black Panther' Defendants," March 18, 1970, DPP 2/4827, 2; "Summary of Facts," in *Regina v. Rupert Francis et al.*, DPP 2/4889, 1–2; Marshall, "Black Power Men Launch Credo."

35. "Summary of Facts," 2.

36. For statistics on the Mangrove Nine, see Vince Hines, *How Black People Overcame Fifty Years of Repression in Britain, 1945–1995*, vol. 1 (London: Zulu, 1998), 138; there were eleven defendants whose national origin was not listed in the court record.

37. Whitfield, *Unhappy Dialogue*, 48.

38. "Persons Charged Following the Black Panther Demonstration on the 2nd March 1970"; *Regina v. Rupert Francis et al.*, DPP 2/4889; ages of defendants are not provided in "The Mangrove Nine Protest" file.

39. U.K. Black Panther Movement, "Organised Action in Self Defence," London, Public Record Office, DPP, 1971–72.

40. The "Organised Action in Self Defence" flier claims that police arrested nineteen of the protestors, while the "Battle for Freedom at the Old Bailey" leaflet cites thirty arrests.

41. Mike Phillips and Trevor Phillips, *Windrush: The Irresistible Rise of Multi-racial Britain* (London: HarperCollins, 1998), 280–81.

42. Detective Sergeant D. Townley, Central Officer's Special Report, Metropolitan Police Criminal Investigation Department, March 30, 1972, in "Black Panther Movement, 'Battle for Freedom at the Old Bailey': Possible Offences for Contempt of Court during the Course of the Trial of the Mangrove Nine," London, Public Record Office, DPP, 1971–72.

43. "Black Panther Movement, 'Battle for Freedom at the Old Bailey': Possible Offences"; Letter from Leslie Boyd, Clerk of Central Criminal Court to Director of Public Prosecutions, December 16, 1971, in London, Public Record Office, DPP 2/5059.

44. Black Panther Movement, "Battle for Freedom at the Old Bailey," December 10, 1971, 1, in London, Public Record Office, DPP 2/5059.

45. Letter from P. J. Palmes to Clerk of Central Criminal Court, April 19, 1972, in London, Public Record Office, DPP 2/5059.

46. Although they are referred to as "coloured" in police records and testimony, Black Panther

defendants refer to themselves in the record as "black." City of London Public Prosecutions, "Queen vs. R. J. Francis, L. Anderson, E. Lecointe, K. Spencer, Black Panther Movement," London, Public Record Office, Marylebone Magistrates' Court, 1970.

47. The police record does not suggest how many officers entered the dance to look for the watch, citing the names of four officers and claiming that "other officers" were present.

48. "Summary of Facts," 1–2.

49. "Black Panther Rioters Get Suspended Sentences," *Times*, June 29, 1971.

50. Black Panther Movement, "Battle for Freedom at the Old Bailey," DPP 2/5059, 1.

51. Black Panther Movement, "Organised Action in Self Defence," DPP 2/4889.

52. Huey Newton and Bobby Seale, inspired by Frantz Fanon's psychoanalytic analysis of Algeria, viewed white police officers as a foreign occupying army. Evidence from Egbuna's writing suggests that Fanon influenced British Panthers as well. See Wendt, "The Roots of Black Power?" 159; Egbuna, *Destroy This Temple*, 154.

53. Black Panther Movement, "The Definition of Black Power," DPP 2/4827; 2/4889.

54. Madeleine Shaw, "Memorandum of a Conviction Entered in the Register of the Old Street Magistrates' Court," January 10, 1973, in *Regina v. Rupert Francis et al.*, DPP 2/4889; Metropolitan Police, "Antecedents of Edmund Lecointe," in *Regina v. Rupert Francis et al.*, DPP 2/4889.

55. Peter Oliver, court cross-examination, DPP 2/4889, 1970.

56. Peter Oliver, "Statement of Witness," September 7, 1970, DPP 2/4889, 1970.

57. Black Panther Movement, "Organised Action in Self Defence," DPP 2/4889.

58. Black Panther Movement, "Battle for Freedom at the Old Bailey," DPP 2/5059, 2.

59. "Case Note," 10–10A, in *Regina v. Rupert Francis et al.*, DPP 2/4889.

60. Black Panther Movement, "Battle for Freedom at the Old Bailey," DPP 2/5059, 2.

61. Black Panther Movement, "Release Bobby Seale, Black People, and All Progressive People in Britain," flier advertising March 2, 1970, demonstration, DPP 2/4827.

62. Egbuna, *Destroy This Temple*, 141.

63. Spencer, "Notes of Evidence," recorded by E. Robey, DPP 2/4827, 4.

64. Black Panther Movement, "Release Bobby Seale," DPP 2/4827.

65. Keith Spencer, "Notes of Evidence," recorded by E. Robey, DPP 2/4827, 4.

66. Black Panther Movement, "Battle for Freedom at the Old Bailey," DPP 2/5059, 2.

67. Jane Grant, "Statements in Case," DPP 2/4827, 4.

68. Black Panther Movement, "Release Bobby Seale," DPP 2/4827. In 1958, *The Listener*, a BBC magazine, reported that "the true progressive was essentially urban and middle class." A 1955 report titled *The Treatment of British P.O.W.'s in Korea* equated the progressive view with communism and claimed that progressives served as mouthpieces for communist propaganda. Both from "progressive, n." *Oxford English Dictionary*, 2nd ed. (Oxford: Oxford University Press, 1989).

69. William VanDeburg, *New Day in Babylon: The Black Power Movement and American Culture, 1965–1975* (Chicago: University of Chicago Press, 1992), 308.

70. Jacqueline Nassy Brown, "Diaspora and Desire: Gendering 'Black America' in Black Liverpool," in *Globalization and Race: Transformations in the Cultural Production of Blackness*, ed. Kamari Maxine Clarke and Deborah A. Thomas (Durham, NC: Duke University Press, 2006), 74. For an extended examination, see also Jacqueline Nassy Brown, *Dropping Anchor, Setting Sail: Geographies of Race in Black Liverpool* (Princeton, NJ: Princeton University Press, 2005).

71. A. Sivanandan, "The Heart Is Where the Battle Is: An Interview with the Author," in

Communities of Resistance: Writings on Black Struggles for Socialism (New York: Verso, 1990), 10.

72. Egbuna, *Destroy This Temple*, 155.

73. In this suggestion I am inspired by Jacquelyn Dowd Hall's desire to chronicle a "Long Civil Rights Movement" that is "harder to simplify, appropriate, and contain." Jacquelyn Dowd Hall, "The Long Civil Rights Movement and the Political Uses of the Past," *Journal of American History* 91 (2005): 1235.

"Glorifying the Jamaican Girl":

The "Ten Types—One People" Beauty

Contest, Racialized Femininities,

and Jamaican Nationalism

Rochelle Rowe

Jamaica, which not only by her own boast, but by world acclaim has long ago
shown the right concept which enables peoples of diverse races to live and
move together as one, has struck the final chord in a unique contest — TEN
TYPES–ONE PEOPLE.
— " 'Miss All-Spice' Winners," *Star*, November 19, 1955

In 1955, Jamaica celebrated a national festival, "Jamaica 300," that commemorated
three hundred years of Jamaica's history as a British colony. A highly visible part of
the year-long celebration was the "Ten Types–One People" female beauty contest,
which attracted three thousand participants and ran in the national tabloid, the *Star*,
from May to December.[1] The contest comprised ten separate competitions, each
of which represented a category for a specific skin tone. "Ten Types" produced ten
winners, one from each competition, who would all reign as beauty queens with no
overall winner presiding. The titles euphemistically pertained to races, ethnicities,
and colors, including "Miss Apple Blossom," "Miss Allspice," and "Miss Ebony."[2]
The ten categories, expressed through the female entrants' bodies, were paraded
alongside each other to suggest a racially harmonious Jamaica.

Radical History Review
Issue 103 (Winter 2009)   DOI 10.1215/01636545-2008-039
© 2009 by MARHO: The Radical Historians' Organization, Inc.

Exceptional for its time, the "Ten Types" beauty contest provides an opportunity to examine the spectacle of the racialized female body in the construction of a multiracial modern Jamaican identity. Though the nationalist planners of the "Jamaica 300" commemorations sought to circumnavigate overt references to British conquest and domination, the celebrations would invoke the legacy of inventing and objectifying racialized female bodies that had begun with the colonial encounter. While nationalists plotted a path to postwar modernity through political and economic development, they in fact figured on the European project of expansion that had launched the age of (European) modernity and that had relied on reading difference onto African female bodies in particular.[3] The "Ten Types" beauty contest symbolically called on the history of (en)gendering race through the bodies of Caribbean women, particularly women of African descent. Thus nationalist enthusiasts would mobilize an inheritance of racialized and gendered constructs to imagine a new Jamaicanness, even as they proposed a multiracial society that had overcome "race." Furthermore, they would use gendered constructs to renegotiate race, specifically African-descended racial identities, to infer Jamaica's departure from colonialism and entrance into the modernity of new nations.

The cultural critic Belinda Edmondson has identified the "New World mythology" of racial harmony and, more particularly, of racial mixing as a symbol of democratization in process. This trope of "hybridity as democracy" has become a paradigm of Caribbeanness, a "Caribbean romance" that, born of colonial invention, yet divorced from its original context, still lingers as a serviceable and iconic postcolonial symbol of the region. Edmondson has poignantly asked how such romances have become so established in the social and political discourse of Caribbeanness, thus revealing the need for historical attention to the construction of New World identities. The anthropologist Donna Goldstein has suggested that similar discourses of racial democracy in Brazil have survived in the popular imagination because of an underinvestigation of the role of gender in the construction of a national mythology. Along these lines, Natasha Barnes has considered Caribbean beauty contests as a historically politicized space, placing these competitions within a range of cultural activities through which contending social and ethnic groups clamored for ownership of the national iconography as prospective self-government loomed.[4]

The present article seeks to build on this work that situates and explores questions of gender in the role of nation building within the context of African diaspora studies. The mid-twentieth-century Jamaican movement for self-government produced a flurry of cultural nationalist programs. This heightened activity in efforts to define the nation provoked a continuum of Jamaican beauty contests where political and cultural elites attempted to deliver a paradigmatic, racially harmonious New World identity through a parade of feminine bodies.[5] At the same time, African-Jamaican cultural elites shared in a trajectory of African diaspora thought concerned with black advancement that problematized the figure of the black woman. They sought to refine an iconic black femininity by placing it in the service of an idea of modern nationhood that would be both proudly black and consummately Western.

Jamaican Cultural Nationalism and the Origins of "Ten Types"

The "Ten Types" contest sprang from the cultural nationalist impulses accompanying the Jamaican and larger West Indian independence movements. Some form of economic and political association among British West Indian colonies had been proposed for three centuries.[6] In 1938, mass labor uprisings throughout the British Caribbean, and the subsequent West Indian Royal Commission into the causes of suffering headed by Lord Moyne, undermined direct crown colony rule from London. The mass uprisings provided the impetus for renewed discussions of the British West Indian Federation and the creation of economically viable self-government for the islands.

This moment of mass political activism provided the initial spur for the formation of new political parties in Jamaica. By the 1950s, however, the two foremost political parties that had emerged, the People's National Party (PNP) and the Jamaica Labour Party (JLP), were dominated by middle-class, urban, educated men. Both parties lacked the participation of the mass of working people who had provided the initial mandate for their existence.[7] Jamaica's social composition reflected its history of "chattel slavery and Crown Colony oligarchy" with a small, white-identified minority of British expatriates, planters, and merchants at the top, a middling business and professional class, predominantly colored, but including Chinese, Syrian, Jewish, and some blacks, and an impoverished agro-proletariat at the bottom, predominantly black but including significant minorities of colored and Indian people.[8] Thus a middle-class proprietorship over the transition to self-government on behalf of a supposedly unready black populous emerged.[9]

Radical black nationalism, such as Marcus Garvey's Pan-Africanist program, failed to secure a place in formal representative politics.[10] Instead, the PNP, the party of Jamaican nationalism, promoted a gendered Victorian ideology of respectability and hard work. It celebrated a masculine image of the industrious black peasant as the wellspring of a decent black citizenry that would mature gradually through the political process. Though much of its membership was originally radicalized by Garveyism, the PNP primarily invested in a plural model that separated racial consciousness from national consciousness. The party engendered an indigenous, "creole" identity that emphasized the uniqueness of Jamaica, vacillating between pronouncements of the Jamaican racial paradise and willing this state into being. Jamaican nationalism, as Deborah Thomas writes, "knotted anti-colonial mobilization to middle-class respectability and cultural creolization."[11]

The idea of a commemorative tercentenary festival originated in 1954 under the JLP administration. The minister of finance Donald Sangster proposed the festival as a means of expanding a long-term economic agenda to combat severe unemployment and underemployment with foreign — specifically North American — investment and tourism. Jamaica's population was still predominantly rural, surviving through seasonal employment, smallholding cultivation, and with little formal welfare provision. Though the economy had grown progressively in the preceding decade, unemployment remained high and was projected to worsen with population growth. Large-scale outward migration had for generations been one of the few outlets for people seeking work, easing pressure on the economy, which was still characterized by a concentration of wealth among the planter and merchant oligarchy.[12]

The JLP initially proposed the celebrations as the commemoration of Jamaica's three hundred years as a British colony. However, they were quickly embarrassed by an outcry from the press and from political opponents who thought the festivities should celebrate the emergent Jamaican nation rather than the departing British rulers. The PNP, which took office in January 1955, promptly revised the tenor of the celebratory plans, changing it from a commemoration of three hundred years of British rule to a celebration of Jamaica's three hundred years as a national entity with a distinctive history, culture, and people. Such a celebration would serve the PNP's program of cultural nationalism, which had thus far included founding welfare associations aimed at community uplift and a cultivation of the "folk" arts.[13] For the PNP, the "Jamaica 300" event provided an opportunity to extend the nationalist spirit beyond its narrow middle-class following to the mass of working people and to encourage the latter to accept the sentiment of a united Jamaican identity.[14]

As part of "Jamaica 300," the "Ten Types" contest was designed to express the idealized model of a plural Jamaica. It reiterated an amenable historical record, something Howard Johnson has described as the selective "amnesia" of the plural Jamaica project.[15] The contest would indicate to both domestic and foreign audiences that Jamaica had resolved the so-called race problem, thereby establishing Jamaican modernity. Much like Brazil's official myth of racial democracy and the melting-pot rhetoric of the United States, "Ten Types" would serve as a metaphor for Jamaica's successful assimilation of once disparate peoples in democratic harmony. Theodore Sealy, the first black editor of the leading national newspaper, the *Daily Gleaner*, was appointed chair of the "Jamaica 300" organizing committee and wrote of "Ten Types": "Jamaica by its climate and geographical position, its past trading and history, has over the centuries become one of those focal points where peoples of diverse races meet and merge. It is from this merging that has developed that consciousness of nationhood reflected in this great modern contest not hitherto conceived in any other country."[16] This attempt to painlessly accommodate the colonial past through a beauty contest figured on an embedded history of making racial meanings through the bodies of women, one that was itself fundamental to the settlement and functioning of Jamaica's plantation economy and colonial society. Jennifer Morgan has used seventeenth-century European travel narratives to show that "ideas and information about brown [Amerindian] and black women" flowed into Europe prior to the settlement of plantations in the New World. Images and accounts, primarily produced by adventurers and prospective planters, informed the new plantation binaries of savage and civilized, African and European, black and white, slave and master. Gender had long served in the praxis of interpreting difference in early modern European society, and with European expansionism, it was the bodies of African women that were "read" primarily for significations of supposedly racial difference that would justify the Atlantic trade.[17]

The Caribbean continued as a "laboratory of European theorization" of presumed racial difference and of the effects of race mixing into the nineteenth and twentieth centuries when Indian and Chinese indentured labor and further European settlement added to the diversity of populations.[18] The female body has been at the forefront of the production of these "meanings," such as in the Victorian "trade in people's likenesses" between anthropologists and ethnographers. This trade produced a typology of racial designations that allowed Victorian gentlemen, for instance, to compare images of the immigrant Indian laborer, "the Cooly Woman," with the creolized, African-descended "Martinique Belle," both illustrating apparent racial "types" dwelling in the West Indies and their relative proximity to, or distance from, whiteness.[19] Given the history of the Caribbean as a place where racial hierarchy was invented and reproduced over centuries, the model of a plural Jamaica and its agent the "Ten Types" pageant marked an attempt to mask and contradict the Jamaican social environment.

"It Is the Women Who Make a Society, and Who Give to It Its Prevailing Tone": The "Miss Jamaica" Beauty Contest and Other Precursors to "Ten Types"

The "Ten Types" pageant was conceived as an alternative to the well-established "Miss Jamaica" beauty contest. "Miss Jamaica" began in 1929 and was sponsored by the *Gleaner*, which was then a publication still closely identified with planter and merchant interests and yet to have its first black editor. The *Gleaner* devised the pageant to boost its circulation, and in turn it provided ample visibility to finalists who gained notoriety and prestige from the event. Though it was well-publicized, the pageant remained an exclusive and essentially private occasion, associated with a close-knit, upper-class social circuit of white families. As Lucille Iremonger recalled in her memoirs, "The prizes were reserved for the daughters of the white planting plutocracy and the other old island families of the dominant caste. My family had come to regard themselves as having almost a prescriptive right to a place on the short list of finalists."[20]

Herbert De Lisser — author, journalist, and politician — produced the annual *Planter's Punch*, a society magazine concerned with upper-class Jamaican life. The *Punch* featured white women on its pages, resident Jamaicans, expatriate British, and touring English and American ladies. Women appeared in posed studio photographs and were eulogized as classical beauties. One feature, "Types of English Beauty," harped on the unchanging quality of Anglo-Saxon beauty through the ages.[21] Another item featured two white Jamaican women, Lucille Parks and Rita Gunter, both alumni of Oxford University, in a discursive tract on the relative merits and faults of (white) Jamaican femininity in contrast to English ladyhood. For upper-class white Jamaicans, the image, behavior, and deportment of the idealized femme were imagined as the yardstick of respectable identity for the community. As Lucille Parks remarked, "It is the women who make a society, and who give to it its prevailing tone."[22] The white-identified minority policed the frontier of race, attempting to preserve intact the prestige of whiteness and to identify whiteness with Jamaicanness, even as constitutional decolonization gradually encroached on white political hegemony.[23]

Brown and black Jamaicans were hardly enthusiastic about the "Miss Jamaica" pageant. The colored Jamaican poet and feminist Una Marson revealed the infamy with which the all-white "Miss Jamaica" contest was regarded among the brown and black middle classes, saying, "Some amount of expense and disappointment could be saved numbers of dusky ladies who year after year enter the beauty competition if the promoters of the contest would announce in the daily press that very dark or black beauties would not be considered." Marson aligned anticolonial nationalism to race and to the notion of the representative bodies of beauty queens. She noted that "there is a growing feeling in many quarters that 'Miss Jamaica' should be a type of girl who is more truly representative of the majority of Jamaicans."[24]

In 1947, such an opportunity seemed to arise. Aimee Webster, a wealthy colored Jamaican, briefly acquired "Miss Jamaica" and incorporated it into her new "Miss British Caribbean" contest. The "Miss British Caribbean" contest was intended to promote Webster's new *Caribbean Post* and, like the publication itself, to support the proposed British West Indian Federation and brought together contestants from West Indian islands.[25] Webster sought to herald the merits of the respectable, "well-born," brown middle-class young woman as a symbol of the modernity, sophistication, and optimism of the postwar West Indian territories.[26]

Under Webster's direction, the winners of both "Miss Jamaica" and "Miss British Caribbean" tended to be light-skinned brown women, the daughters of colored lawyers and civil servants. Racially mixed identities in the Caribbean were not static but broadly defined and varied according to the social context in which a body was being read. Brown beauty queens were considered the best examples of upper middle-class, mixed-raced society, and they tended to be the wealthiest and most light-skinned of the candidates. They were selected as finalists because they happened to possess phenotypes associated with whiteness and therefore with beauty, and yet they also emblemized the emerging potency of "coloredness" as a new political force in the Caribbean. Phyllis Wong, a contestant of colored and Chinese heritage, was chosen as "Miss Trinidad" for 1947 and described in the *Post* as "a true cross-section of Trinidad's cosmopolitan population" and the authentic choice of a multiracial audience that "instinctively recognized [Wong] as typifying the exotic West Indian of tomorrow."[27] "Raven-haired and olive-complexioned" Phyllis Woolford of Guyana, the colored daughter of a Queen's Council barrister, Sir Eustace Woolford, was crowned "Miss British Caribbean 1948."[28] For the *Caribbean Post*, Woolford and Wong typified "the blending of racial characteristics that has resulted today in a very definite West Indian type."[29]

Webster's *Post* and the "Miss British Caribbean" contest revealed the beginnings of the marriage of the project of cultural nationalism to the ideal of mixed-raced female beauty. The progressive West Indian identity Webster espoused was literally resolved through the female mixed-raced body; furthermore, colored femininity carried a special purchase over West Indianness itself. This rhetoric would be deployed in the "Ten Types" beauty contest and in its aftermath, specifically in relation to Jamaican identity. However, after Webster's short management of the "Miss Jamaica" contest, the pageant fell briefly into a lapse and was later resurrected by the Bodybuilder's Association in 1954, a private health society managed by the colored businessman Keith Rhino. The Jamaica Tourist Board, a government-funded entity, partnered with the Bodybuilder's Association to sponsor the pageant. They together invested more money into the contest than previous franchise holders and professionalized the role of "Miss Jamaica" as both a national representative and a cultural ambassador.[30] "Miss Jamaica" titleholders won lucrative prizes, foreign trips, and began to attend "Miss World" and other international beauty competitions. In this format the brown participants who had been singled out by Webster's contest lost status, unable to compete with white Jamaicans and to rise above the occasional place in the final lineup. Black women, meanwhile, continued to be altogether absent from the contest.

While "Miss Jamaica" continued to represent the ideals of a white Jamaica, the PNP, much like Webster, demonstrated that it was alert to the possibilities of elaborating the party's project of economic and cultural nationalism through a beauty contest. In 1950, it sponsored a contest that divided the city of Kingston by area. Titles included "Miss West Kingston" and "Miss East Kingston," the winners of both of whom were featured in the *Caribbean Post* as "Dark Beauties" alongside a column of beauty advice tailored to women of dark complexions, from "chocolate to Ebony."[31] These contests, which were local and directly addressed Kingston's black populations, were presumed to be a good vehicle for aiding the PNP's project of cultural nationalism among the poor. In 1955, the Kingston and St. Andrew Corporation, a PNP developmental organization, proposed a "Miss City of Kingston" competition to showcase Kingston as the "premier metropolis of the British Caribbean" as part of the national festival "Jamaica 300."[32]

In the same year, Theodore Sealy used his editorial in the *Gleaner* to reproach "Miss Jamaica" organizers for appointing yet another white "queen" in

Marlene Fenton. Sealy called it irresponsible to encourage foreigners to associate the better part of Jamaican society with whiteness and refinement at the expense of the wider population, whom he feared was still imagined as backward. As the organizer of the "Ten Types," Sealy set about creating a Jamaican ideal that placed the entire population on a par with the social cache of whiteness and would therefore cast Jamaicans as progressive and modern.[33]

Ten Types: "Uncovering a Wealth of Feminine Charm"
The *Star* launched "Ten Types" in May 1955 as a uniquely inclusive beauty contest, the first of its kind, with a plural political message and a cleverly implied critique of the all-white "Miss Jamaica" contest summarized in the "Ten Types" slogan, "Every lassie has an equal chance."[34] While it is important to distinguish "Ten Types" from the racially exclusive "Miss Jamaica," both pageants represented the interests and tactics of the establishment, relying as they did on commercial sponsorship, press exposure, and the involvement of the Jamaica Tourist Board. Publicity for "Ten Types" appeared regularly in the *Star* and the *Gleaner* and revealed the grand scale of the contest and the organizers' commitment to demonstrating its national scope. The "Ten Types" competition would tour the island, "uncovering a wealth of feminine charm," almost scouring the countryside for Jamaica's hidden beauties.[35] There would be seven months of preliminaries between the launch of the contest in May and the final unveiling of the winners at Christmas. To do this work the *Star* staffed a caravan with its representatives, including a photographer, a reporter, and members of the Jamaica Federation of Women to act as chaperones and to encourage participants to enter.

The Jamaica Federation of Women was modeled after the Women's Institute, which had strongholds in Canada and the United Kingdom and preached a conservative feminism. It was committed to the sort of social work among the rural black poor prescribed by the Moyne Commission and by subsequent expert advice on development in the West Indies. The commission recommended that middle-class women should encourage working black women to adopt housewifery, thereby stabilizing a nuclear family and providing essential welfare. The federation, among many other projects, organized mass weddings and the formal registration of fathers. Its organizational ranks generally duplicated social hierarchies, and though black working women could become members, they were also viewed as the natural constituency of the organization in need of help and guidance.[36] The federation's involvement in "Ten Types" not only lent respectability to the contest's proceedings but also dovetailed with the racialized and gendered project of uplift that was the professed aim of plural nationalism.

The press published the schedule of the "Star Beauty Caravan" for visits to Jamaica's villages and towns and employed local correspondents to distribute leaflets. As a rule, judging panels had to include some members drawn from the color group they were assigned to judge. Throughout the competition, the public was invited to vote for its favorites on the basis of the published photographs of entrants. Final judging took place in private, not before an audience, contrary to beauty contest custom. The process resulted in ten separate beauty queens, each one crowned alongside her fellow queens as a national representative:

Miss Ebony—A Jamaican girl of black complexion.
Miss Mahogany—A Jamaican Girl of Cocoa-brown Complexion.
Miss Satinwood—A Jamaican Girl of Coffee-and-Milk Complexion.
Miss Golden Apple—A Jamaican Girl of Peaches-and-Cream Complexion.
Miss Apple Blossom—A Jamaican Girl of European Parentage.
Miss Pomegranate—A Jamaican girl of White-Mediterranean Parentage.
Miss Sandalwood—A Jamaican Girl of Pure Indian Parentage.
Miss Lotus—A Jamaican Girl of Pure Chinese Parentage.
Miss Jasmine—A Jamaican Girl of Part Chinese Parentage.
Miss Allspice—A Jamaican Girl of Part Indian Parentage.

"Ten Types" attempted to universalize a feminine standard by showing that women of differently raced bodies could conform to a recognizable Western ideal. The selected beauty queens were all, unsurprisingly, slim and petite in frame. In the photograph they are posed in a row, tiptoed, hands on hips, heads turned to face the camera (fig. 1). The array of slim-figured women in identical poses reframed discourses of racialized othering. It suggested instead a universal beauty standard to which all Jamaican women could conform, and furthermore that the differently raced ethnic groups of Jamaica could assimilate to modernity.[37]

The imagined color categories of the "Ten Types" parade appeared to decimalize the Jamaican demographic profile. That is, they appeared to give some measured proportionality to the division of Jamaican society into tenths, as though each category represented a tenth of the diverse whole of the population. In the process, they confined the most frequently occurring skin shade—the dark brown skin of obvious African descent—to only one of these categories. Moreover, the visual array gave primacy to the categories that referenced obvious racial mixes, those that reflected the ethnic composition of the colored middle class. In the parade of feminine beauty, brownness was imagined expansively and occupied a number of the given categories. The array of light brown beauty queens suggested the preeminence of brownness as a social category in the ascendancy, worthy of broad national representation. The "Ten Types" panorama of feminine beauty, which attempted to deliver a multiracial model of plural Jamaica, was therefore weakened by what it revealed about the persistent unease with the place of blackness in the new political order at this heightened moment of cultural nationalism.

Miss Ebony   Miss Mahogany   Miss Satinwood   Miss Allspice   Miss Sandalwood   Miss Golden Apple   Miss Jasmine   Miss Pomegranate   Miss Lotus   Miss Appleblossom

A spectrum of Jamaican beauty displayed before a cannon of Fort Charles, Port Royal. 'Ten types: one people' was the heading of this contest, run in 1955 as part of the 'Jamaica 300' celebrations

Figure 1. "Ten Types, 1955." Stationery Office, London

Miss Ebony: Imagining Black Femininity in Modern Jamaica

Though the categories provided an array of Jamaican identities that seemed to spell out the project of a plural Jamaica, the most striking element of the "Ten Types" contest to contemporary audiences was the novelty of a category for dark-skinned African Jamaican women. In 1959, "Ten Types" was relaunched as an annual competition for each of the color categories. The "Miss Ebony" contest, now renamed as a competition for "coal-black or cool-black girls," was placed at the head of the proceedings and allocated the first year, with "Miss Mahogany" to follow in 1960, and so on through each category.[38] The exceptional attention paid to "Miss Ebony" makes it worthy of further exploration in this discussion.

Dark-skinned women were in 1959 largely missing from beauty contests, just as they were largely invisible as figures of feminine desirability in newspaper advertising, glossy publications, and cinema.[39] African-descended women seeking glamorous careers were restricted by the confines of racialized binaries that had always accompanied their presence in the New World. Black and brown women were typically called on to perform the polar opposite to the ideal of chaste white femininity: the libidinous and primal Other. Those brown women who did manage to achieve some success as actresses, models, and entertainers were celebrated for their ability to break through these racial barriers. The Jamaican press closely followed the rise of the "brownskin" model in U.S. advertising and proudly reported on the smattering of light-brown actresses, such as Eartha Kitt and Lena Horne, who had breached Hollywood.[40] However, most women of African descent working in the entertainment industry, whether dark or light-skinned, seldom appeared in the press and were usually nightclub dancers in Caribbean resorts or in North American and European cities.[41] By contrast, the "Miss Ebony" contest raised the possibility of a desirable and respectable black femininity that an entire community of dark-skinned, black-identified Jamaicans, both male and female, could share in and were expected to aspire toward. Moreover, the "Miss Ebony" contest positioned black women as figurative symbols of Jamaican blackness and as "exemplar[s] of social, sexual, and racial parity."[42]

As part of the PNP's project of cultural nationalism and uplift policy among poor black people, the "Miss Ebony" contest also served as a particularly important symbol of blacks' capacity for dignity and progress: to show that a black woman could perform ably in a supposedly white space. Through "Miss Ebony," the *Star* inferred the promise of progression for the black "race" itself. It was a bold departure and yet also a necessary fixture, showing that the Jamaican nation happily accommodated all within it. The "Ten Types" panorama, with the novelty of "Miss Ebony" attached, was essentially a gesture at fair play.

Black male middle-class leaders were the primary public discussants of the "Miss Ebony" contest, and their commentary is particularly revealing of a gendered ideology of color — the symbolic path to Jamaica's progression — under construction. There is some evidence that black women supported the "Ten Types" contests, not least the many women who entered the competitions and whose voices are missing from the historical record. Furthermore there is some indication that nationalist-minded women shared in the political rhetoric of cultural nationalism articulated through feminine beauty. Marson had been bold enough to critique "Miss Jamaica" for its exclusion of black women, and Webster had organized her own pageant. Lady Allan, the widow of the black politician Lord Allan, was assigned to judge the "Miss Ebony" category and praised the contest for its attention to black women, saying, "it brings out some of our really good-looking Jamaican girls — if I use the term natives they might not like it, but that is what I mean — it brings out the girls who would otherwise not get a chance."[43] The apparent support among some women of color for more inclusive beauty competitions, rather than a straightforward opposition to beauty competitions in general as exploitative of women, reflects a trajectory of black feminist thought concerned with restoring selfhood to black women, what Barnes has called the "desire to be fully constituted as 'women' in a Western conceptual categorization that has traditionally made women of color its 'Other.'"[44]

The publisher Evon Blake, the editor of the *Spotlight* and *Newday* news magazines, seized on the slim evidence of brown women's successes in beauty contests as a sign of wider social improvements in Jamaica and elsewhere in the British Caribbean. Blake subscribed to the project of a plural Jamaica and praised the "Miss

Ebony" contest as a progressive social project delivering self-respect to black women. Like Sealy, his seniority as a black professional made him a rare figure whose career breached a world dominated by white businessmen and colored professionals. A self-made man who had overcome considerable odds, Blake posed himself as a "Race Man" and a "champion" of antiracist campaigning and yet as a disciplinarian of the "Negro element." He challenged racism—such as racist employment policy—but he rebuked black nationalism. Blake endorsed the plural project as one that imbibed liberal principles of equality of opportunity for all.[45]

Spotlight featured Miss Ebony 1959, Doreen Bryan, on its front cover. Blake praised the contest's "sociological import," its ability "to give black girls a firm consciousness of their own beauty." He suggested that black women were "victims of post-slavery propaganda that projected 'whites' as superior and 'blacks' as inferior" and that they thus had a particular susceptibility to a racial inferiority complex. Blake reproduced an account, apparently from a contest organizer, of the diminished racial pride of the "typical" black "office girl," a "type" who, it was alleged, had avoided the contest in droves: "The coal-black Civil Servant girl would consider it an insult if you called her ebony. She tries desperately to lighten her shade and will not face up to the fact that she is wasting her time for her best bet is to cultivate her own type of beauty."[46] This comment is more important as a figurative rhetorical anecdote than as the verbatim account of an organizer, or indeed as a reflection of any black women's responses to the contest. Blake used this example to underline what he regarded as the psychological victimization of the black woman, a person who bore a pathological denial of her essential self, something that would, by implication, eventually inhibit the progress of the race.

Blake's attack on the figure of the black woman haunted by her color echoes a Fanonian gendering of the black struggle. Lola Young has shown that Frantz Fanon absented the black female subject in *Black Skin, White Masks*, relying on fictionalized accounts of black women to cast them as complicit in the potential annihilation of the black race through their own misplaced desire for whiteness. Michelle Wright has identified this absenting of the black female subject as consistent with a trajectory of black intellectual thought in which black women appear as caricatures.[47] Similarly, in his characterization of the black struggle, Blake constructs an allegorical "choice" for black women: to serve either as symbolic figures of progress or as ones of paralysis. Either they willingly cast themselves as proud black women or languish in a state of self-hatred that inhibits the wider (male) progress of the race.

While Blake chastised the unproud "office girl," an allegory for the black middle-class woman, he praised the transformation, with the aid of "brush and comb," of "country girls" into beauties fit to be seen in a national contest. Blake reveled in the novelty of the "Cinderella-like transformation" of the black finalists now stepping into the limelight. He embellished the *Star*'s account of searching the country for beauties. The "Miss Ebonies," he suggested, were "unsophisticated country girls" from the "humblest" backgrounds, buried deep in the countryside. In fact the eventual winner, Bryan, was a secretary and a resident of Mountain View, St. Andrew, a new development in the suburban hinterland of Kingston.[48]

Blake's praise for the "country girls" who became beauty contestants reveals something of the appetite among the ambitious black, male-dominated, middle-class leadership to place black feminine icons at the service of the cause of black advancement. African Jamaican welfare organizations welcomed the "Ten Types" competition and "Miss Ebony" in particular. With it, they embraced the beauty contest format as a new means of challenging racial discrimination. The Afro–West Indian Welfare League petitioned the Bodybuilder's Association to alter "Miss Jamaica" along the lines of "Ten Types," so that black women would be included in the contest. The league even offered to sponsor "dark-skinned" candidates "of beauty, poise, and intelligence" and to provide two black Jamaicans for the judging panel. In 1960, the Jamaican branch of the United Negro Improvement Association (UNIA), the movement founded by Marcus Garvey, proposed its own socially conscious beauty competition. The UNIA aimed at the "Social and Economic uplift of the colored peoples of the world to a status of respectability and responsibility." Its contest would offer prizes geared toward educating and training women out of poverty.[49]

So important were beauty contests as symbols of power that in 1961, Millard Johnson, a radical black nationalist and an embarrassment to the new political establishment, picketed the rounds of "Miss Jamaica." Since 1959, "Miss Jamaica" had begun a glacial pace of change by crowning very light-skinned colored winners. Johnson protested the contest's racial discrimination against the black majority with placards reading "Jamaica is Black," "Who do these girls represent?" "Down with Color Discrimination," and, most significant to the search for black feminine icons, "Beauty is Black."[50]

As a response to Johnson's campaign, the acerbic *Spotlight* columnist Sylvia Slade (perhaps a pseudonym) endorsed Johnson's argument against "Miss Jamaica" for its continued exclusion of darker Jamaican women. Slade agreed this was a potent metaphor of exclusion at a vital moment of political transition when independence was imminent. Jamaica elected by referendum to leave the British West Indian Federation in 1961 and was set to pursue political independence alone. Slade itemized the remaining problems with the "Miss Jamaica" contest, but unlike Johnson, she did not critique the project of plural nationalism. Instead, Slade heaped praise on "Ten Types" as the worthy alternative to "Miss Jamaica" and suggested that nationalizing the latter contest would secure a fairer deal.[51]

In 1962, the black *Gleaner* sports writer Alva Ramsay suggested in a public letter that in the year of Jamaican independence, a dark-skinned black woman should be crowned "Miss Jamaica": "I suggest either we go into the hedges and byways and select a Negro girl as 'Miss Jamaica' for the independence year or we adopt a modified Star ["Ten Types"] pattern and have four queens, — one a negro girl, one a white girl, one a Chinese and one an Indian."[52] In seeking a relatively untainted image of black femaleness to elevate to the level of feminine icon, Ramsay summoned the trope of the rural innocent. Ramsay drew on the black intellectual tradition that privileged the image of the industrious black peasant to situate blackness in the political landscape of a Jamaican future.

Two years later, Ramsay and his organization, the Council for Afro-Jamaican Affairs, began its own "Miss Jamaica Nation" contest to rival "Miss Jamaica." The "Miss Jamaica Nation" contest combined imagery of an upright peasantry with gendered articulations of a new blackness linked to Africa. Black beauty queens were verbally depicted as unadulterated country dwellers, in keeping with an ennobled category of black peasantry, even as they delivered an accomplished feminine performance of groomed appearance, deportment, and mannerisms that were predicated on their consumption of Western beauty culture. These articulate, dark-skinned black women would be sent to Africa as unofficial cultural ambassadors and as agents of mutual learning as new African nations emerged independent from the British Empire. The first winner, Yvonne Whyte, came from a middle-class professional background but was praised at her crowning by Senator Kenneth McNeill as "the first real country girl to win a beauty contest."[53] Whyte, who had an enthusiastic following among black Jamaicans, made a visit to the independence celebrations of Nyasaland, soon to be Malawi. Thus Whyte represented a figurative link between decolonizing Africa and blacks emerging from colonial Jamaica. The "Miss Jamaica Nation" pageant therefore mobilized Africa as a "symbolic referent" of what Deborah Thomas has called "modern blackness," which both "engaged and rejected Western visions of progress and development."[54]

Black middle-class men, who took varying positions on nationalism — from those adopting the plural model, which attempted to mask racial inequality and prescribed uplift as a social leveler, to those concerned about a crisis of racial disempowerment — sought iconic imagery of black femininity. They regarded the black beauty queen as an essential allegory of black advancement but showed lingering unease about how this figure should look and perform. This vein of black thought, which mobilized black femininity as political tool, had a precedent in Jamaica and beyond. In 1895, Robert Love, a Bahamian-born black nationalist and Garvey's mentor, had called for the betterment of black women who would become the cultured wives of a new generation of black male leaders. Garvey himself praised an ideal black womanhood, for example in his 1927 poem "The Black Woman." In the United States, the African American leadership had a similar preoccupation with the idealized figure of black femininity. From the late nineteenth century on, the black press organized beauty competitions and constructed a black feminine ideal, the "New Negro Woman," as an instructive guide for its readership.[55]

Paradoxically, the sought-after black feminine icon would not, like the "office girl," succumb to normative values for feminine desirability, that is, she would not mimic "white beauty." The ideal black woman would somehow embody these normative values, the very essence of the beauty-contest format, but not appear ashamed of her African features. As the figure of Miss Ebony marked a dramatic transformation from country girl to beauty queen, so, too, would the mass of Jamaican people undergo transformation. The iconic black femme acquired modernity and sophistication just as she had acquired "beauty, poise and charm," and she did so on behalf of the nation. The allegorical black femininity of the "Miss Ebony" contest found a welcome reception among the black leadership, who saw it less as an agent for the project of plural Jamaica than as a motif of black progress in Jamaica.

Responses to "Ten Types" from Abroad

"Ten Types" soon aroused the interest of media voices from overseas. Journalists were enthralled by questions of race in the New World at this transitional moment of civil rights activism and antiapartheid struggles. For the U.S. journalist Edward Scott, writing for the *Havana Post* in Cuba, the "Miss Ebony" competition most exemplified the essence of the "Ten Types" message of nonconfrontational racial politics and of black political ambition. Scott described "Ten Types" as a model of racial tolerance and reserved particular praise for the humility shown by Miss Ebony: "I do not know who made up that list of ten names, but it is a masterpiece of poetry, dignity and good taste. The various qualifications are beautifully prepared and I find myself admiring particularly the little Jamaican girl who does not protest that it is undemocratic to have a class for 'Miss Apple Blossom,' but who readily admits that she is 'a Jamaican girl of black complexion' and proudly enters her name in the competition for 'Miss Ebony.'"[56] Scott's response engaged with the subtext of restraint in the model of a plural Jamaica, the ethos of the "Jamaica 300" festival. As with the "office girl," who should learn to cultivate her own type of beauty, black claims for full democratic representation ought to be managed and contained. Black political ambition threatened the status quo. The work of the "Ten Types" contest to decimalize the Jamaican racial profile in this way was to suggest the sublimation of blackness, where blackness signified a dangerous presence that threatened to overturn white privilege.

The visiting South African writer Peter Abrahams asked wryly whether an overall national representative was to be chosen from the "Ten Types" array of women: "With fine subtlety, the contest was both racial and multiracial. . . . Black girls competed amongst themselves; Chinese and Chinese-colored amongst themselves; the fair competed only against the fair . . . . I wondered and asked, whether the organizers would, after they had chosen the winners from the ten types, choose a reigning queen from one of the ten. No one knew. People tended to shy away from this."[57] The North American press audience found in the decimalization of the Jamaican demographic profile an appealing message. *Time* and *Life* magazines, both with million-strong circulations, emphasized the mythology. *Life* reproduced its "Ten Types" feature in its international edition. *Time* informed its readers that "because of the tangled racial mixture of the island colony's population of 1,500,000," ten beauty queens would be chosen "for each of ten racial-color groups."[58] To some commentators, "Ten Types" was so successful in dispersing the threat of black political power and in anesthetizing racial conflict that it was also interpreted as the visual display of the end of racism.

Unlike those who looked for reassurance of a black political threat quelled, the African American society magazine *Ebony* sought proof of a racial paradise that might offer hope for a U.S. black bourgeoisie. *Ebony* sent both its chief photographer and its managing editor to Jamaica to cover the finals of the competition. The *Ebony* team was hosted by a Jamaica Tourist Board eager to show off the "Ten Types" success story. Marshall Wilson, *Ebony*'s white photographer, took "Ten Types" as a model of Jamaican racial harmony with the power to convert racists:

[Jamaica is] making an invaluable contribution to the development of better race relations in the United States. . . . Travelers coming to the island from the United States . . . are very much interested to find that discrimination does not exist in Jamaican hotels or night clubs. Those Americans who believe in equality of races are able to point to the island as an example of how various peoples can live together in harmony. Those who are in favor of segregation are at first amazed—and often converted. By mixing on a social level with cultured colored persons, even the most die-hard believer in segregation begins to have doubts about his convictions.[59]

Ebony frequently looked to the Caribbean for evidence of racial harmony and black advancement. Beauty queens featured prominently in these readings. If there was a crisis of race in the United States, then at least elsewhere in the African diaspora, specifically in the Americas, race—and, implicitly, blackness—was not only happily accommodated in society but also apparently represented in democratic leadership.

Following its "Ten Types" coverage, *Ebony* produced an article on Dutch-controlled Suriname, which, like Jamaica, was a postemancipation, postindenture American society with a diverse population, rival ethnic nationalisms, and a degree of internal self-government. *Ebony* featured an array of Surinamese beauty queens from separate ethnic competitions, declared Suriname a racial paradise, and pondered whether the country welcomed African American migrants. That *Ebony* sought a utopia for a black bourgeoisie indicates not only a wider diasporic concern for the future path of a modern black race but also that the solutions were to be found within the New World African diaspora itself.[60]

For the Jamaica Tourist Board, "Ten Types" provided a new vernacular of fair dealing. Presumably buoyed by the positive responses from abroad, the board used the approach and influence of "Ten Types" to answer persistent criticism of unfair employment policies, as when it announced in *Spotlight* that it had recruited a new batch of female clerical staff:

TYPICAL JAMAICAN STAFF greet visitors to Jamaican Tourist Board headquarters in Kingston. Ranging in shade from mahogany to pale pink, each is a honey—and a clipper in efficiency. To get this eye-filling cross-section Chairman Abe Issa and Secretary Phillip Barker-Benfield last year fine-screened 400-odd applicants. Said Abe: We could easily have filled the jobs with all fair-complexioned girls. But we wanted none of that. As an agency spending public funds, we felt obligated to set an example of drawing our staff from all the various color shades represented in the islands, because efficiency is no respecter of race or color.[61]

Clearly, the "Ten Types" competition had done much to popularize the notion of a plural Jamaica abroad. But despite its ability to represent a racial democracy, the contest also revealed both a persistent unease with the African female body and an attempt to contain the political energies of the black population. Ultimately, the overriding image of "Ten Types" was an expansive representation of brownness that suggested brown identity as the natural representative motif of Jamaica.

Conclusion: "Miss Jamaica" and Brown Femininity as National Motif

Though the "Ten Types" competition stimulated accusations of racial discrimination in the older "Miss Jamaica" contest, the "Miss Jamaica" competition continued as the most prestigious and lucrative of beauty contests on the island. Dark-skinned contestants of "Ten Types" competitions did not fare well in the "Miss Jamaica" contest. In 1959, the first of a slew of light-skinned women triumphed. Sheila Chong was celebrated in the now-familiar language of harmonious race relations exemplified in feminine beauty. Chong was of Chinese and colored parentage. Her diverse racial heritage dominated the press coverage; she was cast as the literal embodiment of Jamaicanness. As *Newday* put it, "This is the first time the queen seemed to please everyone. Sheila Chong is a typical Jamaican girl. A Negro-Chinese-Syrian composite."[62] Light-skinned brown women dominated the pageant, with few exceptions, for the next two decades and beyond. The light-brown Miss Jamaica combined an image of femininity that met dominant aesthetic values and satisfied calls for typicality and cultural authenticity in a national representative.

Brown femininity had become *the* leitmotif of Jamaican identity. The new women's glossy press, *Vanity* and *Jamaican Housewife*, featured brown cover girls almost without exception. They glorified the "golden-brown" skin tones of aspiring models, actresses, and singers. One *Vanity* travel writer in Africa, grasping for a reference to counterpose against the beauty of Senegalese women, summarized this iconic role, "the Jamaican woman of mixed blood is the most beautiful I know in the

Caribbean."[63] On the eve of independence, in August 1962, the *Gleaner* columnist Frank Hill suggested that members of Jamaica's brown population were the only people who were truly indigenous to the island, "the only group created out of the Jamaican environment."[64]

Nationalists who promoted a plural Jamaica unconsciously revealed the weakness of the model for delivering their essential message: that the critical harmonizing element of racial democracy was in fact the presence of a mixed-racial group. Where plural Jamaica was the official message, one that masked racism, the trope of hybridity, the seemingly natural realization of racial democracy, was increasingly literalized through the body of the brown woman of mixed racial heritage. From the "Ten Types" color spectrum of beauty queens, nationalists inferred the racelessness of Jamaican society. The brown Miss Jamaica ultimately summarized this supposedly raceless ideal.

Fittingly, the "Ten Types" contest assumed pride of place in projecting the mythology of Jamaican racial democracy into the postindependence era. Sealy won a lead role in organizing another Jamaican national event, the celebrations to mark Jamaican independence on August 6, 1962. Sealy took part in formulating the new national motto announced as "Out of Many, One People." He later tentatively acknowledged the role of the "Ten Types — One People" beauty competitions in shaping the motto. He recalled, "the contest . . . was so popular that the concept entered the public consciousness and it was probably by force of habit that the members of the Legislature in 1962 chose the expression, 'Out of Many, One People.' "[65] Sealy's assessment is not entirely accurate, for the Legislative Council was not in session when the national motto was announced in April 1962. Rather, the phrase was urged on by the Working Committee who needed a motto for publication on promotional material, suggesting a more direct input from Sealy as the "Ten Types" organizer and committee chair.[66] In his handwritten unfinished manuscript, the outgoing chief minister Norman Manley at first suggested the national motto was his own idea, but he later corrected this assertion to write that he was only "part-author."[67] Just as "Ten Types" had crowned a first Jamaican national festival, "Jamaica 300," so had "Miss Jamaica" alos entered the national embrace, becoming the glamorous centerpiece of the government's new annual "Jamaica Festival" from 1963 onward.

The "Ten Types" competition replaced race with a gendered ideology of color in which brownness symbolically desensitized racial confrontation and blackness was marginalized. Black leadership engaged with the national project took up the beauty contest as an antiracist campaigning tool, but it struggled to reconnect racial and national consciousness through the body of the idealized black beauty queen. Displaying a persistent unease with the ability of the African (female) body to represent modernity, a black, male middle-class leadership ultimately idealized a darker complexioned black femininity as representing the potential for the transformation of a primitive and politically unready black populace. From the decimalizing array of "Ten Types" however, brown femininity, expansively represented, emerged as the figurative shorthand for modern Jamaica.

Notes

I am grateful for the many suggestions and observations offered during the course of my research in Jamaica, particularly for the support of James Robertson, David Dodman, Mark Figueroa, Swithin Wilmot, and Carolyn Cooper at the University of the West Indies. Thank you to the anonymous readers and editors of *RHR* for their thoughtful contributions to this essay. Thanks also to Mary Ellen Curtin, Rivke Jaffe, Peter Gurney, Cathryn Wilson, and Annette Arthur. Thank you to the National Library of Jamaica. This essay was first presented at the Department of Geography "brown bag" seminar at the University of the West Indies, Mona, and at a symposium at the Victoria and Albert Museum, "Dress and the African Diaspora: Tensions and Flows." I am grateful for the comments made at these gatherings.

1.   Theodore Sealy, "How We Celebrated Our First Independence: A Personal Recollection," *Jamaica Journal* 46 (1982): 2–13. The "Ten Types" competition began in 1955 and resumed in 1959 until its demise in 1963. The *Gleaner* claimed that six thousand women had their photographs taken for entry into the competitions ("LaYacona Takes Top Award in Photo Competition," *Gleaner*, July 29, 1985). It is likely that the figure of six thousand participants relates to the number of women attracted to the pageant over its entire lifetime from 1955 to 1963. Hereafter, the "Ten Types — One People" beauty contest is referred to as "Ten Types." Thanks to the Arts and Science Research Council.

2.   I make reference to "white," "colored" or "brown," and "black" or "Negro" people throughout this essay. These were the contemporary color identifiers used in Jamaican society, where *white* referred to British expatriates and the descendants of European settlers including Sephardic Jews, *colored* referred to racially mixed people of a variety of complexions, though they were usually light-skinned, and *Negro* referred to dark-skinned Jamaicans of predominantly African descent. It is also noteworthy that to some extent the predominant white-colored-black social matrix absorbed certain "immigrant" identities such as Jewish, Indian, or Chinese insofar as these individuals acquired wealth and status or intermarried with members of the white-colored-black matrix. Racial terminology was (and is) unstable and varied according to context, both in the Jamaican vernacular and in print; however, the term *colored* refers mostly to a racially mixed, light-skinned, and usually middle-class identity, therefore carrying both class and color connotations. Unlike in the United States, the term *colored* was used less frequently as an umbrella term for all African-descended people. Coloredness or brownness was a broad social category a degree, or a number of degrees, removed from that of dark-skinned African Jamaicans at this time, depending on whether the individual in question was particularly light-skinned and/or wealthy or darker brown in complexion and lower middle-class, respectively. However, it is also apparent from the historical source material that the term *black* was imprecise in printed material and was used on occasion to refer to all people of African descent regardless of skin color. This reveals historical dynamism in racial terminology and quite possibly marks the influence of North America — where binaries of black and white predominate — on the Caribbean.

3.   Eudine Barriteau has discussed the postwar developmental program of Caribbean nations in terms of its reproduction of patriarchal systems without reference to a critique of the liberal ideology of the European Enlightenment that framed colonialism. Barriteau, "Theorising Gender Systems and the Project of Modernity in the Twentieth-Century Caribbean," *Feminist Review*, no. 9 (1998): 186–210.

4.   Belinda Edmondson, introduction to *Caribbean Romance: The Politics of Regional Representation*, ed. Edmondson (Charlottesville: University Press of Virginia, 1999), 2. There are many possibilities for further historical inquiry into the differences between and the similarities of articulations of gender, race, and nation in different locations. The following cultural critics have initiated important discussions in this regard: Patricia Pinha, "Afro-Aesthetics in Brazil," in *Beautiful/Ugly: African and Diaspora Aesthetics*, ed. Sarah Nuttall (Durham, NC: Duke University Press, 2006), 266–89; Rita Barnard, "Contesting Beauty," in *Senses of Culture: South African Culture Studies*, ed. Sarah Nuttall and Chery-Ann Michael (Oxford University Press, 2000), 343–62; Zimitri Erasmus, "Hair Politics," in Nuttall and Michael, *Senses of Culture*, 380–92. Goldstein specifically suggests that a "colour-blind erotic democracy" has persisted in Brazil, which masks racism (Donna Goldstein, "'Interracial' Sex and Racial Democracy in Brazil: Twin Concepts?" *American Anthropologist* 101 [1999]: 563–78). For more of Natasha Barnes's discussions of beauty contests, see "Face of the Nation: Race, Nationalisms, and Identities in Jamaican Beauty Pageants" in *The Gender and Consumer Culture Reader*, ed. Jennifer Scanlon (New York: New York University Press, 2000), 355–71, and *Cultural Conundrums: Gender, Race, Nation, and the Making of Caribbean Cultural Politics* (Ann Arbor: University of Michigan Press, 2006).

5.   This study draws on examinations of mass consumption and specifically of the culture of the beauty industry, including Kathy Peiss's work on the growth of the mass beauty industry in the United States, Sarah Banet-Weiser's study of Miss America as a platform for shaping and articulating national ideals, and Maxine Craig's work on the African American beauty contest tradition as a means of antiracism campaigning and "racial re-articulation." It takes up a feminist treatment of the beauty contest seen as the assertion of community or national ideals delivered through feminine performance, that is, through those learned skills and practices that enact femininity. See Kathy Peiss, *Hope in a Jar: The Making of America's Beauty Culture* (New York: Metropolitan, 1998); Sarah Banet-Weiser, *The Most Beautiful Girl in the World: Beauty Pageants and National Identity* (Berkeley: University of California Press, 1999); Maxine Leeds Craig, *Ain't I a Beauty Queen? Black Women, Beauty, and the Politics of Race* (Oxford: Oxford University Press, 2002); and Deborah L. Madsen, "Performing Community through the Feminine Body: The Beauty Pageant in Transnational Contexts," home.adm.unige.ch/~madsen/Zurich_pageants.htm (accessed August 11, 2007). Additionally, it is influenced by a wider background of feminist theory on the body, including black and postcolonial feminist criticism, which has examined the construction of black bodies and black sexuality as Other and has confronted this both within feminist criticism and in mass culture. See bell hooks, *Black Looks: Race and Representation* (London: Turnaround, 1992); Susan Willis, "I Shop Therefore I Am: Is There a Place for Afro-American Culture in Commodity Culture?" in *Feminisms: An Anthology of Literary Theory and Criticism*, ed. Robyn R. Warhol and Diane Price Herndl (Basingstoke, UK: Macmillan, 1997).

6.   Elisabeth Wallace, *The British Caribbean: From the Decline of Colonialism to the End of Federation* (Toronto: University of Toronto Press, 1977), 85–91.

7.   Trevor Munroe, *The Politics of Constitutional Decolonisation: Jamaica, 1944–62* (Kingston: Institute for Social and Economic Research, University of the West Indies, 1983), 75–95.

8.   Ibid., 1.

9.   For discussions of the roles of women in political activism and of attempts to exclude women from Jamaican politics, see Joan French, "Colonial Policy towards Women after the 1938 Uprising: The Case of Jamaica," *Caribbean Quarterly* 34 (1988): 38–61; and Linette

Vassell, "Women of the Masses: Daphne Campbell and 'Left' Politics in Jamaica in the 1950s," in *Engendering History: Caribbean Women in Historical Perspective*, ed. Verene Shepherd, Bridget Brereton, and Barbara Bailey (Kingston: Ian Randle, 1995), 318–36.

10. Marcus Garvey, the founder of the international United Negro Improvement Association, contested the 1930 elections but did not win a seat.

11. Deborah Thomas, *Modern Blackness: Nationalism, Globalization, and the Politics of Culture in Jamaica* (Durham, NC: Duke University Press, 2004), 29–57.

12. Munroe, *Politics of Constitutional Decolonisation*, 102–5.

13. Thomas, *Modern Blackness*, 52.

14. Howard Johnson, "The 'Jamaica 300' Celebrations of 1955: Commemoration in a Colonial Polity," in *Journal of Imperial and Commonwealth History* 26 (1998): 120–37.

15. Ibid., 123–24.

16. "'Miss Pomegranate,' 'Miss Lotus' Prizewinners," *Star*, November 19, 1955, 1.

17. Jennifer Morgan, *Labouring Women: Reproduction and Gender in New World Slavery* (Philadelphia: University of Pennsylvania Press, 2004), 49, 47.

18. Mimi Sheller, *Consuming the Caribbean: From Arawaks to Zombies* (London: Routledge, 2003), 111.

19. Ibid., 128. *Cooly* was the derogatory term for an Indian-Caribbean indentured laborer.

20. Lucille Iremonger, *Yes, My Darling Daughter* (London: Secker and Warburg, 1964), 65.

21. "Types of English Beauty," *Planter's Punch* 3 (1933–34): 4.

22. Lucille Parks and Rita Gunter, "English and Jamaican Society—Two Views," *Planter's Punch* 4 (1938–39): 57.

23. Natasha Barnes's discussion elaborates on the appearance of the white beauty queen in the Caribbean as marking a new departure for a colonial elite feeling its hegemony impinged on by the transition to self-government. The parade of white femininity veils a more masculinist impulse to assert the primacy of white masculinity over the colonial enterprise (Barnes, *Cultural Conundrums*, 50–70).

24. Una Marson, "Kurrent Komments," *Cosmopolitan*, April 1931, 20.

25. "Editorial: Beauty and Federation: The Meaning of *Post*'s Miss British Caribbean Contests," *Caribbean Post*, May–June 1948, 2.

26. See Aimee Webster, "My View of It," *Vanity*, Summer 1961, 40–41; Webster, "My View of It," *Vanity*, Summer 1960, 13. "Miss British Caribbean" ran from 1947 to 1950 and appears to have dwindled in 1951. Webster wrote later that she passed the "Miss British Caribbean" franchise to another manager in Trinidad who allowed it to lapse by the mid-1950s.

27. "West Indian Nebulae: Phyllis Wong of Trinidad, no. 11," *Caribbean Post*, February 1948, 19.

28. Betty Bachus, "A Good Queen," *Caribbean Post*, July 1948, 10.

29. Betty Bachus, "Carib, Spanish, and Negro," *Caribbean Post*, 1949, 10. Please note that the National Library of Jamaica's holdings of the *Caribbean Post* are incomplete and in a poor state of repair. The publication was short-lived and increasingly sporadic. I have provided all available information for the issues that appeared intermittently from 1949 on.

30. Barnes, "Face of the Nation," 358.

31. "One Hundred Percent for Dark Girls," *Caribbean Post*, 1950, 12–13.

32. Johnson, "Jamaica 300," 122; "Our Girls," *Star*, December 6, 1955.

33. "Miss Jamaica," *Gleaner*, December 5, 1955. Sealy took issue with the image of the peasant "woman on the donkey," the market woman of colonial imagery that had been popularized by the United Fruit Company on postcards as an emblem of unthreatening and compliant black peasantry. This image of the black peasantry contended with a nationalist ideology that romanticized a Victorian patriarchal model of the peasant family and identified the

peasantry with independence, not colonial subjection. For a further discussion of the woman-on-the-donkey imagery, see Krista Thomas, "Black Skin, Blue Eyes: Visualizing Blackness in Jamaican Art, 1922–1944," *Small Axe* 8 (2004): 1–31.

34. "Every Lassie Has an Equal Chance," *Star*, September 1, 1955.

35. "Star Beauty Caravan Taking the Country By Storm," *Star*, July 29, 1955.

36. French, "Colonial Policy," 50–53; Linette Vassell, "Voluntary Women's Associations in Jamaica: The Jamaica Federation of Women" (MPhil diss., University of West Indies at Mona, 1993), 158.

37. See "Black Beauty," *Spotlight*, December 1959, 32; "Rules," *Star*, September 1, 1955; "Glorifying the Jamaican Girl of All Types," *Star*, July 23, 1955. The lack of an audience for the final judging could have been a money-saving measure. Discourses of racialized othering had, for instance, historically cast African women as excessively muscular and as lavishly proportioned, indications of their fitness for plantation labor and of their reproductive capacities.

38. "Miss Jamaica 1959—Ebony Year," *Star*, May 19, 1955. In fact, only five of the intended ten competitions took place after the relaunch: "Miss Ebony" in 1959, "Miss Mahogany" in 1960, "Miss Satinwood" in 1961, "Miss Golden Apple" in 1962, and "Miss Apple Blossom" in 1963.

39. This is with the notable exception of the PNP's earlier attempts at organizing the local Kingston competitions mentioned before.

40. *Brownskin* was the African American euphemism for light-skinned women, used to describe the women who increasingly appeared in the postwar era as models and occasionally as actresses, including Dorothy Dandridge and Lena Horne. For a discussion of the rise of the brownskin model, see Laila Haidarali, "Polishing Brown Diamonds: African American Women, Popular Magazines, and the Advent of Modeling in Early Postwar America," *Journal of Women's History* 17 (2005): 10–37.

41. The *Star*, racier than its sister paper the *Gleaner*, reported the success of "Abu La Fleur," a topless Jamaican dancer named Jeeni Sherman who, while working in London, had managed to secure the role of lead dancer in a popular variety show, *Toujours l'amour*. "Black and White," *Star*, May 15, 1959.

42. Haidarali, "Polishing Brown Diamonds" 10.

43. "Black Beauty," *Spotlight*, December 1959, 32.

44. Barnes, *Cultural Conundrums*, 93.

45. See "Black Beauty," 33; "Black Shadow over 'Paradise Isle,'" *Newday*, June 1961, 19–21; "A Man Called Spotlight," *Spotlight*, December 1956, 32–35.

46. "Black Beauty," 33.

47. Lola Young, "Missing Persons: Fantasizing Black Women in *Black Skin, White Masks*," in *The Fact of Blackness*, ed. Alan Read (London: Institute of Contemporary Arts, Institute of International Visual Arts, 1996), 87–97; Michelle Wright, *Becoming Black: Creating Identity in the African Diaspora* (Durham, NC: Duke University Press, 2004), 124–35.

48. "Black Beauty," 12, 33.

49. "Should Follow the Star," *Star*, September 5, 1955; UNIA (Jamaica Chapter), press release, October 10, 1960, National Library of Jamaica.

50. "Ten Strikes against the 'Miss Jamaica' Contest," *Newday*, June 1961, 36.

51. Ibid.

52. Alva Ramsay, "Miss Jamaica 1962," *Gleaner*, July 13, 1962.

53. "Portland Beauty Chosen for Nyasaland," *Gleaner*, June 8, 1964.

54. Thomas, *Modern Blackness*, 266.

55. Love quoted in Belinda Edmondson, "Public Spectacles: Caribbean Women and the Politics of Public Performances," *Small Axe*, no. 13 (March 2003): 1; Garvey wrote "The Black Woman" from prison in 1927 (reprinted in *Jamaican Housewife*, Spring 1965, 17). For more on the African American context, see Peiss, *Hope in a Jar*, 205; Craig, *Ain't I a Beauty Queen*, 45–64; Noliwe Rooks, *Ladies Pages: African American Women's Magazines and the Culture that Made Them* (New Brunswick, NJ: Rutgers University Press, 2004), 16–29; Megan E. Williams, "The *Crisis* Cover Girl: Lena Horne, the NAACP, and Representations of African American Femininity, 1941–1945," *American Periodicals* 16 (2006): 200–218.

56. Edward Scott, "Beauty Contest of a 'Revolutionary Quality,'" *Gleaner*, August 10, 1955.

57. Peter Abrahams, *Jamaica: An Island Mosaic* (London: Stationary Office, 1957), 198–99.

58. "Jamaica—Skin Deep," *Time*, November 28, 1955.

59. "Jamaica's Tourist Industry Seen as an Aid to Racial Understanding," *Star*, November 30, 1955.

60. "Suriname: Multiracial Paradise at the Crossroads," *Ebony*, February 1967, www.buku.nl/ebony.html.

61. "Travel News," *Spotlight*, October 1955, 6.

62. "Sheila's Big Break," *Newday*, June 1959, 73.

63. "Senegal," *Vanity*, Spring 1966, 41.

64. Frank Hill, "Jamaica: Its People and Institutions," *Sunday Gleaner*, July 28, 1962.

65. Sealy, "How We Celebrated," 4.

66. "Jamaica's Motto Will Be: Out of Many—One People," *Gleaner*, April 4, 1962.

67. Norman Washington Manley, "Second Autobiography," June 6–July 21, 1969, unpublished manuscript, National Library of Jamaica.

Visible Men: African American Boxers, the New Negro, and the Global Color Line

Theresa Runstedtler

What with the ostracising of coloured pugs in America and Australia, France remains the only hunting ground for them. Interracial contests will not be tolerated in England, so that we may, before the passing of many moons, see Paris occupied by the blacks. Already, and with but a slight pull on the imagination, one might easily fancy oneself in bad old Benin.
—F. H. Lucas, "Black Paris," *Boxing*, January 4, 1913

In 1908, the French sportswriter Jacques Mortane mused, "One must believe that our treatment of the niggers is more pleasant for them than it is in America."[1] His proof was the recent influx of African American fighters to the French capital, beginning in 1907 with the appearance of the heavyweight Sam McVea, affectionately dubbed "L'Idole de Paris."[2] Like McVea, the infamous Jack Johnson had also left the United States, crossing the Atlantic in pursuit of a World Heavyweight Championship match against the Canadian Tommy Burns. Moreover, Joe Jeannette, the self-declared mulatto from Hoboken, New Jersey, had traveled to France in search of more lucrative bouts. As Mortane acknowledged, these men left behind the pervasive racial segregation in U.S. boxing, where black American pugilists often had to fight each other repeatedly for second-rate purses in front of sparse and unenthusiastic audiences.

Radical History Review
Issue 103 (Winter 2009)   DOI 10.1215/01636545-2008-031

Struggling to gain notoriety and wealth, and to find challengers worthy of their skills, African American boxers found themselves drawn to the City of Light. Popular myths of French racial tolerance had long circulated in black communities throughout the United States. The well-publicized foreign successes of African American athletes like the renowned cyclist Marshall "Major" Taylor had also convinced many black sportsmen that France was a color-blind nation in which they could live in exile, free from the ravages of white American racism.[3]

However, in reality, questions of color were at the very heart of African American boxers' great popularity in France in the years before World War I. The presence of men like McVea, Jeannette, and Johnson inspired French sports enthusiasts to publicly reflect on their own conceptions of race, manhood, civilization, and the place of Western empire in the modern world. These black American athletes provided French fans with a comfortable abstraction of the colonial question, enabling them to project a public image of enlightened benevolence.

In turn, African American pugilists capitalized on this French fascination with black manhood. They not only articulated their own vision of what it meant to be a New Negro—a proud and assertive black man rather than a meek and submissive Sambo—but also publicly critiqued the backwardness of U.S. race relations. Not to be left out of this international conversation on race, white American journalists mocked the "peculiar" French adoration of African American boxers. Apparently, Frenchmen's joie de vivre, coupled with their Latin effeminacy, had rendered them incapable of shouldering the white man's burden.[4] Moreover, black American sportsmen, unaccustomed to such white adulation, seemed to be developing swelled heads. Thus, while the personal circumstances of black boxers often improved when they arrived in Paris, they remained tangled in the web of a transnational culture of race.

The circulating debates surrounding the exploits of African American pugilists in France provide an alternative vantage point from which to investigate the ongoing fight over the racialized terms of modernity in the early twentieth century. Rather than focusing on the radical internationalist critiques of white supremacy forwarded by black political and cultural elites of the 1920s and 1930s, this article examines the many challenges facing black sportsmen as some of the earliest and most famous "organic intellectuals" of the African diaspora.[5] Even before World War I, mass migration, urbanization, and the broadening reach of the mass-culture industries were reshaping notions of race in a variety of spaces. In other words, to view the rise of the New Negro through the lens of popular culture obliges us to acknowledge how the mobility of black cultural products and of cultural workers helped dramatize the transnational dimensions of race, gender, empire, and biopolitics for regular people on both sides of the color line.[6]

Although African American athletes often left the United States to escape Jim Crow segregation, the flows of commercial culture were already creating an expanding sense of "whiteness" that defied not only national borders but also eth-nic and class lines.[7] In this way, the performances of black American prizefighters in rings and theaters around the world must be placed in the context of what the historian Robert Rydell has called the "broader universe of white supremacist enter-tainments," including blackface minstrelsy, world's fairs, and so-called Wild West Shows.[8] These spectacles of race put nonwhite men and women on display for the curiosity and exotic satisfaction of white audiences, while also enacting visual nar-ratives of white conquest over primitive peoples of color both at home and abroad. Employing many of the same theatrical conventions, boxing and other forms of body culture provided useful justifications for the exclusion of people of color from main-stream politics and society, as "fitness" for citizenship became rooted in a muscular, white, male ideal.[9] Not only did black men have to fight for their place in the ring alongside white men, but once in the ring they were often viewed by white specta-tors as anthropological specimens. The accepted ideal remained that of the superior white male body, even if this racial fiction could not always be sustained in the unscripted realm of the boxing ring.

Yet even as boxing exhibitions and Wild West Shows helped cement these widening coalitions of whiteness, a transnational counterculture of blackness was also emerging in the same pathways of interimperial exchange. Touring black ath-letes and performers had a mobile platform from which to challenge these white-washed visions of modernity. Because of their access to the press and their physical competition with white men, African American boxers were able to push the hypoc-risy of white supremacy into public view wherever they, or news and images of them, traveled.

Far from the bourgeois politics of the early Pan-African Conferences, working-class men like McVea, Jeannette, and Johnson represent a vector of modern black internationalism rarely examined by historians.[10] Scores of African American box-ers traveled along the routes of imperialism and industrialism, gaining firsthand knowledge of the global race "problem." Many began their pugilistic careers as they labored on commercial and military ships, in the dockyards of international ports, and in the underground life of the city. Often eschewing backbreaking manual labor in favor of more lucrative opportunities in the field of popular entertainment, they became ever more ubiquitous figures of fear and desire.

McVea spent so much of his career abroad in England, France, Belgium, Aus-tralia, and the Americas that he gained the moniker "Colored Globe Trotter." Jean-nette's career also took off when he left for Paris in 1909, and over the following ten years he visited a variety of cities from London to Montreal.[11] By the time Johnson won the World Heavyweight Championship in 1908, he had already fought in places as far off as Australia and England, and after his conviction under the federal Mann Act against white slave trafficking in 1913, he lingered in exile throughout Europe and the Americas until surrendering to U.S. authorities in 1920.

From their position outside the United States, black boxers became cultural conduits through which African Americans and other colonized peoples could contemplate the role of race and empire in the wider world. Johnson's expansive boxing career even inspired the New Negro statesman James Weldon Johnson to ponder the biopolitics of the global color line in the shadow of the white man's burden. Writing in 1915, Weldon Johnson declared that the black heavyweight's ring successes were "a racial asset," for despite "its vaunted civilization," the white race definitely paid "more respect to the argument of force than any other race in the world." Referring to the Russo-Japanese War (1904–5), the statesman maintained, "as soon as Japan showed that it could fight, it immediately gained the respect and admiration in an individual way."[12] Similarly, an editorialist for the *New York Amsterdam News* pointed to the transnational implications of Johnson's sporting victories, arguing that the black champion's "individual achievements in the ring had put new life and backbone in the colored races from the China Wall to Niagara's [*sic*] Falls."[13]

Clearly, highbrow periodicals and newspapers were not the only impetus for the rise of black diasporic sensibilities or for transnational racial formations more generally. As the historian Davarian Baldwin argues, black films, sports teams, and art "became ironic positions of strength in the creation of a New Negro consciousness" not only in the United States but across the African diaspora. In particular, black sporting participation "exalted personality, sexuality, and the physical exterior as the expression of a new race consciousness," one that was decidedly masculine, militant, and antibourgeois. In describing the U.S. "Negro Problem" for Russian readers in 1923, the Harlem Renaissance writer and leftist activist Claude McKay acknowledged that pugilists like Jack Johnson usually came out of "a milieu of the very poor proletariat" and were hailed as heroes in all the "Negro billiard halls, barbershops, and nightclubs of American cities." Indeed, the performativity of boxing had a special appeal for the dark proletariat, allowing its members to claim a sense of control over the colored body and its gendered representations at a moment when prevailing ideas of citizenship and the nation were intertwined with images of white manhood.[14]

Nevertheless, while visual imagery and performance certainly helped translate counterhegemonic ideas of race across national borders, they were also susceptible to their own distortions and elisions. As they became some of the most infamous stand-ins for an imagined community of colored peoples across the globe, the hypervisibility of touring African American sportsmen had real implications for the gendering of black nationalisms and transnationalisms in subsequent decades.[15] At the same time, the growing prominence of African American images of blackness throughout the diaspora also complicated later attempts to build transnational racial solidarity.

Black American sportsmen ventured abroad precisely because they found profitable markets for their performances. Race was a commodity to be performed and consumed, and the ability of African American boxers to stage a particular brand of masculine blackness was integral to their survival in this marketplace of race.[16] Although modern black subjectivity or the universal "Negro" had first emerged in an earlier age of slavery and colonialism, the traveling spectacles of African Americans further solidified this process, making certain kinds of blackness highly visible and others invisible.[17]

Black Boxers and the Biopolitics of Modernism

Long before the famed African American performer Josephine Baker arrived in the French capital in 1925, spectacles of black manhood had already become a hot commodity in the Parisian sporting scene.[18] Although vilified and feared in their own nation, African American boxers became huge celebrities in France: they challenged white men in the ring, endorsed a variety of products, published articles in sporting magazines, toured the French provinces, participated in the underground nightlife of the Parisian dancehall scene, and even gained the admiration of the European avant-garde. The early French boxing scene revolved around the life and fights of African American heavyweights, and they emerged as central figures in the racialized and gendered aesthetics of transatlantic modernism.[19]

Ironically, as black American prizefighters searched for a safe space from which not only to make a living but also to publicly critique the injustices of white American Negrophobia, they found their interests aligned with those of French spectators. Parisian fans used their embrace of African American boxers to claim the moral high ground over their Anglo-Saxon contemporaries. They argued that their celebration of black prizefighters illustrated their greater modernity and, by extension, their more sophisticated relationship with the colonial world.[20]

The French sporting establishment actively promoted Paris as the one place where black men could thrive in an unprejudiced boxing ring. According to a *Washington Post* report, "Tales true enough of McVey's easy money from knocking out French champions . . . [had] reached America and tempted several others to enter the game."[21] In particular, McVea's successes as both a fighter and a businessman had convinced many African Americans that "Paris was a paradise for negro pugilists." As the report noted, "McVey, a Paris resident, manages himself, being clear-headed and taking advice from a Paris law firm."[22] McVea was a quintessential New Negro—tough, determined, and independent. Yet regardless of such positive stories, the African American boxer's popularity with French fans ultimately stemmed from his embodiment of primal black physicality.

Unlike their white American and British counterparts, Parisian fans did not seem to fear black male physicality, but rather reveled in spectacles of black strength. McVea's early matches against white fighters exemplified this growing fetishism of the black male body. When L'Idole de Paris knocked out the English fighter Jack Scales in January 1908, his physical stature and boxing skills mesmerized French spectators. As Mortane recounted in colorful detail, with McVea's "avalanche" of blows, Scales's head had "oscillated three or four times from front to back, as if the shock would remove it from his trunk."[23]

For McVea, who found himself shut out of mainstream U.S. boxing when first-rate white American pugilists refused to fight him, French journalists' graphic description and public celebration of his interracial triumphs must have seemed extraordinary. For close to two years, L'Idole de Paris was an invincible hero, beating white opponent after white opponent. A French advertisement for Sen-Sen chewing gum featured a smiling blackface caricature of McVea next to a battered and disfigured white fighter with the caption, "Me always winner, always smiling, never knocked out, because me always chewing."[24] In the French boxing scene, black male physicality and primitiveness were saleable commodities and sources of humor, rather than causes for alarm.

While Negro (black-on-black) matches had little mainstream marketability in the United States, they formed the centerpiece of the French boxing industry. In 1909, a series of fights between McVea and Jeannette captured the attention of Parisian sports fans, provoking passionate debates about race and modernity. Through these matches, sports enthusiasts not only discussed the nature of black masculinity, physicality, savagery, and solidarity; they also pondered the intimate relationship between the survival of the French Republic and its African colonies. In doing so, they eagerly consumed many of the same essentialist images of blackness that circulated in the white American and British media, adapting them to suit their local cultural and political needs. As the McVea-Jeannette fight series linked sport with popular science, politics, and aesthetics, the boxing ring emerged as an important cultural "contact zone" in which all of these racialized themes intertwined.[25]

The two African American pugilists traveled to Paris at a moment when calls for white physical regeneration in the face of modern decadence gripped the popular consciousness. While French fears of white degeneration centered on their declining birthrate, particularly given the German demographic explosion and the threat of German invasion, the African colonies emerged as the ultimate resource for national revival. Writing in 1910, Colonel Charles Mangin argued that France possessed an untapped human reserve, "la force noire" (the black force), which would help to sustain the strength of the imperial nation.[26] "All the French will understand that France does not stop in the Mediterranean, nor in the Sahara," the colonel explained, "that it extends to Congo; that it constitutes an empire vaster than Europe."[27] Despite Mangin's rhetoric of inclusion, this "expansion" would not only demand continued white French stewardship but also keep the majority of black subjects safely contained within colonial borders. Rather than an endorsement of black sovereignty, Mangin's faith in the *force noire* had more to do with prevailing beliefs about the revivifying effects of primitive manhood. Thus the consumption of blackness, as embodied by men like McVea and Jeannette, offered a means to regenerate *white* French manhood, and by extension the French imperial nation, in the safety of the metropolitan capital.[28]

The amazing feats of African American prizefighters often did more to support the French *mission civilisatrice*, the so-called civilizing mission, than to undermine it. The public fascination with men like McVea was, arguably, an extension of France's already well-established culture of imperial spectacle. African American boxers embodied the full range of African stereotypes already in operation in the French capital. By the late nineteenth century, Parisian theater had taken to sensationalizing the French conquest of Dahomey through staged reenactments of battles and ethnographic scenes involving "authentic natives."[29] Alongside these depictions of black colonial barbarity, the image of the African *tirailleur* (soldier) emerged as the epitome of the French civilizing process: a physically robust yet domesticated savage who had not only been tamed but also trained to happily serve in the defense of French interests.[30] Much like the African *tirailleur*, black American prizefighters exemplified the same duality of controlled ferocity, except this time in the service of white French amusement.

Moreover, the McVea-Jeannette series coincided with the rise of l'Art nègre, as avant-garde artists like Henri Matisse and Pablo Picasso began to experiment with the aesthetics of primitivism. Matisse and others employed African motifs to shock viewers and disrupt conventions, thereby critiquing what they saw as the stultifying conformity of white French civilization.[31] Several artists were even known to frequent the matches of African American boxers, using them as a source of creative inspiration. "Since 1910, I had been attracted to boxing matches," the cubist painter André Dunoyer de Segonzac later recounted; "the black heavyweight champions Sam MacVea, Sam Langford, and Joe Jeannette amazed French sporting youth."[32] Therefore, even as the French tried to dissociate themselves from the imperial politics of their Anglo-Saxon counterparts, they actively participated in the very same biopolitical discourses of white male supremacy.

The announcement of the first McVea-Jeannette match had reportedly "revolutionized the world of Parisian sporting men." A month and a half before the scheduled fight of February 20, 1909, fans had already begun to inquire about tickets. "It is the question of the day," one journalist observed, "and in all the boxing clubs and athletic milieus, we discuss this subject with passion."[33] As another sportswriter claimed, "It is not just Paris but all the regions (departments) and even abroad that are interested in the *great event* of February 20." Ticket requests had come to *L'auto* from "London, Brussels, Liège, Anvers, Geneva, Roubaix, Lille, Troyes, Rouen, Reims, Orléans, and even Bordeaux."[34]

The extensive publicity surrounding the match had ethnographic and social Darwinistic undercurrents, exposing prevailing French views on the inherent physicality of black people, along with their evolutionary separation from white civilization. Parisian spectators seemed to revel in the African American competitors' imagined brutality as an antidote to their own effete and effeminate modernity. Referring to McVea and Jeannette as the "two terrible niggers," French sportswriters promised the match would be more gruesome than any other fight in the capital.[35]

This French eroticism of the virile, black male body not only drew scores of fans (both men and women) to the African American fighters' training camps but also inspired the publication of countless pictures and the brisk sale of souvenirs. In describing Jeannette's first public workout, one sportswriter exclaimed, "I will not surprise anyone by saying that his musculature is superb: his large shoulders and supple, elegant legs."[36] Alongside Jeannette's "extraordinary virtuosity," he also touted McVea's "extraordinary power and speed."[37] Many Parisian sporting magazines showcased photos of McVea and Jeannette in just their boxing trunks, baring their powerful chests. The dark-skinned McVea had a stocky, muscular build, while the biracial Jeannette had a much leaner, chiseled physique. French fans could even treat themselves to figurines and silhouettes of the two African American pugilists, especially crafted for the occasion by local artists.[38]

Minstrel stereotypes, neolithic caricatures, and simian tropes abounded in the prefight publicity, betraying the exotic, paternalistic gaze of French spectators. Although McVea and Jeannette differed greatly in color and appearance, one cartoon reduced them both to white eyes and lips against a black background, while others featured the same markers of savagery including dragging knuckles, exaggerated lips, jutting jawbones, and overhanging foreheads. One popular French cartoonist depicted McVea as a menacing gorilla, while also poking fun at Jeannette's seeming inability to find human sparring partners strong enough to train with him.[39] Even though Jeannette often publicly declared that he was a "mulatto" rather than a "nigger," European artists still defined him by the racial tropes of the day.[40] As many caricatures of them suggested, both African American fighters seemed to possess an unrivaled, animalistic strength.

On the evening of February 20, hundreds of sportsmen waited anxiously outside the Cirque de Paris on Motte-Picquet Avenue well before the start of the fight card. Although the modern venue had a capacity of over four thousand spectators, several thousand fans still had to be turned away. Many prominent European sportsmen attended alongside icons of the theater, arts, and letters. Political and scientific leaders were also on hand, from dukes to marquises to doctors. Yet this historic match was not just the domain of the rich and famous, for the promoters had set aside a section of seats for the city's less fortunate. They had also expanded the betting services to accommodate the large number of transactions coming from every sector of society. In the end, the box office alone garnered a record-breaking eighty-five thousand francs.[41]

La Patrie called it "the greatest match . . . ever seen in Paris." French journalists portrayed the fight as almost titillatingly pornographic in its brutality. "For more than an hour, a half-breed as handsome as Hercules [Jeannette] and the strongest of the Ethiopians [McVea] worked patiently and furiously to send one another to dreamland," the writer Georges Dupuy poetically recounted; "it was the assault of a tiger against a bison." Jeannette, the "tiger," was "agile, supple, powerful, aggressive and perfectly composed," while McVea, the "unbeatable black bison," possessed a rock-hard forehead and enormous neck. With his many feints and dodges, Jeannette made his slower opponent look awkward at times; however, McVea also hit Jeannette with pounding blows, knocking him to the canvas. Throughout the fight, McVea struggled to counter Jeannette's assiduous technique with crushing force, and after twenty rounds, he emerged the winner by referee's decision. The celebration of McVea's victory spilled into the streets of the capital.[42]

Yet with the Negro match ending by decision rather than by knockout, many spectators felt cheated. After all, in the weeks before the fight, French fans had anticipated "a butchering capable of causing future prohibitions" of boxing in Paris. From the streets to the pages of sporting magazines, there was a flurry of discussion over whether the McVea-Jeannette match had been faked. Some believed that the two black fighters had made a secret "entente." As one correspondent complained, they had not only "lacked determination and hate" but had also failed to bring "enough passion" to the ring. Countering such opinions, another fan wrote a blistering defense of the fight, maintaining that those who questioned the match's veracity were simply uncivilized people "whose keen desire was to see a boxing ring transformed into a bullfighting arena." As this fan so astutely observed, underlying this controversy were basic assumptions about the inherent savagery of black men and about the viciousness of African combat, especially since these allegations almost never arose in response to matches involving white boxers.[43]

Ironically, this "circus match between two negroes" had served to highlight the vital importance of physical training, particularly of boxing, for the reinvigoration of the French imperial body politic.[44] It had provided white French sportsmen with an excellent example of two primitive adversaries, stripped of all weapons, fighting to their maximum ability. While France now appeared to be in the midst of a sporting renaissance, over the past half century Frenchmen had allowed their scorn for physical activity to make them lose sight of the importance of their muscles. Given the growing threat of war with Germany, boxing seemed to offer young Frenchmen the opportunity not only to revitalize their bodies but also to acquire the critical skills of concentration, precision, and persistence necessary for survival in the modern world.[45]

Back by popular demand, the second McVea-Jeannette match took place on the night of April 17, 1909, at the Cirque de Paris. To ensure a definitive result and, hopefully, a more ardent battle, the fight promoters arranged a "match au finish," for a purse of thirty thousand francs. Guaranteed to test the limits of black physicality, the fight could only end in knockout or submission, rather than by referee's decision.

Such matches had long been illegal both in the United States and in Britain, and even in France white boxers rarely fought under such harsh conditions. Nevertheless, the second time around, the African American pugilists delivered, treating the audience to an exciting match, which continued for forty-nine rounds until a battered McVea threw in the towel. The arduous fight had lasted so long that many of the spectators had already left for the night by the time McVea surrendered. As Dupuy exclaimed, "the rematch . . . was not only the most beautiful we have ever seen in France but perhaps the most terrible and the most savage in the history of boxing throughout the world."[46]

For many spectators, white "civilization" had triumphed over black "savagery." As Dunoyer de Segonzac contended, "I admired Joe Jeannette, the 'yellow' black, a learned boxer, more scientific than his pure black brothers." Another Parisian sportswriter had juxtaposed Jeannette, the "Greek athlete," with McVea, "the eldest son of a grand barbarian king." "In a boxing ring, with rules and care, the art and the energy of Joe triumphed," he maintained; "in a forest, the instinct of Sam would have overcome." With its ten-second knockdown rule, rests in between rounds, the use of gloves, and the help of trainers, the regulated match had apparently given the more civilized Jeannette a distinct advantage over his primitive opponent. Moreover, the French writer Tristan Bernard forwarded his own anthropological analysis, arguing that McVea's submission had exemplified the "lack of perseverance inherent in the [black] race." The dark-skinned fighter's inability to go in for the kill stemmed from "a certain timidity" and the "habit of subservience" also characteristic of African people. In other words, regardless of the black male's superior physique, he still needed the guidance of white civilization. Thus even as McVea and Jeannette generated astounding praise and profits during their Parisian sojourn, they quickly discovered the very real limits of French racial tolerance. A vital part of the racial and gendered circuits of transatlantic modernism, traveling black athletes nevertheless continued to experience what W. E. B. Du Bois described as "double consciousness." They emerged not only as potent symbols in the cultural regeneration of white French manhood but also as popular embodiments of the New Negro. Although their physical performance of primitive black manhood made them international celebrities, they refused to allow this limited vision of blackness to define them. Instead they used their ambivalent position to forward a cogent critique of the global color line.[47]

Black Boxers and the Masculine Counterculture of Modernity

Adding to this sense of "twoness," the precariousness of African American sportsmen's social position gave them a glimpse of both the best and the worst of French racial politics. Unlike members of the black American intelligentsia, these rough-and-tumble men often experienced the full brunt of European racism. Although McVea had become a popular "professor" at Grognet's school of boxing in Paris, where he instructed French students in the "American method," his large black entourage quickly became a bone of contention with the school's director.[48] Grognet openly despised the "army of negroes" that always followed McVea around, calling them both "cumbersome and unpleasant."[49] When the director finally banned "these innumerable 'coloured men'" from the boxing school, McVea decided to take his business elsewhere rather than yield to Grognet's discrimination. While Frenchmen enjoyed watching and taking lessons from famed African American fighters, most did not want their social spaces to be overrun with black men.

Writing from the Hotel des Deux Gares in Paris in April 1914, a well-traveled African American named Ernest Stevens confided, "I have not seen many Afro-Americans and I would not advise anyone to come here looking to better their financial condition, as there are very few avenues of employment open to them."[50] As Stevens told the *Chicago Defender*, "The only exception, perhaps are theatrical folks and prizefighters, and even the latter is not advisable, Paris having been over-run with fistic aspirants of every shade and kind." Apparently, African Americans had been relegated to the field of popular entertainment for the amusement of white European audiences.

Although riddled with class pretension, Stevens's observations seem to confirm that African American working-class men were frequent sojourners in Europe during the early 1900s. As Stevens argued, "If there was a better cultured class [of Negroes] in England than there is they could demand better positions and respect from the English people."[51] Stevens also claimed that while there were not many African Americans currently living in Holland and Germany, the few that did were "of the unfortunate type that [gave] the dominant race a bad impression of the whole."

Uncharacteristically negative in his assessment of life abroad, Stevens advised *Defender* readers that they were better off staying home. "There is only one Afro-American in Paris who can say that he is happy and that is Jack Johnson," he argued. The writer recounted his visit to the black world champion's home in Asnières, a "fashionable suburb" about ten miles outside the city. Johnson looked "robust and healthy," occupying a grand residence that included a large playground and poultry yard, along with a garage housing "several first-class cars." However, to maintain this home, the African American heavyweight was constantly on the move with boxing exhibitions and theatrical performances in various countries. Despite Johnson's ostensible success, he was slipping further and further into debt. Johnson himself advised his black fans to "remain in America," where they could "become good and influential citizens" and could "get one hundred cents worth for every dollar they spend."[52] Although the African American world champion was certainly better off than the average black athlete or entertainer in Europe, he recognized the instability of his own status.

Regardless of these practical realities, African American pugilists still managed to use the French public's cultural embrace of black masculinity to launch a transnational critique of the white man's burden. Their special access to the foreign press and to performance venues enabled them to forward their own protests of the racial and imperial status quo in the years before World War I. Black boxers played against prevailing discourses of race, manhood, and the body in a variety of often contradicting ways, not only speaking back to popular tropes of black savagery but also critiquing the rigid discipline of bourgeois life.

In January 1911, the sporting weekly *La vie au grand air* (*Life in the Great Outdoors*) provided its first installment of Johnson's life story, titled "Ma vie et mes combats" ("My Life and Battles"), and the serial continued for the next five months. Johnson was already enough of a French celebrity for the publishers, Pierre Lafitte and Company, to introduce his autobiography as one of the magazine's most important acquisitions of the year. Greeting readers with a page-sized photo of the black heavyweight's fist, a preview for the series boasted that the story would be told by none other than Johnson himself.[53]

While Geoffrey Ward, Johnson's most recent biographer, includes a passage from this French serial story, historians have yet to plumb this important document for its insights into black working-class understandings of the global color line.[54] In many respects, the black heavyweight's French memoir was a quintessential text of African American exile and protest, a kind of New Negro manifesto that predated the start of World War I and the Harlem Renaissance. "Ma vie et mes combats" was the only autobiographical treatment of Johnson published during his career, and there appears to have been no contemporary English translation. In 1914, Pierre Lafitte and Company rereleased the fourteen-part series as a book (*Mes combats*) to capitalize on the publicity surrounding Johnson's scheduled match against the white American fighter Frank Moran in Paris.[55] While Johnson could recount his life for a foreign audience interested in his struggles as a black man in the United States, such a story was apparently too incendiary to be printed back home.

Although not tied to any specific political project, Johnson's French memoirs demonstrate that his transnational career and working-class origins enabled him to develop a particular critique of Western modernity. Prefiguring the wandering, nautical narratives of Claude McKay, Johnson depicted a life characterized by masculine pursuits and geographic mobility.[56] His narrative not only indicted white American Negrophobia but also pointed to the global contours of white supremacy. Johnson refashioned the negative legacy of black slavery into a story of triumph, questioning the gendered justifications for the white man's burden. Moreover, Johnson's life story spoke explicitly to the challenges of working-class African Americans, casting them as agents in the fight against the color line. Even though Johnson had attained the financial trappings of sporting success and celebrity, he continued to identify with the urban culture of the black proletariat.

The first episode of "Ma vie et mes combats" was surprisingly polemical, providing a sharp critique both of Jim Crow segregation and of prevailing ideas about the superiority of white Western civilization. As Johnson began, "When a white man writes his memoirs, as I will try to do here, it is customary to start with the history of his family from its earliest times."[57] The African American heavyweight disputed the popular belief that black people had no history of which to be proud. "Our memories are passed down, above all, by the tradition of father to son," Johnson explained; "whites don't believe it, but we are also proud of our ancestors and during the long days and even longer nights, when we knew neither schools nor books, we still passed on our memories from past centuries." Addressing his readers as "les hommes blancs" (white men), Johnson argued that while it made white men proud to connect themselves to the noble soldiers of the Crusades, his ancestors had actually built the grand architecture the Europeans had discovered during their missions in Palestine. "Who constructed the Pyramids 40 centuries ago?" Johnson challenged. "Which race built the Egyptian monuments before such things were known in Europe, where the inhabitants, wearing animal skins, lived a miserable existence in caves?" Embracing the wonders of ancient Egypt as a usable past, the black heavyweight questioned the historical foundations of white supremacy.

Moreover, turning a past of servitude into a virtue, Johnson declared that the physical trials of his enslaved forefathers had actually helped make him world champion. "Undoubtedly, it is from my long list of ancestors who were all hard workers, men of the open air, that I have my size, the strength of my arms and the quality of my muscles," the black heavyweight asserted—"all my inherited traits that make me just as proud as others would be of a baron's coronet." In turn, Johnson argued that his rough childhood had only made him stronger. As he recalled, "There were some very hard times in our small home in Galveston, [Texas,] and as soon as I was big enough, my father took me to help him because his job as a porter kept him very busy. At that time, we did not know carpet-sweepers or the vacuum cleaner. There were only old-fashioned brooms, with which I swept. I swept the entire day." As the black champion declared, "I believe that it was this sweeping . . . that strengthened my back and shoulder muscles." In this way, Johnson engaged with turn-of-the-century ideas about the benefits of physical culture. Ironically, while French sportsmen—alongside the likes of Theodore Roosevelt and other proponents of the "strenuous life"—contemplated the need for vigorous exercise and a return to nature to regenerate the white race, Johnson claimed that black men's myriad struggles against white domination had already made them more powerful and robust.[58]

Johnson also used his childhood narrative to counter prevailing ideas about the basic immorality and indolence of black working men. As the African American heavyweight maintained, he came from a tight-knit family and therefore endeavored to improve his station to provide them with a more comfortable life. He spoke lovingly of his mother as a woman with "too good of a heart" and of his older sister Lucy, whose job it was to keep him in line. "Life was not easy in our small house in Galveston and the days when we had empty stomachs were far more frequent than the feast days. Often my mother had worries and I sought to comfort her," Johnson explained.[59]

The black champion portrayed himself as an ambitious and resourceful young man looking for a chance to better himself despite the odds. "[At] nine years of age," Johnson recounted, "I thought about earning my living. Pushing a broom behind my father hardly suited me. I wanted to go out and work on my own account." It was in the boxing ring, rather than in the more respectable realms of education or business, that he gained more control over his own economic destiny and self-representation. Yet even during his early days as a professional prizefighter, he regularly fought on an empty stomach. As the heavyweight claimed, "I was sustained by the idea that I had to earn money if I wanted to assist my poor mother, who still had a whole brood of children to feed."[60]

Alongside this more righteous narrative of sacrifice and self-reliance, Johnson also looked back fondly on the less savory aspects of his boyhood. He described a youth punctuated by street fights, gambling, and confrontations with white policemen as he roamed about Galveston's dockyards with his group of black friends. The African American heavyweight recalled being drawn to the large ships in the port. As an adolescent, he wandered from Galveston to Key West to Boston, first as a stowaway and, after being discovered, as a helper to the ship's cook. Moreover, he eschewed formal education, preferring to experiment with a slew of different occupations, including stable boy, horse trainer, bicyclist, and house painter.[61] Even after he set his sights on becoming a championship boxer, homelessness and a lack of money continued to plague him. Yet Johnson claimed that these rough and roving years had prepared him for the vagaries of professional prizefighting: "I cannot tell you how happy I am now that I had to protect myself against hardship and understand poverty as intimately as I did."[62]

Johnson's mobility increased as his boxing career took off. His later travels throughout Australia and Europe undoubtedly alerted him to the broader cultural climate of the white man's burden. He maintained that the "color question" had caused the "saddest moments" of his fighting career.[63] In recalling the widespread controversy over his 1910 defeat of Jim Jeffries, Johnson questioned the validity of the color line, whether in or out of the boxing ring. To make his point, he included a short verse for his French readers:

For there is neither east nor west,
Border nor breed nor birth,
When two strong men stand face to face,
Though they come from the ends of the earth.[64]

While these may have been the words of the famed British poet Rudyard Kipling's "Ballad of East and West," Johnson remembered learning them from one of his boxing trainers.[65] With a deep sense of irony, the black American heavyweight used the imperial writer's appeal to prevailing ideas of gender to critique his unde-served plight. Johnson maintained that he had chosen to operate above the arbitrary color line, for he viewed his title match against Jeffries as a question of manhood, rather than one of race.

This masculine image of colored success had a particular significance for subaltern resistance. The exploits of African American boxers both in and out of the ring suggested a more accessible and immediate form of social mobility, one located outside the regular channels of politics, education, and business. The body was a democratic space through which black athletes could assert and express themselves in ways that challenged the central tenets of black inferiority. Moreover, African American prizefighters' extensive travels, along with the increasingly transnational reach of their press stories, pictures, and films, helped transmit this vision of the New Negro to men of color in urban spaces across the globe.

The New Negro beyond the Ring

When Claude McKay traveled to London in 1919, he was forced to contend with the legacy of touring black athletes like Johnson. During McKay's first encounter with his literary hero George Bernard Shaw, the English writer declared, "It must be tragic for a sensitive Negro to be a poet. Why didn't you choose pugilism instead of poetry for a profession? . . . You might have developed into a successful boxer with training. Poets remain poor, unless they have an empire to glorify and popular-ize like Kipling."[66] While Shaw's assumptions about black male physicality and its profitability certainly annoyed McKay, the gendered aesthetics of African American boxers had helped lay the groundwork for the black transnational protest culture of the interwar years. The athletes' overseas journeys not only revealed the ubiquity of white racism but also pointed to the need for colored alliances across borders. Not surprisingly, boxing was quickly becoming one of the most popular pastimes of radical men's organizations. As McKay recalled, several African American prize-fighters had joined the International Club, a multiracial political group in London that counted Jews, Italians, Irish, East Indians, and West Indians among its diverse membership. Sparring exhibitions were a regular part of the club's social calendar.[67] Apparently boxing spoke to the masculine imagination of proletarian revolt.

In the early 1920s, the French Senegalese light heavyweight Battling Siki rose to pugilistic stardom. In many respects, the African fighter seemed to model himself after his flamboyant predecessor Johnson, for he was just as audacious in his public defiance of the constraints of colonial etiquette. The *New York Times* even dubbed him "the French Jack Johnson," claiming that Siki needed to be put in his place.[68] The Senegalese fighter loved big-city excitement, fashionable suits, absinthe, wine, and cigarettes, exotic pets, and most of all, white women.[69] The African Amer-ican boxer Bob Scanlon recalled running into a crowd of Parisians surrounding Siki as he stood "with two big Great Danes and a revolver firing it in the air and trying to make the dogs do tricks."[70] For the most part, white writers argued that Siki's brash behavior simply showed that he was unfit for civilization. As one of Siki's opponents, Harry Reeve, told *Boxing*, the Senegalese was "like a wild man let loose in Europe," a kind of "nigger minstrel" in both his dress and mannerisms.[71]

As a black veteran of the Great War and a successful black boxer in an era of primitivist modernism and mounting black militancy, Siki embodied the transnational debates over white supremacy and Western imperialism in the 1920s. He became a stand-in for the colonial world, albeit a rather extreme example of black male savagery. Yet while white journalists in the United States and Europe painted Siki as a "child of the jungle," his life story actually pointed to the blurring boundaries between Europe and Africa, white and nonwhite, and citizen and subject in the modern world. "A lot of newspaper people have written that I have a jungle style of fighting — that I am a chimpanzee who has been taught to wear gloves," Siki complained; "that kind of thing hurts me. I was never anywhere but in a big city in my life. I have never even *seen* a jungle."[72]

However, as much as Siki felt slighted by the white media, he was also keenly aware that the masculine aesthetics of black primitivism paid big dividends. The African prizefighter accentuated his exotic physicality and sexuality to the delight of white Parisian fans. Yet Siki's performance of unbridled black manhood ultimately tested the limits of French racial tolerance. When the popular French champion Georges Carpentier initially declined to meet Siki in the ring, a disappointed African American correspondent for the radical *Messenger* questioned, "Has the uncultured American, bigoted, uninformed, and unsportsmanlike — become the ideal of the former gentleman Carpentier, the national motto of whose country is '*Liberty*, *Equality* and *Fraternity*?' If so, France is rapidly becoming Americanized."[73] Given the recent influx of white American soldiers and tourists, this transformation was hardly surprising. "Wherever they go, they carry their propaganda of race prejudice," the black reporter observed; "France's imperialism is bad enough without her taking on any more of our bad American customs."

After his defeat of Carpentier in September 1922, Siki came up against an even more widespread and intense white backlash. Effectively barred from fighting in various countries and stripped of all his titles, Siki emerged as a transnational symbol of colored resistance.[74] Blaise Diagne, a Senegalese member of the French Chamber of Deputies, insisted on bringing Siki's case before his white colleagues. According to Diagne, the French Boxing Federation had unjustly punished the Senegalese prizefighter for celebrating his victory in the cafés of Paris.[75] There was an obvious double standard at work since nobody complained when white boxers did the same. As Diagne charged, "These men who are as French as you are, though they are of different color, have a right to the same justice as you," and he cautioned his fellow deputies about the danger of giving the impression that France had two, *unequal* forms of justice — one for white Frenchmen and another for colored subjects.[76]

Indeed, Siki's difficulties in France served to highlight the global dimensions of the color line, inspiring none other than McKay to critique the conservative, nationalist agendas of the black bourgeoisie in the United States and France. "The black intelligentsia of America looks upon France as the foremost cultured nation of the world," McKay declared, "the single great country where all citizens enjoy equal rights before the law, without respect to race or skin color." Closing their eyes to the "vile exploitation of Africans by the French," American Negroes had begun to believe that "one imperialist exploiter" could be "better than another."[77] However, Siki's troubles were like a slap in the face to the black bourgeoisie. For McKay, this white uproar over black victory in the boxing ring was ultimately connected to the sport's gendered meanings. "Jack Johnson beat James Jeffries in America, and the American bourgeoisie never could forgive the insult which was done to his dignity by a black man," McKay explained, continuing, "the Negro must not show himself capable of fighting and winning; it is not entirely safe for capitalistic America, which makes twenty million Negroes bow down."[78] Black boxers publicly challenged the gendered logic at the very core of the white man's burden.

The Vietnamese anticolonialist and communist leader Ho Chi Minh made many of the same arguments in the radical journal *Le Paria*, as he pondered the larger significance of Siki's defeat of Carpentier and the white backlash it inspired. Even though they operated on different cultural terrains, Ho saw Siki and René Maran, the Martiniquan author of the anticolonial novel *Batouala*, as making similar contributions to the fight against white supremacy. "Following Maran's ironical pen," Ho declared, "Siki's gloves have stirred everything, including even the political sphere." As Ho claimed, "a Carpentier-Siki match is worth more than one hundred gubernatorial speeches to prove to our subjects and protégés that we want to apply to the letter the principle of equality between races." In turn, he criticized the British Home Office's decision to ban the scheduled match between Siki and the English fighter Joe Beckett. "This does not surprise us," Ho mocked, "as His British Excellency could digest neither [Mustafa] Kemal's croissant nor [Mahatma] Gandhi's chocolate, he wants to have Battling Siki swallow his purge even though the latter is a Frenchman." While on a much smaller scale, Siki's troubles were symbolic of the continued capitalist and imperialist exploitation of the world's "indigenous proletarians."[79]

While not explicitly "political," black boxers embodied a New Negro masculinity grounded in physical culture and a working-class sensibility that influenced the radical critiques of white supremacy later put forward by intellectuals and artists of the Harlem Renaissance and the Nègritude movement. When African American pugilists began arriving in Paris in the early 1900s, they found a profitable market for their displays of black manhood. Yet even as men like McVea, Jeannette, and Johnson traveled to Europe to escape the repression of Jim Crow segregation, they remained caught in the commercial flows of a transnational race culture. Although Parisian sportsmen embraced black boxers in an effort to claim that France was an antiracist and benevolent imperial nation, they were by no means color-blind. Much like their Anglo-Saxon counterparts, they believed that black people were inherently primitive, existing on the margins of white civilization. Because of African American boxers' ironic position, as black celebrities *and* as emblems of black primitivism, they experienced firsthand the double-edged sword of European racial politics. Through their well-publicized travels, these organic intellectuals of the African diaspora not only saw for themselves but also made visible for others the New Negro's fight with the global color line.

Notes

The author thanks Erica Ball, Melina Pappademos, Michelle Stephens, the two anonymous referees, and the members of the Buffalo Seminar on Racial Justice at the University of Buffalo, whose comments and suggestions greatly improved this article.

1. Jacques Mortane, "Tous les nègres en Europe" ("All the Niggers in Europe"), *La vie au grand air* (*Life in the Great Outdoors*), May 9, 1908, 292. Several scholars have noted the difficulty of translating the French word *nègre* into its English equivalent. Despite its visual similarity to "negro," *nègre* was still a derogatory term in the early 1900s whose meaning was likely closer to that of the word *nigger*. See Brent Edwards, *The Practice of Diaspora: Literature, Translation, and the Rise of Black Internationalism* (Cambridge, MA: Harvard University Press, 2003), 25–38; Jack Johnson, *My Life and Battles*, trans. Chris Rivers (Westport, CT: Praeger, 2007), xv–xvi.

2. Sam McVea's name had a number of popular spellings including McVey and MacVea.

3. For more on Taylor's extensive travels, see Andrew Ritchie, *Major Taylor: The Extraordinary Career of a Champion Bicycle Racer* (Baltimore: Johns Hopkins University Press, 1988).

4. See, for example, "La Caricature à l'Étranger: 'Boxing One of Most Popular Sports in France Just Now,'" *Boxe et les boxeurs* (*Boxing and Boxers*), June 7, 1911, 2025. A reprint from a New York newspaper, this cartoon lampooned French sports fans for their fascination with black boxers.

5. Much of the historical scholarship on black diasporic politics remains focused on the efforts of African American activists, intellectuals, and writers, particularly during and after World War I. See, for example, Edwards, *Practice of Diaspora*; Paul Gilroy, *Black Atlantic: Modernity and Double Consciousness* (Cambridge, MA: Harvard University Press, 1993); Brenda Gayle Plummer, *Rising Wind: Black Americans and U.S. Foreign Affairs, 1935–1960* (Chapel Hill: University of North Carolina Press, 1996); Michelle Stephens, *Black Empire: The Masculine Global Imaginary of Caribbean Intellectuals in the United States, 1914–1962* (Durham, NC: Duke University Press, 2005); Penny Von Eschen, *Race against Empire: Black Americans and Anticolonialism, 1937–1957* (Ithaca, NY: Cornell University Press, 1997). Antonio Gramsci's concept of the "organic intellectual" provides a helpful framework for understanding the importance of traveling African American sportsmen in the rise of a popular black internationalism. See Antonio Gramsci, *Selections from Prison Notebooks*, ed. and trans. Quintin Hoare and Geoffrey Nowell Smith (New York: International Publishers, 1971).

6. On the importance of the culture industries for the shaping of modern racial formations, see Davarian Baldwin, *Chicago's New Negroes: Modernity, the Great Migration, and Black Urban Life* (Chapel Hill: University of North Carolina Press, 2007), 8–9.

7.   The expansion of whiteness as a racial category was not simply a U.S. phenomenon. On the transatlantic discourses of whiteness and Anglo-Saxonism in this period, see Stuart Anderson, *Race and Rapprochement: Anglo-Saxonism and Anglo-American Relations, 1895–1904* (East Brunswick, NJ: Associated University Presses, 1981); Paul Kramer, "Empires, Exceptions, and Anglo-Saxons: Race and Rule between the British and United States Empires, 1880–1910," *Journal of American History* 88 (2002): 1315–53.

8.   Robert Rydell, *All the World's a Fair: Visions of Empire at American International Exhibitions, 1876–1916* (Chicago: University of Chicago Press, 1984), 6. Also see Robert Rydell and Rob Kroes, *Buffalo Bill in Bologna: The Americanization of the World, 1869–1922* (Chicago: University of Chicago Press, 2005).

9.   On the turn-of-the-century fascination with white male bodies (their aesthetics and abilities), see Gail Bederman, *Manliness and Civilization: A Cultural History of Gender and Race in the United States, 1880–1917* (Chicago: University of Chicago Press, 1995); Michael A. Budd, *The Sculpture Machine: Physical Culture and Body Politics in the Age of Empire* (New York: New York University Press, 1997); Lisa Grunberger, "Bernarr MacFadden's Physical Culture: Muscles, Morals, and the Millennium" (PhD diss., University of Chicago, 1997); John F. Kasson, *Houdini, Tarzan, and the Perfect Man: The White Male Body and the Challenge of Modernity in America* (New York: Hill and Wang, 2001); Clifford Putney, *Muscular Christianity: Manhood and Sports in Protestant America, 1880–1920* (Cambridge, MA: Harvard University Press, 2001).

10. The role of the black working class in the making of the Atlantic world is beginning to receive more attention. See, for example, Jeffrey Bolster, *Black Jacks: African American Seamen in the Age of Sail* (Cambridge, MA: Harvard University Press, 1997); Edwards, *Practice of Diaspora*, 187–240; Peter Linebaugh and Marcus Rediker, *Many-Headed Hydra: Sailors, Slaves, Commoners, and the Hidden History of the Revolutionary Atlantic* (Boston: Beacon, 2000); Stephens, *Black Empire*, 167–203.

11. Nat Fleischer, *"Fighting Furies," Story of the Golden Era of Jack Johnson, Sam Langford and Their Negro Contemporaries*, vol. 4 of *Black Dynamite: The Story of the Negro in the Prize Ring from 1782 to 1938* (New York: O'Brien, 1938), 173–74, 194–201.

12. James Weldon Johnson, "The Passing of Jack Johnson," *New York Age*, April 8, 1915.

13. "Laying Down His Crown," *New York Amsterdam News*, April 9, 1915.

14. In *The Practice of Diaspora*, Edwards masterfully explores the budding print culture of the black diaspora, focusing on the inherent problems associated with the translation of language and ideas across borders. Although Baldwin's study focuses on Chicago, the mass consumer marketplace was also creating spaces of protest for people of color outside the United States (*Chicago's New Negroes*, 13, 195). See also Claude McKay, "Negroes in Sports," in *The Negroes in America*, ed. Alan L. McLeod (Port Washington, NY: Kennikat, 1979), 54. On the development of modern black masculinity alongside consumer culture, see Martin Summers, *Manliness and Its Discontents: The Black Middle Class and the Transformation of Masculinity, 1900–1930* (Chapel Hill: University of North Carolina Press, 2004).

15. On the gendering of the African diaspora, see Jacqueline Nassy-Brown, "Black Liverpool, Black America, and the Gendering of Diasporic Space," *Cultural Anthropology* 13 (1998): 291–325; Stephens, *Black Empire*.

16. For a discussion of race as fetish and commodity, see Frantz Fanon, "The Fact of Blackness," in *Black Skin, White Masks*, trans. Charles Lam Markmann (New York: Grove, 1967), 109–40; Anne McClintock, *Imperial Leather: Race, Gender, and Sexuality in the Colonial Contest* (New York: Routledge, 1995), 207–31.

17. See Louis Chude-Sokei, *The Last "Darky": Bert Williams, Black-on-Black Minstrelsy, and the African Diaspora* (Durham, NC: Duke University Press, 2005), 58, 114, 141; Ifeoma Kiddoe Nwankwo, *Black Cosmopolitanism: Racial Consciousness and Transnational Identity in the Nineteenth-Century Americas* (Philadelphia: University of Pennsylvania Press, 2005), 9–13. In his discussion of the famed blackface entertainer Bert Williams, Chude-Sokei contends that "the 'universal' status of . . . the 'stage Negro' enabled the specifics of the African American context to masquerade . . . as globally representative in ways that were ironically supported by the cultural power of the United States" (58).

18. Much of the literature on African American performers and artists in France still focuses on the interwar years. See, for example, Brett Berliner, *Ambivalent Desire: The Exotic Black Other in Jazz-Age France* (Amherst: University of Massachusetts Press, 2002); William Shack, *Harlem in Montmartre: A Paris Jazz Story between the Great Wars* (Berkeley: University of California Press, 2001); Tyler Stovall, *Paris Noir: African Americans in the City of Light* (New York: Houghton Mifflin, 1996).

19. See Sieglinde Lemke, *Primitivist Modernism: Black Culture and the Origins of Transatlantic Modernism* (New York: Oxford University Press, 1998). Lemke describes primitivist modernism as a hybrid, multiracial, and transatlantic cultural formation.

20. Shawn Michelle Smith's exploration of French praise for W. E. B. Du Bois's photographic exhibition of the American Negro at the 1900 Paris Exposition exposes the same dynamic. See Shawn Michelle Smith, *Photography on the Color Line: W. E. B. Du Bois, Race, and Visual Culture* (Durham, NC: Duke University Press, 2004).

21. "French Call Fight a Fake Unless a Knock-Out Ends It," *Washington Post*, February 19, 1911.

22. French newspaper reports corroborate this story of black American independence. McVea took his white manager to court and then took over the management of his own affairs. See "Sam Mac Vea devant le tribunal" ("Sam Mac Vea before the Court"), *L'auto*, March 28, 1909; "Sam Mac Vea Manager," *L'auto*, October 15, 1909.

23. Jacques Mortane, "Athlétisme: Un beau combat de boxe" ("A Beautiful Boxing Match"), *La vie au grand air*, January 11, 1908, 26.

24. "Après le match—Sen-Sen chewing gum" ("After the Match: Sen-Sen Chewing Gum"), *L'auto*, March 28, 1909. McVea's caption was written in the same pidgin French (*petit nègre*) spoken by many of the African *tirailleurs*. On the importance of language in the maintenance of the racial division between white and black in the French military, see Berliner, *Ambivalent Desire*, 14.

25. For a discussion of "contact zones," see Mary Louise Pratt, *Imperial Eyes: Travel Writing and Transculturation* (New York: Routledge, 1992).

26. Sylvie Chalaye, *Nègres en images* (*Negroes in Imagery*) (Paris: L'Harmattan, 2002), 110–11; Berliner, *Ambivalent Desire*, 9–10.

27. Charles Mangin, *La force noire* (*The Black Force*) (Paris: Hachette, 1910), 355.

28. On the existence of a similar racial dynamic in the United States, see Bederman, *Manliness and Civilization*, 170–215. Bederman illustrates that Theodore Roosevelt and other white American middle-class adherents of the "strenuous life" appropriated the Wild West and images of primitive Native American manhood to combat the supposed feminizing tendencies of modern life. Building on Bederman's analysis, I argue that this discursive relationship among race, manhood, and the body was not just a U.S. phenomenon but rather a fundamental part of the broader geopolitical climate of the white man's burden.

29. Chalaye, *Nègres en images*, 99–101.

30. Ibid., 103. Also see Dana S. Hale, "French Images of Race on Product Trademarks during the Third Republic," and Richard Fogarty and Michael Osbourne, "The Constructions and Functions of Race in French Military Medicine, 1830–1920," in *The Color of Liberty: Histories of Race in France*, ed. Sue Peabody and Tyler Stovall (Durham, NC: Duke University Press, 2003), 131–46, 206–36; and Hale, *Races on Display: French Representations of Colonized Peoples, 1886–1940* (Bloomington: Indiana University Press, 2008), 91–99; Berliner, *Ambivalent Desire*, 9–36.

31. Patricia Leighten, "The White Peril and L'Art Nègre: Picasso, Primitivism, and Anticolonialism," *Art Bulletin* 72 (1990): 609–30; Jennifer Boittin, "Soleil Noir: Race, Gender, and Colonialism in Interwar Paris" (PhD diss., Yale University, 2005), 16.

32. André Dunoyer de Segonzac, qtd. in Claude Meunier, *Ring noir: Quand Apollinaire, Cendrars et Picabia découvraient les boxeurs nègres* (*Black Ring: How Apollinaire, Cendrars, and Picabia Discovered the Black Boxers*) (Paris: PLON, 1992), 35.

33. L. Manaud, "Un véritable championnat du monde" ("A True Championship of the World"), *L'auto*, January 6, 1909.

34. "Comment s'entraînent Jeannette et Mac Vea" ("How Jeannette and Mac Vea Train"), *L'auto*, February 12, 1909.

35. See, for example, "Les deux terribles nègres s'entraînent avec ardeur" ("The Two Terrible Niggers Train with Ardor"), *L'auto*, January 15, 1909.

36. L. Manaud, "Joe Jeannette au travail" ("Joe Jeannette at Work"), *L'auto*, January 9, 1909. Also see L. Manaud, "Le grand match—Sam Mac Vea contre Joe Jeannette" ("The Grand Match—Sam Mac Vea against Joe Jeannette"), *L'auto*, February 19, 1909; Jacques Mortane, "Joe Jeannette à l'entraînement" ("Joe Jeannette in Training"), *La vie au grand air*, February 13, 1909, 106.

37. "Les deux terribles nègres."

38. G. Dubois, "Leurs mensurations" ("Their Measurements"), *L'auto*, February 18, 1909; "Silhouettes des combattants" ("Silhouettes of the Fighters"), *L'auto*, February 20, 1909.

39. "Joe Jeannette à Paris" ("Joe Jeannette in Paris"), *L'auto*, January 8, 1909; "Les grands combats de boxe" ("Great Boxing Matches"), *L'auto*, January 14, 1909; Mich, "Joe Jeannette ne trouve plus d'adversaires!" ("Joe Jeannette Can't Find Any More Adversaries!"), *L'auto*, January 29, 1909; Mich, "Les grands champions" ("The Great Champions"), *L'auto*, February 1, 1909. The caricature of Jeannette shows the black fighter squaring off against a bucking horse.

40. Regarding his race, Jeannette wrote in a British sporting magazine, "Although I have been called a Canadian, I was born in Hoboken, N.J., of a white mother. I am the happy father of two children, also begot of white blood, so that we are none of us of the race known as 'niggers'" ("That World's Title," *Boxing: New Year's Annual 1914* [London, 1914], 43). While one could argue that Jeannette expressed an alarming level of racial self-hatred, his marketing of himself as a mulatto fighter certainly played into the prevailing narratives of whiteness and civilization in Europe, where the one-drop rule was less applicable than in the United States.

41. "Les deux terribles nègres"; "L'opinion de la presse" ("The Opinion of the Press"), *L'auto*, February 22, 1909; "Le grand match de samedi prochain" ("Next Saturday's Great Match"), *L'auto*, February 17, 1909; "Une grande soirée pugilistique" ("A Great Pugilistic Evening"), *L'auto*, February 21, 1909; "Ce Grand combat aura lieu le samedi 20 février" ("The Big Fight Will Take Place on Saturday, February 20"), *L'auto*, January 16, 1909; "Le chiffre de la recette" ("The Revenue"), *L'auto*, February 22, 1909.

42. *La Patrie*, qtd. in "L'opinion de la presse"; Georges Dupuy, "Le tigre et le bison" ("The Tiger and the Bison"), *L'auto*, February 21, 1909; "A coups de confetti" ("With Throws of Confetti"), *L'auto*, February 24, 1909.

43. *La vie illustrée* (*The Illustrated Life*), qtd. in "Après le grand match: Que dit-on de la rencontre" ("After the Big Match: What are we saying of the match?"), *L'auto*, February 23, 1909; J. Joseph-Renaud, "Un cinématographe? . . . !" ("A Cinematograph? . . . !") *L'auto*, February 24, 1909; Tristan Bernard, "Après le grand match: Sam et Joe" ("After the Big Match: Sam and Joe"), *L'auto*, February 22, 1909; "Les jaloux" ("The Jealous"), *L'auto*, March 3, 1909.

44. Marcel Prévost of *Figaro*, qtd. in "L'opinion de la presse."

45. Boxing and physical culture had already gained greater respectability as character-building activities for modern men in the United States and in Britain. See Bederman, *Manliness and Civilization*, 170–215; Elliot Gorn, *The Manly Art: Bare-Knuckle Prize Fighting in America* (Ithaca, NY: Cornell University Press, 1986), 179–206.

46. "La revanche aura lieu!" ("The Rematch Will Take Place!"), *L'auto*, March 30, 1909 ; Meunier, *Ring noir*, 33–34; Georges Dupuy, "Sam Mac Vea contre Joe Jeannette: Après le grand match" ("Sam Mac Vea against Joe Jeannette: After the Big Match"), *L'auto*, April 19, 1909.

47. Dunoyer de Segonzac, qtd. in Meunier, *Ring Noir*, 35–36; "Après le grand match: Impressions d'un monsieur chauve" ("After the Big Match: Impressions of a Bald Gentleman"), *L'auto*, April 20, 1909; Tristan Bernard, "Le plus beau combat" ("The Most Beautiful Fight"), *L'auto*, April 19, 1909. On "double consciousness," see W. E. B. Du Bois, "Of Our Spiritual Strivings," in *The Souls of Black Folk*, ed. Henry Louis Gates Jr. and Terry Hume Oliver (New York: Norton, 1999), 11. As Du Bois wrote, "It is a peculiar sensation, this double-consciousness, this sense of always looking at one's self through the eyes of others, of measuring one's soul by the tape of a world that looks on in amused contempt and pity."

48. For descriptions of Grognet's school, see L. Manaud, "Le rendez-vous des combattants" ("The Meeting of Fighters"), *L'auto*, September 30, 1909 ; and "Maitres et champions: Un grand établissement sportif à Paris," ("Masters and Champions: A Great Sporting Establishment in Paris"), *L'auto*, September 16, 1909.

49. *La boxe et les boxeurs*, December 22, 1909, 67; "A vous touché," *La boxe et les boxeurs*, December 15, 1909, 41–42.

50. "Ernest Stevens Visits Jack Johnson in Paris," *Chicago Defender*, April 25, 1914. Stevens had sent a series of letters to the *Chicago Defender* describing his visits to places like Brazil, Argentina, England, Germany, and other European countries.

51. Ibid.

52. Ibid.; Geoffrey Ward, *Unforgivable Blackness: The Rise and Fall of Jack Johnson* (New York: Knopf, 2004), 358.

53. "Une publication sensationelle" ("A Sensational Publication"), *La vie au grand air*, January 14, 1911, 21.

54. Ward, *Unforgivable Blackness*, 4–5.

55. Jack Johnson, *Mes combats* (*My Battles*) (Paris: Lafitte, 1914). There is now a composite English translation of the series of articles and this book: Jack Johnson, *My Life and Battles*, trans. Chris Rivers (Westport, CT: Praeger, 2007). Johnson's first English autobiography did not appear until later. See Jack Johnson, *In the Ring—And Out* (1927; New York: Citadel, 1992).

56. McKay's works, *Banjo* and *A Long Way from Home*, have emerged as two of the most examined texts of early twentieth-century black American, particularly working-class, travel.

See Edwards, *Practice of Diaspora*, 187–240; Stephens, *Black Empire*, 129–203. *Banjo* describes the multiracial, working-class environment of the French port city of Marseilles, while McKay's autobiography traces his own international wanderings. Claude McKay, *Banjo: A Story without a Plot* (1929; New York: Harcourt Brace, 1957); Claude McKay, *A Long Way from Home: An Autobiography* (1937; London: Pluto, 1985).

57. Jack Johnson, "Ma vie et mes combats" ("My Life and Battles"), *La vie au grand air*, January 21, 1911, 47.

58. Ibid. On Roosevelt's ideas of the "strenuous life," see Bederman, *Manliness and Civilization*, 170–215.

59. Johnson, "Ma vie et mes combats," January 21, 1911, 48.

60. Ibid.; Jack Johnson, "Ma vie et mes combats," *La vie au grand air*, February 4, 1911, 79.

61. Jack Johnson, "Ma vie et mes combats," *La vie au grand air*, January 28, 1911, 64.

62. Jack Johnson, "Ma vie et mes combats," *La vie au grand air*, February 18, 1911, 114.

63. Ibid.

64. Jack Johnson, "Ma vie et mes combats," *La vie au grand air*, April 29, 1911, 275. *La vie au grand air* printed the English verse and then translated it for readers.

65. Kipling was one of Johnson's favorite poets. Ward, *Unforgivable Blackness*, 329.

66. McKay, *A Long Way from Home*, 61.

67. Ibid., 69–70.

68. *New York Times*, March 18, 1923, qtd. in Peter Benson, *Battling Siki: A Tale of Ring Fixes, Race, and Murder in the 1920s* (Fayetteville: University of Arkansas Press, 2006), 12.

69. Ibid., 12–14, 25–26, 37–39.

70. Bob Scanlon, "The Record of a Negro Boxer," in *Negro: An Anthology*, ed. Nancy Cunard (New York: Ungar, 1970), 210.

71. Harry Reeve, "My Impressions of Battling Siki: A Good Man But a Wild One," *Boxing*, November 15, 1922, 215–16.

72. Dan Schocket, "Battling Siki—the Man They Turned into a Joke," *World Boxing*, September 1974, qtd. in Benson, *Battling Siki*, 89. Also see Ed Cunningham, "Siki Denies Coming from Jungle," *The Ring*, August 1925, 28.

73. "Americanism in France," *Messenger*, September 1922, 477.

74. "Battling Siki Suspended," *London Times*, November 11, 1922; J. Bissell, "The Bar Up to Siki," *Boxing World, Mirror of Life, and Sporting Observer*, November 18, 1922; "Italian Boxing Clubs Close Their Doors to Battling Siki," *New York Times*, November 15, 1922; "Major Arnold Wilson's Attitude," *London Times*, November 11, 1922; "Opens Competition for Siki's Title," *New York Times*, November 23, 1922; "Siki's License Is Canceled by French Boxing Federation," *New York Times*, November 22, 1922; "Siki Is Deprived of French Title," *New York Times*, November 10, 1922; "Siki Now Barred from Boxing Here," *New York Times*, November 11, 1922. Also see Benson, *Battling Siki*, 251, 253–55.

75. "Siki Case to Be Aired in French Chamber," *New York Times*, November 30, 1922. Also see Gerald Early, "Battling Siki: The Boxer as Natural Man," in *The Culture of Bruising: Essays on Prizefighting, Literature, and Modern American Culture* (Hopewell, NJ: Ecco, 1994), 73.

76. "Dark-Hued Deputy Loses Plea for Siki," *New York Times*, December 1, 1922.

77. McKay, "Negroes in Sports," 50–52.

78. Ibid., 53.

79. "De Siki à la révolution mondiale" ("Of Siki and the Worldwide Revolution"), *Le Paria*, November 1922. Apparently, film producers were considering hiring Siki to star in a moving picture version of *Batuoula*. See "Siki's Victory Stirs Americans in France to Protest Equality," *Chicago Defender*, October 7, 1922.

The Violence of Diaspora:

Governmentality, Class Cultures,

and Circulations

Deborah A. Thomas

One of the problematics haunting much of the scholarship on the African diaspora has to do with how, when, and why questions regarding the state often seem to drop out of our analytic frames. This is not to say that there has not been a long history of diaspora scholarship that has taken the political economies of black folks' relations to particular states as its foundational rubric. Think here not only of classic texts such as W. E. B. Du Bois's *Black Reconstruction* (1935) or *The Philadelphia Negro* (1899), for example, but also of canonical histories of black Marxisms and even of contemporary explorations of particular sites of pan-Africanist or internationalist mobilization.[1] Of course, one of the points of using diaspora as a rubric for analysis is to get outside the limiting framework of nation-states for understanding modes of communication and the creation of political and cultural communities.

Yet what is often missing in these accounts is a sense of the transnational, indeed transimperial, dimensions of particular governmental projects. This sense is also absent from the bulk of culturalist scholarship that became hegemonic in African diaspora studies in the mid-twentieth-century United States. This body of work, on the one hand, elaborated an analysis of cultural continuities, retentions, and syncretisms—in other words, an analysis of Africanisms within American societies. On the other hand, it focused on comparative diasporic cultures, the kind of "black folk here and there" approach often associated with St. Clair Drake.[2]

Radical History Review

Issue 103 (Winter 2009)   DOI 10.1215/01636545-2008-032

© 2009 by MARHO: The Radical Historians' Organization, Inc.

I argue here that a focus on modes of governmentality across empires helps us (1) maintain a critical dialogue between the two registers in which we mobilize the term *diaspora*—both as an instantiation of a worldwide black community that is the result of the transatlantic slave trade and as the community formations resulting from contemporary transnational migrations; and (2) clarify how particular state projects were imagined and developed transnationally. A better understanding of these two dimensions would clarify the ways gender and sexual norms are mobilized by states in ways that reproduce class hierarchies through the idea of "culture." The specific project that will concern me in this essay has to do with the attempts to characterize and manage diverse class cultures within black American populations by way of the discourse of dysfunction that arose in relation to black family formation in the United States and the West Indies in the post–World War II period. I am interested in this discourse first, because of what it can tell us about how links were posited—and institutionalized through policy—between the economy, family, and political participation for communities of African descent in a range of locations at a particular moment. Second, I want to investigate how these links have produced a kind of epistemological violence that continues to pervade contemporary popular analyses of actually existing violence among black populations at home and abroad, even though the political and economic basis for these links has shifted fairly radically.

Specifically, I want to think through the proliferation of discourse about the so-called culture of violence seen to characterize particular Caribbean societies and to accompany migrants from these societies into diasporic locales. I will argue that the culture of violence discourse has its roots in the earlier mobilization of the culture of poverty trope, itself the result of a culturalist approach to understanding inequality that became solidified in the aftermath of World War II. This is an approach in which difference is mapped in terms of culture, and culture itself then becomes reified, a static term that is seen to determine the behavior, outlook, and potential of entire groups. I will show that the development of culturalist discourse vis-à-vis black family formation was transnational, having particular but related effects among different diasporic (in the sense of worldwide black community) populations and that this discourse also moves with people as they create diasporas (in the sense of transnational migrant communities). Ultimately, my aim in this essay is to build on the work of scholars like Hazel Carby, M. Jacqui Alexander, Ann Stoler, and Elizabeth Povinelli to show how the classed and gendered dimensions of state projects are entangled, and that this entanglement is both reproduced by and reproduces culturalist-oriented scholarship, even in the face of much transformed ways of organizing global relatedness in economic and political spheres.[3] That is, I am interested in black people's relationships to states across imperial and generational moments, and specifically in how the movement from a mid-twentieth-century emphasis on state-centered industrial modernization to a late twentieth-/

early twenty-first-century movement toward global neoliberalism has affected the ways black masculinity and black family formation are positioned in relation to development paradigms.

Discourses of Depravity: Jamaicans and the Culture of Violence

Let me start with two true stories. Early in the morning on Good Friday 2005, a close friend of mine called Vinny was killed, ambushed by gunmen at the gate of his yard as he was on his way out to pasture his goat.[4] Vinny was someone I had come to know very well during my initial PhD fieldwork in a rural hillside community just outside Kingston in the mid- and late 1990s, and he was someone with whom I had kept in close touch ever since. The gunmen had come for his licensed firearm to fuel the unprecedented gang war that had quickly enveloped the community over the previous year or two. When Vinny did not produce the gun immediately, the three youth pulled their own, eventually shooting him eight times and dumping his body in the gully behind the house. They took the gun and ran off, leaving Vinny's family to search for his body. I flew to Jamaica to help Vinny's wife, Winsome, prepare for his funeral and for the nine-night celebration that would precede it.[5] We went up to the house (which, after Vinny's murder, had been abandoned by family members who had scattered for safety) to pack up some of Vinny's personal things and then traveled to the funeral home to drop off his burial clothing. As we waited to see his embalmed body, we watched as the police brought in a body attached to a wooden cross. It was not clear whether the person had been killed before the de facto crucifixion or not, but the specter of his dangling, bloody limbs was obviously meant to serve as a public example and warning. This kind of exemplary spectacularity was repeated in a different form over the weekend, as two men were murdered and their bodies set ablaze beneath a heap of rubber tires in an open lot in West Kingston. For a national community becoming lamentably accustomed to these sorts of performative acts of brutality, the following incident—my second example—nevertheless provoked alarm and outcry.

On October 5, 2005, several armed men firebombed a dwelling in southwest St. Andrew near downtown Kingston, possibly as part of a feud between men from two areas in the district. Four people were killed in the blaze; they were unable to escape the burning house due to the padlock that secured the veranda's iron grille. One of these four was ten-year-old Sasha-Kay Brown, who spent her last moments pleading for help from her neighbors. "The little girl climbed up on the grille and called out the names of almost everybody who lived on Barnes Avenue, begging them to come and help her," one woman recalled. "But when we ran out of our houses and tried to assist her, the gunmen fired at us. The last thing we heard the little girl said [*sic*] was that the fire was burning her, then her voice just faded."[6] The gunmen also shot and killed the family's dog, whose body was later found in the burnt-out yard.

For Kingstonians inured to the day-to-day violence that surrounds them, this quadruple murder was nonetheless stunning. For many newspaper and radio-show commentators, it marked a new level of brutality and cruelty — "cold and ruthless death squads" using children in the settling of scores between grown men. Cedric Wilson, an economist and a guest columnist for the *Gleaner* (one of two daily newspapers in Jamaica), argued that the quadruple murder signaled a new phase of war. "The ruthlessness of the crimes being committed are the acts of twisted supermen," he stated. "This is [a] new breed of criminals without soul or conscience, evil men for whom the conception of good and evil is irrelevant." Garth Rattray, a frequent columnist for the *Gleaner*, went a step further, arguing that by devaluing each other's humanity in such dramatic ways, we are no better than the imperialist slave masters of yore:

These murderers exhibit the same brand of selfish, insular, tribal thinking that landed our forefathers here in the first place. . . . We used to enslave each other for conquest; now we enslave each other out of lust for power. We used to sell our fellowman to the Europeans for baubles, glass and metal; now we sell out our fellowman to crime bosses for drugs and money. We may not like to admit it, but as long as people have to live in fear, as long as people are internally displaced by violence, as long as people are being eliminated, we are still an enslaved nation.[7]

Of course, these two examples are not the only ones I could have cited, but they are the kinds of spectacular killings that are usually given as evidence of Jamaica's culture of violence. This phrase itself is so taken for granted that it is commonly used as if its meaning were universally understood and agreed on. In the Executive Summary of 2005's National Security Strategy green paper, for example, it appears thusly: "The continuous growth in the number of violent incidents causes many Jamaicans at home to live in fear, and influence [*sic*] those in the diaspora to abandon their dream of resettling on the 'rock.' It is now conceded that Jamaica has spawned a culture of violence in its most negative form, which is abhorrent to its values and stands in the way of every kind of social progress." For many commentators, Jamaica is seen as a "killing society," to use the words of Hermione McKenzie, the president of the Association of Women's Organizations in Jamaica, and crime is seen to be a way of life in which the gun constitutes a symbol of manhood. By corollary, sexual violence, according to Women's Media Watch, is normalized as a part of an overall "inner-city" culture of violence characterized by political violence, drugs, and gangs, a culture that is then glorified through the media and thereby reproduced.[8]

Though it now extends across the country, this violence is understood as having initially been concentrated in the capital city of Kingston and its surrounding areas. This is, in part, because the so-called inner-city communities whose names evoke the landscape of political and drug-related violence that is ordinarily a defining feature of gang warfare in Jamaica—Southside, Grants Pen, Tivoli Gardens, August Town—are located there. Historically, these communities have been referred to as "garrisons," a term originally used by the demographer Carl Stone to denote political strongholds led by "top rankings" in which any significant social, economic, or cultural development only occurred under the auspices of the dominant party leadership and where residents seeking to oppose or organize against the dominant political party risked suffering personal injury and property damage. Most analysts trace the development of garrison communities to post–World War II urbanization and the disruption of traditional social orders and networks. With the urban economy unable to absorb the rapidly expanding labor market, unemployment rose dramatically, and growing discontent among new migrants was fueled by what Stone called an "expectations gap." The new population of "sufferers" became vulnerable to politicians who discovered that they could be enticed to become party loyalists with promises of political spoils. As the opposing parties built their cadres of supporters willing to win elections by any means necessary, political gangs with the intention of intimidating voters and of cementing political garrisons also appeared. Leaders of these gangs maintained close links with politicians, creating a situation of democratic clientelism also known as political tribalism.[9]

By the mid-1970s, the "sufferers'" physical neighborhoods were polarized, as units in newly constructed large-scale housing developments downtown were given only to supporters of one or the other political candidate; thus, Tivoli Gardens developed as a Jamaica Labour Party (JLP) enclave, and Arnett Gardens, for example, developed as a People's National Party (PNP) enclave. Within these communities, party activists pushed out minority party supporters, in many cases forcing them to set up squatter communities elsewhere. Since residents of garrison communities operate with a profound distrust of the police, the "dons" or area leaders become the political authorities in the area, performing statelike functions such as security, the mediation of domestic and other disputes, and the determination of guilt and punishment; they also help with access to health care and education. This kind of assistance is crucial in spaces where the neoliberal state has abandoned people to what one resident in a World Bank–funded study on violence in inner-city communities termed "bare survival." In other words, as several academic and editorial commentators have noted, "the hard core garrison communities exhibit an element of autonomy, in that they are states within a state. The Jamaican state has no authority or power except in as far as its forces are able to invade in the form of police and military raids."[10]

Though the locations of the original so-called garrison communities have remained constant through the years, the social organization of crime began changing in the mid-1970s. At that time, the more intense export trade in ganja coincided with the oil crisis and the foreign exchange and balance of payments crises. The concomitant implementation of structural adjustment policies also worsened patterns of inequality and increased poverty. During the late 1970s and the early 1980s, growing unemployment and an increased cost of living prompted a move from political partisan violence to turf violence. In other words, people became less beholden to politicians, though they still remained loyal to their party. In part, this was because after the 1980 elections, which were particularly bloody (over eight hundred of the almost one thousand murders that year were attributed to political campaigning), several area dons were sent abroad, while others began pursuing full-time criminal activity in Jamaica. The clamping down on the ganja trade and the newly transnational organization of political gangs led many to go into cocaine and crack distribution, both in the United States (principally in New York and Miami) and in Jamaica. The hard-drug business also generated a trade in illegal high-powered weapons, which has ensured easier access to guns for the general population.[11]

This new organization of violence has had a major effect on the residential location patterns of the urban poor, many of whom are forced to flee deteriorating war zones and the destruction of their homes and places of employment. Because rival politically affiliated gangs continue to challenge the state's claims to legitimacy and authority (already challenged, of course, by various leaders' own involvement in the industries of violence in Jamaica), several crime-reduction plans have been initiated in the past decade, and task forces have been commissioned to write reports and give suggestions about how to reduce political and gang violence. Despite these efforts, however, by 2004 the murder rate in Jamaica reached 60 per 100,000 people, the highest in the world. Moreover, by the end of 2007, 843 murders had been committed compared to 756 during the comparable period in 2006, an increase of about 14 percent. In July alone within the capital city of Kingston and the two surrounding parishes of St. Andrew and St. Catherine, 89 people were killed, an 82–percent increase over July 2006, which saw 49 murders. Part of this increase might be attributed to political campaigning, as general elections were held on September 3, 2007.[12]

Crime and violence have thus become an integral part of the fabric of day-to-day life in Jamaica—not only within the so-called inner-city communities that were first politicized during the 1960s and then mobilized by drug dons in the 1980s but throughout society as a whole. As a result, some Jamaicans and outside observers alike have come to understand violence as a primordial aspect of Jamaican culture, an essentialist view in which it is "not merely that the violence has an internal semiotic (and therefore to understand the violence one has to understand the culture)," as David Scott has written, "but that the semiotic of the culture is—at least in part—violence, and *therefore* to understand the culture, one has to understand the violence."[13] In other words, the notion of a culture of violence presupposes a kind of savagery that hearkens back to earlier scientific racisms. This is a vision not only held by Jamaicans in Jamaica but also by those living abroad, a point made clear by the fact that crime was one of the biggest agenda issues during the June 2006 Jamaica Diaspora Foundation conference in Kingston—where overseas Jamaicans identified crime as the number one factor inhibiting their own return and their ability to conduct business in Jamaica—and by the decision in late 2005 to stop reporting weekly crime statistics in the newspaper and to remove crime reportage from the front page of the *Gleaner*. This last action was taken in part because Jamaicans living abroad complained that constant front-page coverage of murders not only made foreigners wary of visiting Jamaica but also made U.S. citizens discriminate against resident Jamaicans on the basis of hailing from such a violent nation. Their concerns highlight how, for many U.S. nationals, the association of violent crime with particular immigrant groups intensifies the nativist and anti-immigrant sentiment that has played so large a role in class and racial formation in the United States.[14]

The sense that Jamaica is a hotbed of out-of-control violent crime is not confined to the U.S. context, but also extends to other Caribbean migrant destinations. For example, in April 2007, Tony Blair publicly stated that "the spate of knife and gun murders in London was not being caused by poverty, but [by] a distinctive black culture," one characterized, in part, by bringing up youth "in a setting that has no rules, no discipline, no proper framework," and no father. This comment ran counter to analyses given by others in his administration, who stressed that black youth were disproportionately impoverished and therefore disproportionately represented within the criminal justice system in England. Blair based his statement on the comments of a black pastor, who later argued that his remark to Blair—"When are we going to start saying this is a problem amongst a section of the black community and not, for reasons of political correctness, pretend that this is nothing to do with it?"—was taken out of context. Blair also advocated an "'intense police focus' on the minority of young black Britons behind the gun and knife attacks," leading many community leaders to fear heightened police profiling and discrimination. Finally, he argued that "we need to stop thinking of this as a society that has gone wrong—it has not—but of specific groups that for specific reasons have gone outside of the proper lines of respect and good conduct towards others and need by specific measures to be brought back into the fold."[15]

In Toronto, Canada, another Caribbean immigrant destination, an exploration of blogs and newspaper editorials that address the 9 percent increase in the city's homicide rate in 2005 reveals a similar anti-immigrant stance. For many of these commentators, and especially for those on the more conservative end of the political spectrum, Jamaicans were seen to be responsible for 80 percent or more of the city's gun crime and certainly for the bulk of the city's murders, although they constituted only 7 percent of the city's population of 2.5 million. Jamaica, in these accounts, is seen as the "birth place for the gang culture now taking hold of the city," and Jamaicans are thus positioned as "utterly ruthless and remorseless psychopaths" who come from "fatherless homes." These Jamaicans bring to Toronto a "'born fi' dead' culture" that is proliferating because of "poorly screened immigration and multiculturalism policies that encourage immigrants to hang onto their culture no matter how dysfunctional or destructive." In this view, Jamaicans are born into a pathological culture of violence that they carry with them as they migrate to Toronto, infecting an otherwise peaceful, tolerant, and by some accounts overly generous Canadian ethos. Yet it is not only within metropolitan centers that the discourse of the Jamaican culture of violence is mobilized. In early twentieth-century Cuba, there was a general criminalization of black migrants who came to work the sugar estates, and recent escalations of violence in Trinidad and Guyana are sometimes anecdotally discussed in terms of the ways local patterns might be becoming "Jamaican-ized."[16]

Violence, in these types of accounts, is not only racialized but also sexualized. This is because the cases I focus on here foreground the impression that black youth have been raised in households that deviate from the normative pattern of sexual relations and family formation and infer that this is one of the principal causal factors of the violence. Even more critical, here violence is positioned as external to the formation of states like the United States, the United Kingdom, and Canada, rather than as constitutive of them. However, as anthropologists, historians, and other social theorists have by now convincingly demonstrated, violence is and has been part and parcel of nationalism—both in the initial struggle for statehood and in the ongoing efforts to construct a notion of citizenship.[17] This is true not only for European states, many of whose consolidation was the result of imperialist expansion and slavery, but also for new states formed in the post–World War II period as the result of anticolonial movements. But by positioning violence as external to the process of state formation, certain commentators reproduce a notion of violence as cultural rather than structural (even though they may identify factors such as poverty as producing violence in particular contexts). They also perpetuate analytic discourses that position New World blacks as culturally deviant and therefore as ultimately unassimilable to the nationalist ideals that characterize the states in which they find themselves. In other words, existing violence both generates and reproduces a particular epistemological violence—one that has become the dominant framework through which many understand the place of black people in relation to states.

Diasporic Silences: The Violence of Discursive Elisions

Because the contexts of knowledge production influence the kind of knowledge that is pursued, most scholars would readily agree that the political, economic, and sociocultural issues and assumptions current at any given moment shape the questions we ask, the arguments we make, and the concepts we use. Brent Edwards's 2001 *Social Text* essay, "The Uses of Diaspora," lays out a genealogy that clarifies some of the context shaping the scholarly turn to diaspora and discusses how uses of the term have changed over time. In the discussion below, I pick up on a few of his points to push us in another direction.

Edwards contends that the use of the term *diaspora* entered scholarly literature in the United States during the 1950s as African American scholars became interested in the transnational black influences on anticolonial movements in Africa. Diaspora, on the one hand, became a way for U.S. scholars to think through differences of opinion regarding "the political scope of *Pan-Africanism* in the independence moment," as well as a way to explore the question of origins. It was thus a concept that was, in his words, "resistant or exorbitant to the frames of nations and continents" in relation to both cultural politics and realpolitik. However, as the Cold War gained speed and as African nations gained independence, diaspora became reduced to its cultural aspects, "rather than precisely a means to theorize both culture and politics at the transnational level."[18] The question of origins became a question of culture, at which point anthropology entered the picture.

While St. Clair Drake advocated a comparative analysis of diaspora populations that was oriented toward the goal of coordinating action to, in his words, "complete the worldwide task of Black Liberation," earlier comparative scholarship on blacks in the New World was shaped by a Boasian focus on acculturation and the diffusion of particular cultural traits across what were then known as "culture areas."[19] Melville Herskovits, Franz Boas's student, was particularly interested in the different degrees to which New World black populations retained, adapted, and reinterpreted cultural practices understood as African in derivation. Friends with many of the Harlem Renaissance bigwigs (Zora Neale Hurston was one of his research assistants), Herskovits felt that clarifying the African derivation of African American cultural practices in particular would counter the claims of those who asserted that black Americans had no significant cultural legacy and therefore contributed nothing culturally or politically to the United States. Herskovits's idea was that providing evidence of this cultural legacy through "scientific" study would not only bolster African American self-esteem but also lessen racial prejudice. The model he developed—the "scale of Africanisms"—has been understood by critics and sympathizers alike as more of a classificatory scheme than a theory. Nevertheless it provided one blueprint for imagining that New World black populations might share a common history and, by implication, might be able to construct a common future.[20]

While the kind of culturalist analysis that Herskovits mobilized provided the basis for a cultural politics that countered the denigration of "things African," it also heralded, as Penny Von Eschen has argued, a "shift from the vocabulary of political economy to the language of moralism." In part, this shift was also due to the move away from biologically based theories of racial difference and toward a framework "that defined differential racial and ethnic characteristics as matters of learned cultural norms" — a move that was itself the result of the post–World War II racial liberalism spurred by the emergent civil rights movement and the Cold War. Yet there were two conservative effects of the anticommunist fervor of the early Cold War period. First, sociological analyses of race and class began to privilege a focus on culture over a focus on socioeconomic inequality. This had both academic and practical effects. Academically, it supported a liberal view of development that naturalized capitalist competition and that positioned the cultural (and sexual) practices of middle-class white Americans as normative. Moreover, racism was then portrayed as "an anachronistic prejudice and a personal and psychological problem, rather than as a systemic problem rooted in specific social practices and pervading relations of political economy and culture." Practically, the cultural model put forward by intellectuals like Michael Harrington (whose book *The Other America* was said to provide the impetus for President Lyndon B. Johnson's War on Poverty) and Daniel Moynihan and Nathan Glazer (whose *Beyond the Melting Pot* was also taken up in policy circles) directed attention away from the overall political economy of American capitalism and of how it "uses, abuses, and divides its poorly organized working class" and toward psychologically oriented assimilationist strategies for eliminating poverty.[21] These strategies emphasized self-help, but not the kind of self-help that looks like grassroots political organization among a class *for itself*.

The second conservative effect of early Cold War anticommunism was that activism toward black liberation began to privilege a focus on nationalism over a focus on internationalism. In Von Eschen's analysis of how the Truman Doctrine and Cold War politics led black Americans to become increasingly exceptionalist to secure their demands for equality in the United States, she argues that liberal African Americans eschewed a previous emphasis on the oppression of black peoples worldwide to secure particular kinds of rights "at home."[22] Of course, as she shows, this was not necessarily a freely made choice among black activist circles; anticolonial activists experienced significant repression at the hands of the government during the early Cold War period. Yet to legitimate the emergent sense that the United States should lead the "free world" and to shape international perceptions of American race relations, the Truman administration and the State Department offered a compromise that narrowed the scope of what constituted a black community.[23]

Herein lies the root of the epistemological violence generated by the turn to culturalist analysis. The question of where black populations stood in relation to states (an important question for black Americans after the failure of Reconstruction and for colonial blacks especially after World War II) became secondary to the question of how blacks in the West were connected to roots, to Africa. And though the language of cultural politics has enabled a critique that is antinationalist, it abandons the impetus within *inter*nationalism toward imagining alternative ways to constitute political community.[24] It also derails a more global political economic analysis that would frame violence in Jamaica within a more historical and relational context.

That is, a culturalist analysis of diaspora tends to obscure a focus on how some imperial and nationalist projects have been developed transnationally, producing similar challenging effects for black populations in the diaspora. Chief among these projects is that which concerned African American family formation and sexuality and which resulted in a discursive labeling of both African American and black Caribbean communities as sharing a culture of poverty as a result of faulty familial organization.

The Culturalization of Poverty and Violence

In the immediate aftermath of the Civil War in the United States, the Freedmen's Bureau—a federal agency established in 1865 to protect and aid emancipated slaves in the South—began to concern itself with family formation. Newly emancipated slaves were not only encouraged to marry but were faced with imprisonment and in some cases denied pension payments if they decided not to. In this way, Roderick Ferguson reminds us, the bureau played an active role in the attempt to "rationalize African American sexuality by imposing heterosexual marriage upon the freedman through the rule of law and as a condition for citizenship."[25] In doing so, the burden of responsibility for former slaves was shifted from the government and former slaveholders to the patriarchal husband, now seen as legally responsible for the well-being of the household. This federal attempt was short-lived, however, as the bureau was discontinued in 1869, though its educational activities continued for an additional three years. Nevertheless, the groundwork was set for linking patterns of family formation to legitimate economic and political participation in a newly united nation-state.

In the West Indies—and in Jamaica in particular—the situation was somewhat different as the colonial state did not involve itself in Afro-Jamaican family formation until much later. Baptists and other missionaries, however, were very much interested in creating respectable Christian blacks out of the masses of freed people after full emancipation in 1838. They imagined legitimate family formation through marriage as an integral part of a series of reforms that would remake former slaves into a nascent middle class, one modeled on middle-class Englishmen—in other words, a middle class that embodied the values of independence, thrift, moderation, modesty, and education.[26] If slavery had created "an unnatural phenomenon, male slaves who were entirely dependent on their masters," in the missionary communities developed after emancipation in Jamaica, black men were now to have the opportunity to be *real* men by casting off dependency and by taking charge of their now legitimate households. As in the United States, because the Jamaican colonial state had depended on the plantations to provide welfare during slavery, this was also a move to socialize in newly freed people the values of working for wages and of paying for medical care and education. In both cases, family structure became a way to measure progress and civilization (that is, assimilation into the postemancipation state), and white heteropatriarchal, middle-class families became the standard against which African American and Afro-Jamaican families were judged. As Ferguson argues, the "demand for a racialized heteronormativity released polymorphous exclusions targeting women, people of color, and gays and lesbians at the same time that it became a regulatory regime, working to inspire conformity among women, people of color, and homosexuals."[27]

Notably, however, black family structure in the West Indies did not become a concern of the imperial government until after the labor rebellions that swept through the region during the late 1930s. Prior to that time, as historian Lara Putnam has demonstrated, Afro-Jamaican promiscuity and the high rates of children born to unmarried women (approximately two-thirds from the period of emancipation through the present) were understood by observers either as signs of blacks' irredeemable savagery and immorality or as the result of victimization and disadvantage. By the 1920s and 1930s, some uplift-oriented middle-class Afro-Caribbean men and women began to pay more attention to family formation and parenting practices. Furthermore, they wrote about their concerns in the West Indian publications that were emerging within Afro-Caribbean migrant destinations throughout Central America in particular. This is significant because migration in this case seems to have prompted a black middle-class activist concern with family patterns among poorer West Indians, just as it did in the United States in the wake of the Great Migration north. Nevertheless, these concerns did not immediately translate into policy recommendations. According to Putnam, despite interest in the sexual mores of Afro-Caribbean populations among observers, missionaries, and Colonial Office bureaucrats, "there was little emphasis placed on the social, cultural, or psychological consequences of Afro-Caribbean domestic forms."[28] Yet by the aftermath of the worldwide economic depression, regionwide labor riots, and the beginning of World War II, West Indian family formation became newly situated as a policy concern in the Colonial Office, and a link was created between poverty and what looked like parental irresponsibility to British middle-class government officials and social welfare workers. This was also the case in the United States.

In part, this shift in policy-oriented attention to lower-class black families in the United States and the West Indies resulted from a move away from the biologically driven understandings of race that undergirded various strands of scientific racism throughout the mid-nineteenth and early twentieth centuries and toward anthropologically and psychologically oriented analyses of human difference. Equally important to this shift, however, was the newly hegemonic industrial-development ideology that positioned the patriarchal family at the heart of economic productivity, the reproduction of labor, and educated consumption.[29] In this context, one that stretched across the Atlantic, the roles were clear—men labored and women reproduced their labor by seeing to the health and welfare of the household—and deviating from this norm was seen as a cultural rather than structural problem, not only in the West Indies but also in the United States. As Ferguson explains, "Within a national context that has historically constructed the heteropatriarchal household as a site that can absorb and withstand material catastrophes, African American poverty was often explained by reverting back to the question of African American intimate relations and denying the irresolvability and historicity of state and capital's own exploitative practices."[30] Studies commissioned at the time reproduced this view, and implicit within these studies were concerns regarding the political futures of African Americans and black Caribbeans at the dusk of the British Empire.

One of these studies, Gunnar Myrdal's *An American Dilemma*, commissioned by the Carnegie Corporation and ultimately published in 1944, was geared toward examining the causes of the continued inequalities between blacks and whites in the United States. Myrdal focused on a number of institutional dimensions of social, economic, and political life, but undergirding his analysis was a concern with the so-called disorganization of African American family structure, a disorganization that "constructed African Americans as figures of nonheteronormativity who could potentially throw the American social order into chaos."[31] Similarly, the West India Royal Commission sent to the West Indies after the labor riots that swept through the region in the late 1930s produced a report (also known as the Moyne Report, after the head of the commission) stating that one of the causes of the region's labor problems was a dysfunctional family structure among poor and working-class black West Indians. This structure was characterized by high rates of illegitimate births, a "loose" family organization, and the "careless" upbringing of children. For the authors of the report, dysfunctional families generated a lack of economic productivity and motivation and therefore also a lack of ability to participate politically in an engaged and thoughtful way. The report ultimately recommended a movement toward independence for the West Indian colonies, as well as the establishment of an Office of Colonial Development and Welfare that would not only see to improvements in housing, education, public health, and land resettlement but would also foster more responsible parenting and sexual restraint.

In Jamaica, the sociologist Thomas Simey became the head of the Office of Colonial Development and Welfare in 1941. His conviction was that sociological studies would lead to a broader understanding of the problematic familial institutions that were prevalent among the majority of the population and, therefore, also to the development of solutions to the problems to facilitate a transfer from crown colony government to self-rule. Simey's own survey of social conditions in Jamaica — *Welfare and Planning in the West Indies* — set the pattern for future family studies by delineating types of mating practices and by arguing that there seemed to be a close correlation between color, occupation or economic level, and family type. These findings were echoed, though modified in various ways, by scholars who Simey invited to study social conditions in the region, including Edith Clarke and Madeline Kerr (whose 1952 study was also influenced by the functionalist psychologically oriented studies of family life in the United States).[32] Of course, later studies modified the value bias and Eurocentric stress on male dominance and the nuclear family by suggesting that lower-class family forms were creatively adaptive and represented solutions to problems faced in other spheres of their lives. Lower-class people, while sharing the general values of the society, also were able to "stretch" these values to make them fit their own circumstances.[33] What is key for my purposes here, however, is that family formation was seen as an issue related to the viability of statehood, and thus black peoples' sexual practices and family organization became problems to be addressed at the highest levels of government, as they also were in the United States during the same period.

In fact, in addition to the emphasis on scholarship, one of the first activities of the Office of Colonial Development and Welfare staff in the West Indies was to visit the mini–New Deal programs of the Roosevelt administration in Puerto Rico and the United States Virgin Islands, visits organized by the Rockefeller Foundation. Unlike Great Britain, the United States did not initially adopt a welfare approach to issues of social development. Instead, U.S. officials took a scientific approach, establishing a policy of population control and institutionalizing home economics education. The home economics movement emerged in the United States at the turn of the twentieth century and was designed, as Rhoda Reddock has argued, to draw households "into relations with the market as a consumption unit and to bring housework in line with capitalist modernization, stressing rationality, professionalism, and scientific principles." By the mid-1950s, based on research conducted in Puerto Rico and Jamaica funded by the U.S. Conservation Foundation, the general agreement was that overpopulation (the result of promiscuity and high illegitimacy rates) was the main reason for the region's economic problems, and the Puerto Rican model (sterilization among lower-class women) was put forward as a solution. Laura Briggs has argued that these kinds of collaborative investigations should direct our attention to the syncretisms between overseas development and domestic welfare or poverty policies. In other words, in both the U.S. and West Indian sociological literature, a link was made between "the poor" (or, in the case of the West Indies, the "lower classes") and "sex patterns," patterns that ultimately became proxies for race. These patterns, then, constituted poor black people as unassimilable to the national mainstream and therefore excluded them from the normative categories of citizenship.[34]

Thus, by the time Oscar Lewis coined the term *culture of poverty*, the sexual and kinship patterns that constituted poor black people as deviating from the idealized cultural norms of the United States and Jamaica were already elaborated through research and policy. However, the traits Lewis listed as characteristic of a culture of poverty—simple language; a great need for sex and excitement; a propensity to rage, aggression, and violence; an inability to be alone and a constant need for sociability; a high incidence of early sexual unions outside of the context of marriage and thus of illegitimate children; an emphasis on appearances; a lack of participation in the major institutions of the larger society (with the exception of jail, the army, or the public welfare system); an orientation to the local and an inability to see beyond immediate problems; and a value on "acting out more than thinking out, self-expression more than self-constraint, pleasure more than productivity, spending more than saving, personal loyalty more than impersonal justice" — served to further entrench the culturalist view of social inequality, in part because his books were published by popular presses and in part because his ideas were reproduced by those in the U.S. policy arena, such as Moynihan.[35]

I am rehashing some of this terrain to point out similarities in terms of how poor black people were positioned in relation to the U.S. government and the newly emergent states within the British West Indies around the same time period. In both the United States and the West Indies during the mid-twentieth century, because "stable" families with male breadwinners were seen as the motors of modern, industrial economic growth, regulating the sexuality of lower-class blacks — and especially of urbanized, industrialized, lower-class blacks — became a key aspect of the state's relationship to black populations. Thus African Americans and Afro–West Indians whose families deviated from the normative model of heteropatriarchy were seen as "reproductive rather than *productive*, heterosexual but never *heteronormative*." They were therefore subjected to a discursive regulation that ultimately, according to the logic of mid- and late twentieth-century development paradigms, blamed them for their own poverty and, after the dismantling of the welfare state in the United States and the implementation of structural adjustment programs in Jamaica, abandoned them to the whims of the market.[36]

Within the current neoliberal moment, however, the family is no longer hegemonically viewed as the engine of economic growth. Instead, growth is believed to be powered by entrepreneurship. And though gendered notions of respectability, as Carla Freeman reminds us, still operate to delimit who might or might not be seen as a legitimate entrepreneur, the entrepreneur *is* a figure that can be — to a degree — extricated from the context of family.[37] This means that the family unit is no longer seen as the most critical factor in relation to economic production, as it was during the mid-twentieth century.

Of course, this does not mean that black family formation — and especially black masculinity — has somehow suddenly become a political nonissue, both in relation to contests for the state in the United States and Jamaica and in terms of the various kinds of black nationalist "common sense" that have emerged in both locations.[38] Instead, as we have seen, the culture of poverty discourse (in which black males are irresponsible, selfishly status-seeking, and incorrigibly undomesticated) has given way to the culture of violence discourse (in which black males — because they have been undomesticated — are susceptible to the pull of gangs and the street, through which they become pathologically incapable of exhibiting empathy or human compassion). Black men have become problematic in new ways, their marginality defined in relation to new institutional configurations. In the first instance, poor black men are "problems" because they are not household heads, stable breadwinners, and actively present (patriarchal) fathers to their children. In the second, poor black men are "problems" because they cannot gain a significant foothold in legitimate entrepreneurial activities (because they were fatherless) and are therefore responsible for the violence that perpetuates poverty and insecurity. In the first case, their pathology is diagnosed in relation to their roles in the family; in the second, it is diagnosed in relation to their roles in the economy. Either way, faulty black masculinity is to blame for economic underdevelopment and persistent poverty.

Nevertheless, there is a real opportunity here. If, due to the nature of global economic shifts, the family is no longer the primary unit of economic productivity and political engagement and a late nineteenth-century sexual division of labor is no longer idealized in the same way that it was during the mid-twentieth century, then (1) we must abandon the idea that the nuclear family is the primary unit through which populations can engage the state; (2) we could successfully chip away at the hegemony of culturalist discourse regarding family formation and faulty black masculinity, even in the face of Christian Right attacks on, among other things, the *Roe v. Wade* decision in the United States, and despite the emergence of the male marginalization discourse in the West Indies; and (3) we must be able to look again at new ways of organizing our political and economic loyalties and of formulating our notions of how transnational and diasporic alliances and commitments are forged, broken, and remade. To do the latter, however, we need more finely honed analyses of how gender, class, generation, race, nation, sexuality, and—yes—the political economy of governmentality constitute each other in diaspora. Otherwise we risk reproducing the hegemony of the kinds of nonholistic culturalist frameworks that are mobilized by popular observers, as well as by some journalists and scholars. As I have attempted to show here, these kinds of frameworks are impoverished lenses through which to analyze social inequality and can only perpetuate discursive violence against black people worldwide.

Notes

1. W. E. B. Du Bois, *Black Reconstruction in America: An Essay toward the History of the Part Which Black Folk Played in the Attempt to Reconstruct Democracy in America, 1860–1880* (New York: Russell and Russell, 1966) and *The Philadelphia Negro: A Social Study* (Philadelphia: University of Pennsylvania Press, 1996). For more on varieties of black Marxism, see Cedric Robinson, *Black Marxism: The Making of the Black Radical Tradition* (Chapel Hill: University of North Carolina Press, 2000); and Robin D. G. Kelley, *Hammer and Hoe: Alabama Communists during the Great Depression* (Chapel Hill: University of North Carolina Press, 1990). Discussions of other forms of internationalism and pan-Africanism include Carole Boyce Davies, *Left of Karl Marx: The Political Life of Black Communist Claudia Jones* (Durham, NC: Duke University Press, 2007); Brent

Hayes Edwards, *The Practice of Diaspora: Literature, Translation, and the Rise of Black Internationalism* (Cambridge, MA: Harvard University Press, 2003); Winston James, *Holding Aloft the Banner of Ethiopia: Caribbean Radicalism in America, 1900–1932* (New York: Verso, 1998); Erik McDuffie, "'[She] Devoted Twenty Minutes Condemning All Other Forms of Government but the Soviet': Black Women Radicals in the Garvey Movement and in the Left during the 1920s," in *Diasporic Africa: A Reader*, ed. Michael A. Gomez (New York: New York University Press, 2006), 219–50; Michelle Ann Stephens, *Black Empire: The Masculine Global Imaginary of Caribbean Intellectuals in the United States, 1914–1962* (Durham, NC: Duke University Press, 2005).

2. St. Clair Drake, "The Black Diaspora in Pan-African Perspective," *Black Scholar* 7 (1975): 2–14; and "Diaspora Studies and Pan-Africanism," in *Global Dimensions of the African Diaspora*, ed. Joseph E. Harris (Washington, DC: Howard University Press, 1982), 341–402.

3. Hazel Carby, *Cultures in Babylon: Black Britain and African America* (New York: Verso, 1999); M. Jacqui Alexander, *Pedagogies of Crossing: Meditations on Feminism, Sexual Politics, Memory, and the Sacred* (Durham, NC: Duke University Press, 2005); "Erotic Autonomy as a Politics of Decolonization: An Anatomy of Feminist and State Practice in the Bahamas Tourist Economy," in *Feminist Genealogies, Colonial Legacies, Democratic Futures*, ed. Chandra T. Mohanty and Alexander (New York: Routledge, 1997), 63–100; and "Redefining Morality: The Postcolonial State and the Sexual Offences Bill of Trinidad and Tobago," in *Third World Women and the Politics of Feminism*, ed. Chandra T. Mohanty, Ann Russo, and Lourdes Torres (Indianapolis: Indiana University Press, 1991), 133–52; Ann Stoler, *Carnal Knowledge and Imperial Power: Race and the Intimate in Colonial Rule* (Berkeley: University of California Press, 2002); Elizabeth Povinelli, *The Empire of Love: Toward a Theory of Intimacy, Genealogy, and Carnality* (Durham, NC: Duke University Press, 2006).

4. I am calling the youth "gunmen" here—an anonymous and ominous term—as that is how they would come to be described in the newspaper and radio reports of the murder. Yet, as in many small-scale face-to-face communities, these youth are known to people, and their families are long-standing community members. In fact, one of the gang leaders (who has since been assassinated) participated in a theater group I ran briefly out of the community center in the village.

5. A "nine night" is a Jamaican funerary ritual, an extended wake that takes place for nine nights after death during which time mourners sit up all night to celebrate the life of the deceased with food, music, and (often) drumming.

6. Glenroy Sinclair, "Thugs Torch Family of Four—Ten-Year-Old's Wail Dies in Blaze," *Daily Gleaner*, October 6, 2005.

7. Betty Ann, Blaine, "Death and the Death of Outrage," *Jamaica Observer*, October 11, 2005; Cedric Wilson, "Broken Windows and Young Minds," *Sunday Gleaner*, October 16, 2005; Garth Rattray, "Are We Dying in Vain?" *Daily Gleaner*, October 11, 2005.

8. "A National Security Strategy for Jamaica," *Sunday Gleaner*, May 7, 2006; Hermione McKenzie, qtd. in Glenroy Sinclair, "Gunmen Murder Six Women in Four Days—One Hundred and Nineteen Since January," *Daily Gleaner*, September 29, 2005. Similar formulations were given in Phyllis Thomas, "Reversing the Culture of Violence in Jamaica," *Sunday Gleaner*, May 2, 2004; in Barry Chevannes, *Learning to Be a Man: Culture, Socialization, and Gender Identity in Five Caribbean Communities* (Mona, Jamaica: University of the West Indies Press, 2001); and in "Why Jamaican Men Rape," *Sunday Gleaner*, March 19, 2006.

9. On the development of garrison communities, see Carl Stone, *Class, State, and Democracy in Jamaica* (New York: Praeger, 1986); *National Committee on Political Tribalism* (Kingston: Government of Jamaica, Constitutional Reform Unit, 1997); Barry Chevannes, "The Formation of Garrison Communities" (paper presented at the symposium "Grassroots Development and the State of the Nation," University of the West Indies at Mona, November 16–17, 1992); Carlene Edie, *Democracy by Default: Dependency and Clientelism in Jamaica* (Boulder, CO: Lynne Rienner, 1991); and Carl Stone, *Democracy and Clientelism in Jamaica* (New Brunswick, NJ: Transaction, 1980); Carl Stone, "Crime and Violence: Socio-political Implications," in *Crime and Violence: Causes and Solutions,* ed. Peter Phillips and Judith Wedderburn (Mona, Jamaica: Department of Government, University of the West Indies, 19–48); Bernard Headley, *A Spade Is Still a Spade: Essays on Crime and the Politics of Jamaica* (Kingston, Jamaica: LMH, 2002).

10. Christopher Charles, "Garrison Communities as Counter Societies: The Case of the 1998 Zeeks' Riot in Jamaica," *Ideaz* 1 (2002): 29–43; Horace Levy, *Urban Poverty and Violence in Jamaica: Report on Research* (Mona, Jamaica: Center for Population, Community, and Social Change, Department of Sociology and Social Work, University of the West Indies, 1995), 43; The quote is from *National Committee on Political Tribalism,* 12.

11. On the transformation of gang violence, see Stone, *Crime and Violence*; Anthony Harriott, "The Changing Social Organization of Crime and Criminals in Jamaica," *Caribbean Quarterly* 42 (1996): 61–81; and "The Jamaican Crime Problem: New Developments and New Challenges for Public Policy," in *Understanding Crime in Jamaica: New Challenges for Public Policy,* ed. Anthony Harriot (Mona, Jamaica: University of the West Indies Press, 2004), 1–12; Levy, *Urban Poverty and Violence in Jamaica*; Charles, "Garrison Communities as Counter Societies," 32; Headley, *A Spade Is Still a Spade,* 72.

12. On the spatial effects of violence, see Alan L. Eyre, "Political Violence and Urban Geography in Kingston, Jamaica," *Geographical Review* 74 (1984): 24–37; and "The Effects of Political Terrorism on the Residential Location of the Poor in the Kingston Urban Region, Jamaica, West Indies," *Urban Geography* 7 (1986): 227–42. Jamaican murder statistics are from Tara Abrahams-Clivio, "Let's Renounce the Title of Murder Capital," *Jamaica Observer,* October 20, 2005. To compare, the murder rate in the United States in 2005 was 5.6 per 100,000 (*Crime in the United States* [Washington, DC: Federal Bureau of Investigation, US Department of Justice, 2005], www.fbi.gov/ucr/05ucis/); in Canada, it was 2 per 100,000 (*The Daily, November 8,* 2006); and in England (and Wales), it was 1.4 per 100,000 people (Alison Walker, Chris Kershaw, and Sian Nicholar, "Crime in England and Wales, 2005/2006," *Home Office Statistical Bulletin,* 2006, www .crimereduction.gov.uk/statistics/statistics50.htm [accessed September 4, 2007]). The latter figure is a count of murders occurring in England and Wales and includes the fifty-two victims of the July 7 subway bombings. See also Mark Beckford, "Murder on the Increase," *Jamaica Gleaner,* August 24, 2007.

13. David Scott, "The 'Culture of Violence' Fallacy," *Small Axe* 1 (1997): 146.

14. Karen Brodkin, "Global Capitalism: What's Race Got to Do with It?" *American Ethnologist* 27 (2000): 237–56.

15. Patrick Wintour and Vikram Dodd, "Blair Blames Spate of Murders on Black Culture," *Guardian,* April 12, 2007. There is, of course, a long history to this kind of discourse in Britain, a discourse that proliferated especially after the report on the Brixton Riots written by Sir Leslie Scarman (*The Scarman Report: The Brixton Disorders, 10–12 April 1981, Report of an Inquiry* [New York: Penguin, 1981]). See also Paul Gilroy, *"There Ain't No Black in the Union Jack": The Cultural Politics of Race and Nation* (Chicago: University of

Chicago Press, 1987). I thank Mary Chamberlain and Faith Smith for directing me to these sources.

16. See John Chuckman, "City at Risk," chuckman.blog.ca/?tag=guns (accessed October 2, 2006); John Macfarlane, the editor of *Toronto Life*, qtd. in Lorrie Goldstein, "Stop Blaming Jamaicans for Gun Crime," *Toronto Sun*, May 7, 2006; Eugene Rivers, "The Sins of the Fathers Are Visited on Black Youth," *Globe and Mail*, December 2, 2005; Bruce Garvey, "Jamaica's 'Born fi Dead' Culture," *National Post*, October 27, 2005. On the animalization of black migrants in early-twentieth-century Cuba, see Alejandro de la Fuente, *A Nation for All: Race, Inequality, and Politics in Twentieth-Century Cuba* (Chapel Hill: University of North Carolina Press, 2000), chap. 3.

17. See Carole Nagengast, "Violence, Terror, and the Crisis of the State," *Annual Review of Anthropology* 23 (1994): 109–36, for an early review essay on the topic.

18. Brent Hayes Edwards, "The Uses of Diaspora," *Social Text* 19 (2001): 49, 55, 52, 55. See Kevin A. Yelvington, "The War in Ethiopia and Trinidad, 1935–1936," in *The Colonial Caribbean in Transition: Essays on Postemancipation Social and Cultural History*, ed. Bridget Brereton and Yelvington (Gainesville: University Press of Florida, 1999), 189–225, for a more nuanced discussion of how the question of origins, or of ethnic subjectivity, is dialectically and mutually constituted by the question of class.

19. St. Clair Drake, "Black Diaspora in Pan-African Perspective," 11.

20. Melville Herskovits, *The Myth of the Negro Past* (New York: Harper, 1941). See also Kevin A. Yelvington, "The Invention of Africa in Latin America and the Caribbean: Political Discourse and Anthropological Praxis, 1920–1940," in *Afro-Atlantic Dialogues: Anthropology in the Diaspora*, ed. Yelvington (Santa Fe, NM: School of American Research Press, 2006), 35–82. Other anthropologists critiqued the notions of acculturation and syncretism and the typology Herskovits developed. Sidney Mintz and Richard Price argued that instead of identifying particular cultural traits that might link New World blacks to African societies, it would be better to conceptualize these linkages as "unconscious 'grammatical' principles" and to analyze the political economy surrounding peoples' efforts to make their worlds by holding on to particular cultural practices and by adapting others to their new circumstances (*The Birth of African-American Culture: An Anthropological Perspective* [Boston: Beacon, 1992], 9). Indeed, Herskovits's vindicationist research agenda and ideas were not politically popular during the 1930s and the 1940s, when many African American leaders contending with the failure of Reconstruction were emphasizing not cultural difference from the American mainstream, but cultural similarity to promote the goals of assimilation, integration, and the extension of the rights of citizenship to the descendants of slaves. In the late 1960s and 1970s, however, Herskovits's ideas were picked up again and applied to the study not only of religion and expressive culture but also of patterns of land tenure, inheritance, and family formation.

21. The quotes about the changing language of race are from Penny M. Von Eschen, *Race against Empire: Black Americans and Anticolonialism, 1937–1957* (Ithaca, NY: Cornell University Press, 1997), 162. For similar analyses of these transformations, see Laura Curran, "The Culture of Race, Class, and Poverty: The Emergence of a Cultural Discourse in Early Cold War Social Work (1946–1963)," *Journal of Sociology and Social Welfare* 30 (2003): 18; and Kamari M. Clarke, *Mapping Yoruba Networks: Power and Agency in the Making of Transnational Communities* (Durham, NC: Duke University Press, 2004). On the development of normative ideas on family formation, see Lara Putnam, "Parenthood at the End of Empire: Great Britain and Its Caribbean Colonies, 1910–1940" (paper presented at the Latin American Labor History Conference, Duke University, Durham,

NC, May 4–5, 2007), and Roderick A. Ferguson, "Nightmares of the Heteronormative: *Go Tell It on the Mountain* versus *An American Dilemma*," in *Aberrations in Black: Toward a Queer of Color Critique* (Minneapolis: University of Minnesota Press, 2004), 82–109; and Von Eschen, *Race against Empire*, 157. The quote about American capitalism and the working class is from Anthony Marcus, "The Culture of Poverty Revisited: Bringing Back the Working Class," *Anthropologica* 47 (2005): 47; Michael Harrington, *The Other America: Poverty in the United States* (1962; New York: Penguin, 1981); Nathan Glazer and Daniel Moynihan, *Beyond the Melting Pot: The Negroes, Puerto Ricans, Jews, Italians, and Irish of New York City* (Cambridge, MA: MIT Press, 1963).

22. The quote is from Von Eschen, *Race against Empire*, 3. Many black intellectuals rued these changes, E. Franklin Frazier chief among them. While Frazier himself deployed a culturalist frame for viewing African American family life (despite the fact that he also emphasized sociostructural factors in his analysis of African American family organization), he saw in the move away from internationalist anticolonial politics a diminished inclination to critique Western society and culture. He also felt that the turn from an analytic framework that privileged the language of political economy inhibited the elaboration of a model of black modernity that was inspired, at least in part, by African independence (see Kevin Gaines, "E. Franklin Frazier's Revenge: Anticolonialism, Nonalignment, and Black Intellectuals' Critiques of Western Culture," *American Literary History* 17 [2005]: 506–29). Frazier's *Black Bourgeoisie*—written and first published in France before being published in the United States in 1957—articulated as scathing a critique of U.S. black middle-class intellectual and political leaders as did Frantz Fanon's *Wretched of the Earth* of the newly postcolonial political leadership. Both saw in bourgeois nationalism a narrowing of focus and an emphasis on culture and assimilation, rather than an impetus toward the radical transformation of the relationships among black people, capitalism, and nation-states (E. Franklin Frazier, *Black Bourgeoisie: The Rise of a New Middle Class* [New York: Free Press, 1957]; Frantz Fanon, *The Wretched of the Earth*, trans. Constance Farrington [New York: Grove, 1963]).

23. St. Clair Drake also identified the Cold War as inspiring a move away from internationalism, but he suggested that it was the *success* of anticolonial movements in Africa that played such a decisive role in turning African Americans away from coordinated political action. He argued that once African countries became nations, the sense of a unity of purpose fractured: "The period of uncomplicated united struggle to secure [African] independence from the white oppressor had ended for each colony as it became a nation. Diaspora blacks had to decide which of various political factions, if any, within the new nations they would support" (Drake, "Diaspora Studies and Pan-Africanism," 351).

24. It is also this antinationalist sense that pervades the use of *diaspora* within British cultural studies, though here we see the maintenance of explicit attention to class and political economy, at least until the publication of Paul Gilroy's *The Black Atlantic: Modernity and Double Consciousness* (Cambridge, MA: Harvard University Press, 1993). This is because within this context, diaspora became a way to identify the relationships between racism and British nationalism.

25. Ferguson, *Aberrations in Black*, 85–86.

26. On "Christian blacks," see Diane Austin-Broos, "Redefining the Moral Order: Interpretations of Christianity in Post-Emancipation Jamaica," in *The Meaning of Freedom: Economics, Politics, and Culture after Slavery*, ed. Frank McGlynn and Seymour Drescher (Pittsburgh, PA: University of Pittsburgh Press, 1992), 221–44. On postemancipation village and family formation, see Catherine Hall, "Gender Politics and Imperial Politics:

Rethinking the Histories of Empire," in *Engendering History: Caribbean Women in Historical Perspective*, ed. Verene Shepherd, Bridget Brereton, and Barbara Bailey (Kingston, Jamaica: Ian Randle, 1995), 48–59; and *Civilising Subjects: Colony and Metropole in the English Imagination, 1830–1867* (Chicago: University of Chicago Press, 2002).

27. Ferguson, *Aberrations in Black*, 85.

28. Putnam, "Parenthood at the End of Empire," 1. For similar analyses of the way migration influenced family structure, see E. Franklin Frazier, *The Negro Family in the United States* (1939; Chicago: University of Chicago Press, 1966); Kevin Gaines, *Uplifting the Race: Black Leadership, Politics, and Culture in the Twentieth Century* (Chapel Hill: University of North Carolina Press, 1996); Evelyn Brooks Higginbotham, *Righteous Discontent: The Women's Movement in the Black Baptist Church, 1880–1920* (Cambridge, MA: Harvard University Press, 1993).

29. M. G. Smith, introduction to *My Mother Who Fathered Me: A Study of the Family in Three Selected Communities in Jamaica*, by Edith Clarke (1957; London: Allen and Unwin, 1966), i–xliv; Rhoda Reddock, *Women, Labour, and Politics in Trinidad and Tobago: A History* (London: Zed, 1994).

30. Ferguson, *Aberrations in Black*, 85.

31. Ibid., 88; Myrdal Gunnar, *An American Problem: The Negro Problem and Modern Democracy* (New York: Harper, 1944).

32. Thomas S. Simey, *Welfare and Planning in the West Indies* (Oxford: Clarendon, 1946); and Clarke, *My Mother Who Fathered Me*; Madeline Kerr, *Personality and Conflict in Jamaica* (Liverpool: Liverpool University Press, 1952). For early family studies in the United States, see John Dollard, *Caste and Class in a Southern Town* (New Haven, CT: Yale University Press, 1937); Hortense Powdermaker, *After Freedom: A Cultural Study in the Deep South* (New York: Viking, 1939); Oliver Cox, *Caste, Class, and Race: A Study in Social Dynamics* (Garden City, NY: Doubleday, 1948); Alison Davis, Burleigh B. Gardner, and Mary R. Gardner, *Deep South: A Social Anthropological Study of Caste and Class* (Chicago: University of Chicago Press, 1941); Lloyd Warner, Buford Junker, and Walter Adams, *Color and Human Nature: Negro Personality Development in a Northern City* (Washington, DC: American Council on Education, 1941).

33. In fact, Simey was himself encouraged to read the sociological literature on African American family structures that was emergent in the United States at the time (Lara Putnam, personal communication, October 12, 2007). For modifications of earlier family research, see Robert Dirks and Virginia Kerns, "Mating Patterns and Adaptive Change in Rum Bay, 1823–1970," *Social and Economic Studies* 25 (1976): 34–54; Nancie Gonzalez, "Towards a Definition of Matrifocality," in *Afro-American Anthropology: Comparative Perspectives*, ed. Norman Whitten and John Szwed (New York: Free Press, 1970), 231–44; Sidney Greenfield, *English Rustics in Black Skin: A Study of Modern Family Forms in a Pre-industrial Society* (New Haven, CT: College and University Press, 1966); Hyman Rodman, "On Understanding Lower-Class Behavior," *Social and Economic Studies* 8 (1959): 441–50; and *Lower-Class Families: The Culture of Poverty in Negro Trinidad* (New York: Oxford University Press, 1971); Hymie Rubenstein, "Conjugal Behavior and Parental Role Flexibility in an Afro-Caribbean Village," *Canadian Review of Sociology and Anthropology* 17 (1980): 331–37; and "Caribbean Family and Household Organization: Some Conceptual Clarifications," *Journal of Comparative Family Studies* 14 (1983): 283–98; Carol Stack, *All Our Kin: Strategies for Survival in a Black Community* (New York: Harper and Row, 1974). A more recent perspective has also developed that returns to

Herskovits's position that West Indian family forms are modifications of West African forms. See, for example, Virginia Kerns, *Women and the Ancestors: Black Carib Kinship and Ritual* (Urbana: University of Illinois Press, 1983); Niara Sudarkasa, "African and Afro-American Family Structure" in *Anthropology for the Nineties*, ed. Johnnetta Cole (New York: Free Press, 1988), 182–210; Constance Sutton, "Africans in the Diaspora: Changing Continuities in West Indian and West African Sex/Gender Systems" (paper presented at the "New Perspectives on Caribbean Studies: Toward the Twenty-First Century" conference, August 29, 1984.

34. Reddock, *Women, Labour, and Politics*, 225. For mid-1950s U.S. research, see Judith Blake, *Family Structure in Jamaica: The Social Context of Reproduction* (Glencoe, IL: Free Press,1961); J. Mayone Stycos and Kurt Back, *The Control of Human Fertility in Jamaica* (Ithaca, NY: Cornell University Press, 1964). For critical perspectives on this research, see Laura Briggs, *Reproducing Empire: Race, Sex, Science, and U.S. Imperialism in Puerto Rico* (Berkeley: University of California Press, 2002), 178, and Ferguson, *Aberrations in Black*.

35. Oscar Lewis, *Five Families: Mexican Case Studies in the Culture of Poverty* (1959; New York: Basic Books, 1975); and *La Vida: A Puerto Rican Family in the Culture of Poverty—San Juan and New York* (New York: Random House, 1965). The quotes are from *La Vida*, xxvi. See also *The Negro Family: The Case for National Action* (Washington, DC: U.S. Department of Labor, 1965). Of course, Lewis's ideas have been widely criticized. Anthropologists and others have taken issue with his use of the culture concept, with the ways his own data sometimes contradicted his theoretical assertions, with the ways he contributed to a racialization and sexualization of poor people, and with the sense that despite his various disclaimers, he ultimately took up the culture of poverty thesis as a way to blame the poor for their own poverty and marginalization. For these critiques, see Eleanor Leacock, ed., *The Culture of Poverty: A Critique* (New York: Simon and Schuster, 1971); Rodman *Lower-Class Families*; Charles Valentine, *Culture and Poverty: Critique and Counter-Proposals* (Chicago: University of Chicago Press, 1968); Briggs, *Reproducing Empire*; Micaela DiLeonardo, *Exotics at Home: Anthropologies, Others, American Modernity* (Chicago: University of Chicago Press, 1998); also, "Book Review: The Children of Sanchez, Pedro Martinez, and La Vida by Oscar Lewis," *Current Anthropology* 8, no. 5 (1967): 480–500. While Lewis's own solutions for poverty tended to emphasize collective action and political protest geared toward achieving the rights and responsibilities of true citizenship, those who took his ideas and ran with them were seen as offering up solutions that emphasized self-help and government nonintervention (see Lewis, *La Vida*, xlvi, l).

36. Ferguson, *Aberrations in Black*, 85.

37. Carla Freeman, "The 'Reputation' of Neoliberalism," *American Ethnologist* 34 (2007): 252–67.

38. Wahneema Lubiano, "Black Nationalism and Black Common Sense: Policing Ourselves and Others," in *The House That Race Built: Black Americans, U.S. Terrain*, ed. Lubiano (New York: Vintage, 1998), 232–52.

Where Blackness Resides:
Afro-Bolivians and the Spatializing and
Racializing of the African Diaspora

Sara Busdiecker

We came from Africa. The Spanish brought us; but who knows in what
year—not even our grandparents could know that. . . .
—Afro-Bolivian female Yungas resident, age eighty-two, 2001

We're from Africa. It's said that we're from the African, from Africa. The race,
every black, is from Africa, all the blacks, no? My parents used to say that, that's
how I know; I've written all those things down in my head.
—Afro-Bolivian male Yungas resident, age eighty-two, 2001

With the increasing use of the term *diaspora* across academic disciplines in recent
years and the growing popularity of African diaspora studies, scholars have offered
varying definitions of just what the concept diaspora encompasses. There is little
argument, however, that at its most basic level it describes a dispersal. In the case
of the African diaspora, this is of course a spatial dispersal of peoples of African
descent outside of the African continent. Consequently, diaspora identities are fundamentally about space and the negotiation of identity in relation to space and place.
While the African diaspora is, in fact, global, all too often a select few geographic
places monopolize conversations about and understandings of the African diaspora.
Despite a global dispersal and presence dating back centuries, people of African

Radical History Review
Issue 103 (Winter 2009)   DOI 10.1215/01636545-2008-033
© 2009 by MARHO: The Radical Historians' Organization, Inc.

descent continue to be perceived as "out of place" (physically, as well as culturally, socially, and historically) in certain circumstances outside the African continent.

Those identified as black in Bolivia are estimated to constitute less than 2 percent of the overwhelmingly Indian and mestizo national population.[1] Despite a continuous presence in Bolivia dating back to the 1500s, when Spaniards brought Africans into the region to work as slaves in the silver mines of Potosí, black Bolivians have been largely ignored by their government, their fellow citizens, and scholars.[2] From the 1851 abolition of slavery to the present, claims about the existence of a distinct Afro-Bolivian ethnic or racial identity have been contested or, more often, overshadowed by a dominant Indian-/mestizo-centric vision of Bolivian history, society, culture, and national identity.[3] What acknowledgment Afro-Bolivians have received has tended to be dismissive, highlighting only their small numbers, their geographic concentration, and a sociocultural identity and historical trajectory that are supposedly indistinguishable from those of the country's majority indigenous population.[4]

Considering the extent to which Afro-Bolivians have been overlooked in their own country, it should come as no surprise that they have suffered the same fate in the larger African diaspora. While the justifications for this exclusion are multiple, this essay, speaking to the aforementioned centrality of space in conceptualizing the African diaspora, examines the geography of this exclusion or, more precisely, the perceptions of geography and how they produce the racialization of place and the spatialization of blackness.

During two years (2000–2002) of anthropological research on contemporary Afro-Bolivian identity and culture and the broader meanings and experiences associated with blackness and race in Bolivia, the significance of space and place to notions of Afro-Bolivianness became increasingly evident to me. This significance emerged in opposition to the prevailing view that there was nothing to Afro-Bolivianness save superficial skin color, a view enabled by the fact that in Bolivia the organization of diversity and the popular, scholarly, and official discourses on difference emphasize socioeconomic class and degrees and kinds of Indianness to the exclusion of other kinds of difference.[5] I spent a large portion of two years living and conducting ethnographic fieldwork in Tocaña, a small Afro-Bolivian village in the Nor Yungas province several hours outside the national capital, La Paz.

Travel to the site proved a challenge due to the poor condition of the roads and the absence of direct, public transportation in and out of Tocaña.[6] However, it is not the challenge of entering the Yungas or the seeming remoteness of the community that compelled reflections on the role of geography in creating and sustaining notions of blackness, for there are far more remote and inaccessible locales to be found in Bolivia. Instead, it was the realization that despite the movement of significant numbers of Afro-Bolivians in and out of the Yungas region over the past twenty years for the purposes of completing their education, finding work, or engaging in periodic commercial activities, the region and even the specific community of Tocaña with its mere 130 residents served, without comment or qualification, as representative of Afro-Bolivianness in general. What is represented as "authentic" Afro-Bolivian identity, culture, and experience—as "quintessential" blackness—in newspaper articles, on postcards, in travel guides, and in conversation, is, in fact, more accurately Afro-*Yungueño* identity, culture, and experience. This means that not only are black-skinned bodies to be found in the Yungas but also that they are to be found in poor rural communities where they engage in the cultivation of the coca and fruit that dominate the Yungas economy and live daily, seasonally, and annually according to that economy, landscape, and rural isolation. Bolivians appear to take for granted the idea that the Yungas is a natural locus for people of African descent. In light of the fact that the history of Afro-Bolivians seemingly ends with abolition (there being virtually no historiographic accounts of the population after 1851 to cite), it is the Yungas that connects the past to the present. Markers of how Bolivians think about blackness are found in the ways in which this connection is written and spoken about.

Locating Blackness in Space, Putting Blackness in (Its) Place

Since no modern census data has been collected (much less circulated) *confirming* the regional presence of Afro-Bolivians in the Yungas, and since the details of Afro-Bolivian history are not widely known by Bolivians in general, "locating blackness" refers to the geographic space blacks inhabit in popular knowledge and in the imagination (of Afro-Bolivians and non–Afro-Bolivians alike) as much as in fact. What imaginary racialized geographies manifest themselves in the limited discourse touching on Bolivia's blacks?[7] Where are Afro-Bolivians in the cultural geography or moral topography of Bolivia?[8] What geographies of identity—understood as the "senses of belonging and subjectivities which are constituted in (and which in turn act to constitute) different spaces and social sites"—operate in the Bolivian context that impact the spatialization of blacks and blackness in such a way that they are peripheralized in the realms of social, cultural, political, scholarly, and activist discourses and participation?[9]

Geographical regions in a nation are but one space vested with senses of belonging and subjectivities; in this instance, it is the regionalizing of race and the racializing of regions that is central for locating this marginalized—even invisible—group. There are several familiar, if general, examples of indigenous groups in Bolivia who are associated with particular places in the nation; the Tupi-Guarani are, for instance, associated with the Amazon region, the Aymara with the highlands, and the Quechua with the valleys. An even more general association that operates throughout the Andes is that of Indians with rural spaces and of mestizos and whites with urban spaces.[10] The major regionalism of Bolivia that pits *colla* (highland dweller) against *camba* (lowland dweller) also involves the association of groups or types with particular geographic spaces; the *colla* is perceived as racially and culturally Indian and the *camba* as mestizo and culturally more European, with both groups subject to unflattering stereotypes by the other.[11] Afro-Bolivians are left out of or are ambiguously positioned in both the association of *campesino*/rural space with Indians and the racialized *colla* versus *camba* regionalism.

Despite the migration of many blacks out of the Yungas over the past twenty years and their increasing presence and visibility in urban areas such as La Paz, Cochabamba, and Santa Cruz, the association of blacks with the Yungas persists in a way that is both naturalized and taken for granted. A deliberate examination of the interplay between geography and identity with respect to Afro-Bolivians reveals specific ways in which the Yungas as a region is implicated in the content of social constructions of blackness and, additionally, in the scarcity of those constructions.

The Yungas, which is divided into the Nor (North) Yungas Province and the Sud (South) Yungas Province, stretch northeast and south from La Paz along the eastern side of the Cordillera Real and the Cordillera Quimsa Cruz in an area of about 9,600 square miles. This semitropical region (*yunkas* means "warm valleys" in Aymara) is characterized by year-round warm temperatures, generous seasonal rainfall, and fertile soil and lush green vegetation covering uneven mountain and valley terrain. This makes for a stark contrast with the neighboring altiplano region that sits at eleven thousand feet to thirteen thousand feet above sea level on the other side of the cordillera; the landscape there includes flat grassland and snow-capped mountain peaks, while the air is thin, cold, and dry. The Yungas is an intermediate zone between this and the more humid and rain-forested Amazon lowlands of Alto Beni, which neighbor the Yungas to the east.

These characteristics of the Yungas region provide the foundation on which geography is implicated in the construction of blackness. There is a notion that the Yungas is somehow environmentally the "closest thing to Africa" in Bolivia and so a "natural place" for black slaves to have ended up and a "natural place" for their descendants to have stayed. With this, an Africa otherwise distant in time, space, and memory makes a rare if abbreviated appearance, its invocation tying Bolivia's blacks to the larger diaspora by virtue of their shared dispersal from the African continent. If any part of Afro-Bolivian history is familiar to both blacks and non-blacks, it is the oft-repeated but brief account that blacks were brought to Bolivia to work the silver mines of Potosí, did not fare well there due to the altitude and cold, and so came to live in the Yungas, where their descendants can still be found, "because those tropical climates are the ones they best tolerate."[12] This account easily ties into the "natural place" myth that surfaces repeatedly in casual conversation, as well as in research and newspaper articles, evident in remarks such as, "The black community or ethnicity in Bolivia . . . has in the Yungas an ideal habitat if it is a question of a warm geographic area and conditions similar to those of the 'mother country.'"[13] Another states, "Whoever visits . . . Chicaloma or Ocabaya [Sud Yungas towns], in the midst of the leafy vegetation, will think they are magically being transplanted to black Africa."[14] The Bolivian cardiologist and university professor Hernán Criales Alcázar has dedicated an entire book, *La raza negra y la altura* (*The Black Race and Altitude*), to arguing for the biological incompatibility of blacks with high altitude such as that found in Potosí (thirteen thousand feet above sea level) and La Paz (twelve thousand feet above sea level). He explains the absence of blacks in these and other locations in Bolivia in biological rather than historical or socioeconomic terms.[15]

Coexisting with the idea that the Yungas offer a more hospitable environment for blacks is the image (more prevalent in past centuries than in the present) of the Yungas as an inhospitable environment in general. One Yungas overseer, Francisco Xavier de Bergara, described the region in the following manner in 1805: "This is a land of the unhealthiest sort known. It has the perverse quality of debilitating the most robust constitution. . . . [The Yungas] are extremely humid and hot. The rains are very continuous. Tertian fever is abundant. . . . Humanity lives exceedingly uncomfortable and annoyed by the multitude of insects that pursue it."[16] Blacks, then, were brought to this region "to attend the diverse plantations that needed rough work and a special resistance for the hot and unhealthy climate."[17] More recently, the British anthropologist Allison Spedding notes that Indian Yungas residents are known to be pallid and yellow compared to people of the high plains in part because of the unhealthy climate and the frequency of parasites in the region. She points out that in pre-Colombian times the Inca state used Yungas coca plantations as penal colonies because of the hard work, the difficulty in accessing the region, and the unhealthy conditions.[18] Bergara and others acknowledge that black slaves and laborers were challenged by the environment of the Yungas, but it was still considered a more suitable and natural place for them, reflecting perceptions of Africa's environment as inhospitable and attitudes that blacks were at once more physically rugged and less human than others. As a result, they were "brought . . . for the agricultural work of the hot regions, where individuals of other races could not endure."[19]

A popular saying heard in Bolivia and possibly dating back centuries, sums up much of the naturalized connection between blacks and the Yungas — "Gallinazo no canta en puna" (The vulture/turkey buzzard doesn't sing in the highlands). *Gallinazo* refers to a large black bird that seldom flies high or far, and while it can be seen in the Yungas it is rarely found in the high plains. This saying, as it is currently uttered by blacks or in reference to blacks, reflects the notion that they, like the *gallinazo*, are to be found in the Yungas and would be out of place in the highlands, where they would likely fall victim to altitude sickness. Sometimes the saying is changed to explicitly state, "*Negro* no canta en puna."[20] All of these suggestions that blacks are physically suited for the Yungas, dating from the colonial period to the present, contribute to the biologizing and thus racializing of blackness, something subsumed in the prevailing scholarly and popular discourse that emphasizes Bolivia's ethnic fluidity and social mobility as independent of characteristics thought of as "racial."

Yet other reminders of the black connection to the Yungas can be heard in popular song lyrics. For instance, Los Kjarkas sing of a "negro ardiente" (passionate black) and his *saya* (a uniquely Afro-Bolivian song and dance expression) "nacida en tierra caliente de los Yungas de La Paz" (born in the hot land of the Yungas of La Paz) in a song frequently heard on radio and television. The lyrics of Afro-Bolivian *saya* music also make reference to the Yungas, as one song announces to the audience, "Somos yungueñitos, señores presentes" (We are people of the Yungas, all of you people present). Among blacks, the Yungas region is consistently invoked in narratives of identity and origins, as in "we, as a people, are from the Yungas," or as the lyrics proclaim, "somos Yungueñitos." The Yungas prove central in establishing (even if unconsciously) a direct link to generations of ancestors and to a shared and particular historical past.

Many Afro-Bolivian migrants to La Paz and elsewhere still have family in the Yungas but have established themselves as full-time city dwellers for many years and may also have children who have never lived in the Yungas. Regardless, the region is still often referred to as if it was every individual's home or place of origin. Family visits maintain ties with the region, and migrant organizations sustain and promote that regional identity. For instance, Afro-Bolivians in Santa Cruz formed the Centro de Residentes Yungueños de Santa Cruz (Center for Yungas Residents of Santa Cruz) in the 1990s. In La Paz, the original members of the first Afro-Bolivian identity organization, Movimiento Cultural Saya Afro-Boliviano (Afro-Bolivian Saya Cultural Movement), formed in 1988, were all migrants from the Nor Yungas region. The practice of asserting a Yungueño identity may take on special significance for blacks as a means of *spatially* establishing their existence and their Bolivianness in the face of not only their small numbers and the national neglect of the salience of blackness but also in the face of the common but mistaken assumption — evidenced in personal anecdotes recounted by many blacks — that blacks seen in La Paz or elsewhere outside the Yungas are probably Brazilian, Peruvian, or from somewhere other than Bolivia. Place is, of course, an important component of many group identities or "imagined communities," whether in a group's own sense of origins or home or in its portrayal as a localized culture or ethnicity. For Bolivian blacks, emphasizing the space and place that is the Yungas is certainly a means of delineating themselves as a united and spatially defined group — a "legitimate" ethnic group by traditional definitions — and literally mapping blackness onto the Bolivian nation.[21]

In the 1990s, a group of urban blacks submitted a petition to reword the national constitution to include mention of their rights as *afrodescendientes* (Afrodescendants) over their "ancestral land." While the Yungas were not explicitly named, they are the only lands in Bolivia that blacks have an "ancestral" connection to, as evidenced in this discussion. The petition came in response to the recent inclusion of the rights of indigenous populations over their *tierras communitarias de origen* (communal lands of origin). The mobilization around land issues of indigenous populations throughout the Americas has, among other things, secured political visibility and a political identity for Indians. The relationship between blacks and land is less clear, but here is a case in which engaging in a rhetoric of ancestral lands could be interpreted as a strategy for gaining a political identity for blacks. The strategy does not, however, seem to have succeeded for Afro-Bolivians; the evidence gathered by the author during fieldwork in Bolivia strongly points to cultural performance as Afro-Bolivians' foothold for a largely apolitical form of national recognition dating from the 1990s. The strategy is, nevertheless, a reminder that there is more at stake in establishing group identity than identity for its own sake. At stake are issues of rights—to property, to livelihood, to political representation, to access to development funds, and so on. Notably, *afrodescendientes* were not explicitly named in the national constitution until December 2007, when it was amended under the administration of Evo Morales (Bolivia's first Indian president).

The Yungas at the Periphery of *lo Andino* and the Diaspora

While claiming a geographic space may help solidify the imaginings of blacks as an ethnic group, that that space is the Yungas may actually explain in part the relative invisibility and neglect of the Afro-Bolivian population. Here, one must consider the implications of the emphasis on *lo andino* for this particular region and its inhabitants. *Lo andino* refers to "that which is Andean," which in scholarship and popular discourse has long been interchangeable with "that which is Indian." In other words, even while there is the general association of Indians with rural areas and of mestizos and whites with urban areas, the Andean region as a whole is associated with Indians and Indianness, in particular with the highland Indian, and the typical/stereotypical highland region most often associated with the Andes mountain range. The image attached to "Andean," both geographically and culturally, actually excludes much of Bolivia's terrain and population, including the Yungas.

That the majority of inhabitants in the region are either Aymara migrants or the not-so-distant descendants of Aymara migrants from the altiplano is a contributing factor in the "nontraditional" image associated with Yungas inhabitants insofar as these Indians are separated from their places of origin and the families, communities, and physical and historical spaces that might solidify their "traditional" ethnic identity. Inhabitants have also long been a part of a market economy. Xavier Albó was compelled to refer to the Aymara of the Yungas as "the 'other' Aymaras" in a 1976 examination of the Sud Yungas region, *Yungas: Los "otros" aymaras*.[22] He wrote that the Yungas resident had less of a sense of Aymara ethnic/cultural identity, less of a connection with an Aymara past and more interest in the present and future, and that issues of "the *indio*," whether positive or negative, were not found in the region as they are in parts of the altiplano or in La Paz. He further attributed group conflicts to economics and class divisions rather than ethnic divisions.

More than twenty years after that assessment, Albó continues to present Yungas inhabitants as nontraditional based on their links to a market economy and their "lesser cultural and linguistic loyalty."[23] Bolivia's blacks are thought to have assimilated into these nontraditional Aymara, and it is frequently stated that Afro-Bolivians have no unique cultural identity of their own but rather that they share the cultural expressions, social and economic realities, and historical experiences of their rural Aymara neighbors. Here again, their location in space—this time in proximity to a majority Aymara population in the Yungas—has impacted understandings of Bolivian blackness. While association with the Yungas biologizes and thus racializes blacks, it simultaneously denies them an ethnicity of their own, the suggestion being that any unique sociocultural identity they might have had was lost once they left Africa. Due to this primary association, blackness is consequently reduced to the mainly somatic and, correspondingly, race is constructed as physically and biologically real.

The discursive marginality of the Yungas in the shadow of *lo andino* explains, then, some of the discursive marginality of blacks in Bolivian identity discourse and beyond Bolivia. Blacks are not only left out of the national discourse of Bolivianness, dependent on Andeanness and Indianness, and focused on the highlands rather than the Yungas, but they are also left out of the international discourse on the African diaspora. Indeed, talk of the African diaspora tends to remain silent on Andean blacks, but in particular on those from present-day Bolivia. Throughout the Americas, people identified as black are often associated with coasts, and they are typically understood as the descendants of slaves working a primarily Atlantic coastal plantation system and over time confronting increasingly mixed (mulatto/mestizo) societies or, in the case of the United States, a largely white immigrant population. By contrast, Bolivia has no coasts. Bolivia's first blacks arrived not to work plantations but to work in mining, and they faced and continue to face a majority indigenous population. So it would appear that Bolivia's blacks are not "traditional" African diaspora types existing in a "typical" diasporan space, just as Aymara Yungueños are not traditional Andean Indians existing in a typical highland space. The Yungas region lies at the margins of *lo andino*, and Bolivia lies at the margins of the African diaspora.

Conclusion

Both the analytical concept of the African diaspora and the lived experiences of African diaspora populations have space and place at their very center. However, it is not merely about spatial *facts*—that is, the points to which African descent populations were dispersed and the locations outside of Africa where they can currently be physically found—but rather, as suggested in this essay, about how those facts are perceived and how those perceptions in turn impact the social construction of blackness in a given historical and sociocultural context. There are clearly assumptions and expectations about when and where people of African descent are to be found outside Africa; blacks and blackness (whether somatic, cultural, political, etc.) can, in other words, be "out of place." This demonstrates that the African diaspora is imagined as a biologized and thus racialized category. What is at stake in recognizing such assumptions and expectations may very well be the undoing of core and peripheral spaces and populations in the African diaspora world, which has undoubtedly led to an incomplete and even skewed (toward the center) understanding of the diaspora and to a peripheralization of populations, experiences, and identities that do not fit or are invisible historically, as in the case of Bolivia's black population.

In a historical and scholarly moment when much is made of global movements, the permeability of borders, and the defiance of space (through the seemingly unprecedented physical and virtual ease with which bodies, goods, services, and ideas travel), the spatialization of identities and experiences that continues to occur *within* the African diaspora (which according to many definitions is no less than the prototypical example of globality and of spatial defiance) is all the more conspicuous. Even as Bolivia's blacks move in and out of the Yungas and increasingly take up residence outside the region, the national imagination continues to locate them there. After more than five hundred years, the descendants of African slaves continue to be identified not simply through somatic characteristics but by associating these characteristics with a particular geographic space; this demonstrates that racialized geographies of imagination and geographies of identity are operating on them, on the historical and sociocultural landscape of Bolivia, and on the African diaspora more broadly.

An incident involving Bolivia's current president encapsulates the (out of) place(ness) of blacks and blackness in Bolivia. During an unsuccessful run for the presidency in 2002, Morales came to the Nor Yungas provincial capital, Coroico, to give a speech at a campaign rally. On that occasion, residents from the nearby Afro-Bolivian community of Tocaña were invited to perform Afro-Bolivian *saya* dance and music. About twenty residents danced, sang, and drummed *saya* around Coroico's central plaza to open the rally and draw together a crowd; then they gathered, front and center, to listen to Morales speak. Nothing in Morales's speech specifically referenced or acknowledged the Afro-Bolivians who had been invited to perform and who stood before him. The only time he acknowledged them was when, after concluding his speech, he danced *saya* around Coroico's central plaza with a young Afro-Bolivian woman on each arm, at which point he commented, "I feel like I'm in Africa." With these words, uttered after a speech silent on Afro-Bolivians (as both Bolivian political and public discourse generally are), Morales expressed something about the place of blackness in Bolivia—that is, *no place*. Morales, like so many Bolivians, had few reference points for the African-descended in Bolivia. So rarely do nonblack Bolivians find themselves surrounded by blacks that distant Africa was invoked to make sense of such a circumstance. Thus Morales's "I feel like I'm in Africa" suggested that Africa's legacy was incompatible with the very Indian or Indian/mestizo Andean nation of Bolivia. Even in the Yungas, then, blacks were "out of place," a people or "race," out of its natural space—which would seem to be, judging by the words of Morales, distant (in space and time) Africa.

Notes

1. Blacks have not been counted as a separate category on the national census since 1900. Published estimates of the population over the past twenty years have ranged anywhere from 2,000 to 250,000.

2. A 1964 article by the German historian Inge Wolff is recognized as the first piece of methodologically and theoretically rigorous scholarly work on slavery in Bolivia. The first full-length works dedicated to the history of Bolivian slavery were published in the 1970s—Alberto Crespo's *Esclavos negros en Bolivia* (*Black Slaves in Bolivia*) (La Paz: Academia Nacional de Ciencias de Bolivia, 1977) and Max Portugal Ortiz's *La esclavitud negra en las épocas colonial y nacional de Bolivia* (*Black Slavery in the Colonial and National Eras of Bolivia*) (La Paz: Instituto Boliviano de Cultura, 1977). In the years since, two more books dedicated to Bolivian slavery have been published—*La mujer negra en Bolivia* (*The Black Woman in Bolivia*) (La Paz: Ministerio de Desarrollo Humano, Secretaría Nacional de Asuntos Etnicos, de Género y Generacionales, Subsecretaría de Asuntos de Género, 1995) by Eugenia Bridikhina, and *María Sisa y María Sosa: La vida de dos empleadas domésticas en la ciudad de La Paz (siglo XVII)* (*María Sisa and María Sosa: The Lives of Two Domestic Servants in the City of La Paz [Seventeenth Century]*) (La Paz: Ministerio de Desarrollo Humano, Secretaría Nacional de Asuntos Etnicos, de Género y Generacionales, Subsecretaría de Asuntos de Género, 1997) by Pilar Mendieta and Eugenia Bridikhina. These books and the few articles that came out in recent years all consider slavery in the colonial period, with little mention of slavery during the republican period beginning in 1825. The history of African-descended Bolivians after their 1851 emancipation remains largely unwritten. This, in turn, gives the impression that they ceased to be distinguished as social actors once they were free or, alternatively, that they ceased to exist all together once slavery was abolished and they were, in theory, able to integrate into the general population.

3. Throughout this essay, the terms *black* and *Afro-Bolivian* are used interchangeably to refer to all Bolivians of African descent. The term *afroboliviano* (Afro-Bolivian) has gained popularity since the early 1990s, largely due to the formation of a black consciousness movement among urban black migrants. These migrants were instrumental in promoting this term to replace *negro* (black) or the more commonly used *negrito* (little black or cute/ dear black) and *moreno* (brown-skinned person or person of dark coloring). *Afroboliviano* is considered more respectful and a means of asserting blackness as a legitimate and distinct ethnic identity, as opposed to the merely phenotypic identity implied by the terms used before the introduction of *afroboliviano*. *Negrito* and *moreno* are still used, particularly among older generations who associate the term *afroboliviano* with those active in the urban black consciousness movement and in the public performance of *saya*, the uniquely

Afro-Bolivian song and dance tradition. While the author addresses in other writings the ways in which this element of expressive culture has come to be viewed as "the last" or "only" evidence of Afro-Bolivian cultural retention, and thus emblematic of the Afro-Bolivian population, for the purposes of this essay *saya* should be understood as a cultural tradition and expression born and nurtured in the rural isolation of the regional space/place here discussed. See Sara Busdiecker, "We Are Bolivians Too: The Experience and Meaning of Blackness in Bolivia" (PhD diss., University of Michigan, 2006).

4. This indigenous majority includes more than thirty recognized Indian ethnic groups, with the largest being Aymara and Quechua. Afro-Bolivians are most often associated with the Aymara population.

5. If the role of place in ethnic fluidity is acknowledged, it becomes apparent that blacks are not the only ones being racialized in Bolivia. An individual referred to as *indio*, or to be more polite, *indígena* or *campesino*, would likely be a rural dweller who labored in agriculture, spoke Aymara or Quechua and spoke Spanish with the accent of an Aymara or Quechua speaker (if able to speak Spanish at all), had limited education, and wore some form of dress that revealed his or her rural and regional origins. If this individual was female and was to leave her rural community to work as a street vendor in a city such as La Paz, she would need to speak Spanish while working but would likely wear a *pollera* skirt and its associated dress items (e.g., bowler hat, shawl, *aguayo* for carrying bundles, etc.). That individual would likely be referred to as *cholita*, a label (*cholo/chola*) applied to an intermediary position between Indian and mestizo. While not always consistently defined and applied, the *cholita* is generally thought to be "in process" or "on the rise." Should this individual have daughters, they could potentially come to be labeled mestizas by speaking Spanish exclusively and well, attaining more education, changing a clearly indigenous surname like Quispe to Gisbert, and abandoning *cholita* dress and braids for contemporary skirts, pants, and hairstyles. Notably, individuals labeled Indian, *cholita*, or mestiza may all have the same "racial" ancestry and the same physical traits; phenotype is not the most important factor—and often not a factor at all—in the application of ethnic labels. All of this offers only a simplified description of what is a common scenario in the context of Bolivia. Cases like this are what lead to the contention that race and racism are of no importance in Bolivia. Ethnicity is fluid; any individual has (supposedly) unrestricted social mobility. Of course, this is provided that the individual sheds less desirable or less valued ethnic traits, which, invariably, are those associated with Indians, and aspires toward traits associated with mestizos and whites—no one tries to take advantage of ethnic fluidity by moving from white to Indian.

6. In 1995, the Inter-American Development Bank designated the road from La Paz into the Yungas "the world's most dangerous road" (*Baltimore Sun*, April 5, 2000). Locally, it is known as "the road of death" due to the numerous accidents that occur along the narrow dirt road that twists and turns as it descends 11,800 feet from La Paz into the heart of the Yungas with thousand-feet precipices on one side and rock overhangs on the other.

7. Jacqueline Nassy Brown, "Black Liverpool, Black America, and the Gendering of Diasporic Space," *Cultural Anthropology* 13 (1998): 291–325.

8. Peter Wade, *Blackness and Race Mixture: The Dynamics of Racial Identity in Colombia* (Baltimore: Johns Hopkins University Press, 1993), 51.

9. Sarah Radcliffe and Sallie Westwood, *Remaking the Nation: Place, Identity, and Politics in Latin America* (London: Routledge, 1996), 27.

10. That the word *campesino* (technically referring to rural peasants, from the root *campo*, meaning "countryside" or "field") is used in place of or interchangeably with *indio* or

indígena is just one manifestation of this association. See Benjamin S. Orlove, "Down to Earth: Race and Substance in the Andes," *Bulletin of Latin American Research* 17 (1998): 207–22.

11. Allyn MacLean Stearman, *Camba and Colla: Migration and Development in Santa Cruz Bolivia* (Orlando: University Presses of Florida, 1985).

12. Felipe Costas Arguedas, "El folklore negro en Bolivia" ("Black Folklore in Bolivia"), *Tradición* 15 (1954): 59.

13. Mario Montaña Aragón, "La familia negra en Bolivia" ("The Black Family in Bolivia"), in *Guía etnográfica y lingüística de Bolivia (Tribus del altiplano y valle)* (*Ethnographic and Linguistic Guide to Bolivia [Tribes of the Plateau and Valley]*) (La Paz: Don Bosco, 1992). All translations from Spanish to English are the author's.

14. "Las poblaciones negras de los Yungas" ("The Black Populations of the Yungas"), *Los tiempos*, December 17, 1978.

15. Hernan Criales Alcázar, *La raza negra y la altura (The Black Race and Altitude)* (La Paz: Facultad de Medicina, Enfermeria, Nutrición, y Tecnología Medica, 1992).

16. Quoted in Crespo, *Esclavos negros en Bolivia*, 2nd ed. (La Paz: Librería Editorial Juventud, 1995), 128.

17. Raul Meneses, "Provincia Sud Yungas" ("South Yungas Province"), in *La Paz en su IV centenario, 1548–1948: Monográfica 1* (*La Paz in Its Fourth Century, 1548–1948: Monograph 1*) (La Paz: Comité Pro IV Centenario de la Fundación de La Paz, 1948), 196.

18. Allison Spedding, *Wachu Wachu: Cultivo de coca e identidad en los Yunkas de La Paz* (*Wachu Wachu: The Culture of Coca and Identity in the Yungas of La Paz*) (La Paz: Centro de Investigación y Promoción del Campesinado, 1994).

19. *Censo Nacional 1900* (*National Census 1900*) (La Paz: Instituto Nacional de Estadística, 1900), 39.

20. Another reminder of the supposed physical incompatibility of blacks with high altitude comes in the form of a widely performed and recognized folk dance in Bolivia called the *morenada*. It is popularly thought to portray newly arrived black slaves on the march to Potosí. Dancers wear black masks with bulging eyes, flared nostrils, and swollen tongue and lips to represent the physical reactions to the dry and thinning air.

21. This de-emphasizes, however, the reality of a separate and increasingly important urban black experience. This is in contrast to what is observed in the Aymara population, where much is made, both in popular discourse and in scholarship, of the urban *cholo* identity as separate and distinct from the rural *indio* identity.

22. Xavier Albó, *Yungas: Los "otros" Aymaras; Diagnóstico económico-socio-cultural de Sud Yungas* (*Yungas: The "Other" Aymaras; A Economic-Social-Cultural Diagnosis of South Yungas*) (La Paz: Equipo CIPCA, 1976).

23. Xavier Albó, *Iguales aunque diferentes: Hacia unas políticas interculturales y lingüísticas para Bolivia* (*Equal though Different: Toward Intercultural and Linguistic Policies for Bolivia*) (La Paz: Ministerio de Educación, UNICEF, CIPCA, 2000).

Active Marooning: Confronting *Mi Negra* and the Bolivarian Revolution

Cristóbal Valencia Ramírez

Never again will we be just anybody's political flag! To be called "mi negra" is something very personal. The old Venezuelan culture where "mi negra" was acceptable is not a liberating culture. This revolution must be extended to the racial aspects of Venezuelan culture.
— Flor Márquez, Afro-Venezuelan activist, July 6, 2007

During the 2006 Venezuelan presidential campaign, Hugo Chávez's opponent, Manuel Rosales, announced a proposal to establish a welfare debit card called *Mi Negra* (My Black). The proposal aimed to deposit $280–$460 once a month into individual debit accounts for about 3 million Venezuelans whose earnings were at and below the minimum-wage level. Rosales claimed that the proposal intended to give marginalized Venezuelans a direct share of the national oil profits. Under criticism from Afro-Venezuelan organizations, Rosales explained the proposal's name as a reference to oil. However, the advertisements associated with the proposal featured almost exclusively black Venezuelans. Some of the ads showed toothless, grinning Afro-Venezuelans hoisting up the black card and singing the praises of Mi Negra and Rosales. The message behind the proposal—that Afro-Venezuelans were indigents—came through both in the images and in discourses surrounding the proposal.

Critiques of the proposal from the Bolivarian Left proved equally troubling. Officials in the Chávez administration criticized the proposal, saying, "Que se vaya

Radical History Review
Issue 103 (Winter 2009)   DOI 10.1215/01636545-2008-034
© 2009 by MARHO: The Radical Historians' Organization, Inc.

'Mi Negra' para los monos" ("Mi Negra" can go back to the jungle).[1] Bolivarian activists critiqued the proposal as an individualistic ploy — a handout — that would prove unpopular in the climate of the collective struggle of the Bolivarian Revolution.[2] Similarly, academics focused on the economic unfeasibility of the proposal and the "political savvy" of Chávez supporters who refused populist handouts in favor of deeper sustainable development.[3] None of these reactions captured or critiqued the racist nature of the proposal, an omission that exposes the systemic racism inherent and naturalized in daily exchanges in Venezuela. For the opposition and the Bolivarian Left, "Mi Negra" was a play on a colloquial term of endearment, not a racial slur or a racist proposal.

Afro-Venezuelan activists launched a critique of the racist nature of the campaign that led to a wider critique of Venezuelan race relations and of the Bolivarian Revolution. The organization, Afro-Descendant Maroons for the Revolution, and the Network of Afro-Venezuelan Organizations issued statements explaining and condemning the racist nature of the proposal. The accusations were submitted to the National Electoral Committee (CNE) for consideration of possible violations of electoral laws that prohibit the use of racist elements in campaign materials. Activists ensured the Rosales campaign and the CNE that they would take further action seeking a judgment of the Venezuelan Supreme Court if the propaganda was not banned. The cofounder of the Network of Afro-Venezuelan Organizations, Luís Perdomo, explained the significance of the event: "In a certain way the proposal propaganda worked. Many desperate and ignorant voters didn't think twice about the racist nature of the proposal. So, we took advantage of the moment to make a critique of the predatory practices of the opposition, the exclusionary practices of the Chávez government and Bolivarian activists to exert our influence as an organized movement. This was a great example of active marooning."[4] The responses surrounding the Mi Negra proposal highlight the tense race relations in Venezuela and, more important, provide an opportunity to explore tensions within the Bolivarian Revolution. In 1999 and 2007, Afro-Venezuelan activists lost the struggle for constitutional recognition and state institutional support. Historic constructions of a criollo culture not only hinder race-based activism but generate criticism of Afro-Venezuelan activists' insistence that racism be a primary concern of the Bolivarian revolution.[5] However, through a sustained politics of self-liberation, a process I call "active marooning," Afro-Venezuelans are transforming notions of a premodern blackness linked to expressive culture by constructing a contemporary Afro-Venezuelan political identity.[6]

This essay uses ethnographic evidence from periodic fieldwork, conducted from 2003 to the present, with Afro-Venezuelan and mestizo Bolivarian activists to discuss active marooning in the context of the Bolivarian Revolution and of the development of twenty-first-century Venezuelan socialism.[7] Anthropology and its ethnographic method rely on history for the contextualization of the contemporary.

In this case, an interdisciplinary approach has proven useful for at least two reasons. First, scholars of diasporic political identity stress that to understand race-based resistance and consciousness, history must be considered an ongoing feature of real life.[8] Second, and in turn, Venezuelan anthropologists argue that the persistence of contemporary ethnic groups—such as Afro-Venezuelans—relies on foregrounding autochthonous histories.[9] I conclude with a discussion of how the Venezuelan case fits into diaspora scholarship regarding African-descended peoples' negotiation of citizenship in the modern state.

Creole Society and Afro-Venezuelans

Venezuela is defined as a nation of mestizos. The majority of inhabitants are a mix of African, indigenous, Spanish, or Portuguese ancestry. Estimates of the contemporary Afro-descendant population range widely between 10 and 60 percent of the total population of 27 million inhabitants.[10] Afro-Venezuelan activists attribute this discrepancy to the absence of racial or ethnic categories on national censuses since the late nineteenth century. In any case, the discrepancy clearly indicates a particular racial politics. Activists argue that government claims of "racial equality" prohibit any scientific studies of the number, location, and social status of Afro-descendants.[11] This claim is reflected in civil society's denial of the existence of a contemporary Afro-Venezuelan identity and population.

The denial of a contemporary Afro-Venezuelan population is largely due to the construction of a Venezuelan *mestizaje* that relies on both the inclusion and the exclusion of Afro-Venezuelans in the formation of the modern nation. Afro-Venezuelans are included in the historic formation of a criollo culture of mestizo citizens as an enslaved labor force largely disappeared through miscegenation, with the exception of a few folkloric retentions and survivals evident in contemporary society. Folkloric contributions are code for "lesser" contributions. Afro-Venezuelan social, economic, and political contributions to contemporary society are denied, safely excluding this population group from the modern nation. The anthropologist Peter Wade describes this condition as the "all-inclusive ideology of exclusion" on which *mestizaje* depends.[12] Several developments facilitate the transfer of official race concepts from the intellectual and political sphere to larger society simultaneously silencing alternatives. These developments include the historical confluence of intellectual and political careers,[13] ownership of key media by racist sociopolitical elites,[14] the absence of a census that accounts for Afro-Venezuelan social, economic, and political realities, and an educational system with racially exclusionary curriculum and disparities in facilities.[15] Furthermore, Afro-Venezuelan identity is hindered by a hemispheric privileging of indigenous identities and activism.

Contemporary scholars of the Bolivarian Revolution rarely offer a race analysis, and if they do, it refers to indigenous Venezuelans.[16] However, many use class as a code for race. The anthropologist Patricia Márquez racializes and criminalizes

Chávez supporters by writing: "When a 'hood' from the barrio murders during an assault, he simultaneously kills what he sees as the oligarchy. For the chavista at heart, everything that he associates with the opposition, money, white skin, *cara de sifrino*, is oligarchy and deserves to be hated."[17] Furthermore, indigenous identity is far more present in government and activist discourses of the Bolivarian Revolution. Indigenous political movements in Latin America are more successful at winning collective rights than are African-descended ones. Of the fifteen Latin American countries that have legally adopted some form of collective rights for ethnic and racial subgroups, only six have extended these rights to Afro-Latinos (Brazil, Colombia, Ecuador, Guatemala, Honduras, and Nicaragua). Generally, scholars explain this phenomenon as a difference in organizational depth, population size, and higher levels of group identity. However, Juliet Hooker argues that this disparity is better explained by lawmakers' conceptions of what is "distinct group identity separate from the national culture" and by a group's ability to effectively express this identity.[18] Venezuelan ethnic diversity in the constitution refers only to the thirty-six indigenous nations within its borders and not to Afro-Venezuelans. Thus indigenous nations obtain particular consideration in state-sponsored programs and in constitutional laws pertaining to land ownership, economic development, and educational and health rights. They are also represented by two seats in the National Assembly and maintain institutional links with the government through the Indigenous National Council of Venezuela (CONIVE) and Misión Guaicaipuro—a state-funded project for restoring indigenous rights. No such rights or institutions are accorded Afro-Venezuelans.

Venezuelan criollo society is not a racial democracy; it simply masks a process of whitening that complicates Afro-Venezuelan organizing. It is a white supremacist project that makes racial difference something that existed in the past and Afro-descendancy something shared by all Venezuelans. Thus discrimination is understood as a set of economic rather than racial disparities. Furthermore, once race ceases to exist in the present, there can be no harm in essentializing a premodern, subordinated black subject such as *mi negra*.[19] More important, blackness—as a social formation—is stripped of its political potential. Afro-Venezuelan activists participating in the Bolivarian Revolution point out that other Bolivarian activists often deny the particularities of their struggle. It is quite common for Bolivarian revolutionaries to dismiss the Afro-Venezuelan movement as divisive, a small minority, and thus unimportant or even nonexistent. Charles Price points out that any "anti-systemic" group must work within the options available to a given population in the processes of identity formation.[20] One cannot easily or effectively claim a status that is incomprehensible or contested by society. This is the situation Afro-Venezuelans face when organizing their participation in the development of twenty-first-century socialism.

Active Marooning

Many Afro-Venezuelan activists around the country use a discourse of contemporary marooning to describe their activism. Perdomo explains: "Our traditions give us the instruments to strengthen our struggle. We don't talk about slaves anymore, but slavery still exists. It is the condition of being forced against your will to live in a certain place, in a certain way. Personally, I consider myself a contemporary maroon."[21] Active marooning is above all a sustained politics and concept of self-liberation characterized by the consolidation of an Afro-descendant identity and consciousness that leads to collective action. It is the process of merging culture and politics into a single entity: a political community.[22] This process involves the revitalization of autochthonous Venezuelan maroon histories and a process of self-reconceptualization that offer a teaching opportunity and organizing tool to contextualize contemporary political action. Active marooning forms the ideological basis of the Afro-Venezuelan movement, the goals of which are recognition, education, democratic participation, and autonomy. The Afro-Venezuelan movement predates the Bolivarian Revolution and is an interconnected struggle for democracy.

Through the linking of histories, Afro-descendant culture, and contemporary politics, Afro-Venezuelan identity and responses emerge in practice.[23] The anthropologists Arlene Torres and Norman Whitten encourage scholars of blackness in Latin America and the Caribbean to focus on the dynamic and creative forces of rebellion and self-liberation.[24] This approach is concerned with how the struggle for liberation is related to and supported by cultural processes of social relations, gendered interaction, symbolism, community formations, and regional and national systems. Furthermore, they emphasize the interaction between processes of liberation and the nature of structures of domination. This framework establishes a concept of race in both analysis and practice as not only oppressive but also, more important, as something positive and uplifting. To render Afro-Venezuelans a distinct and recognizable contemporary population, active marooning involves a complex process of identity formation. Identity emerges through social relationships across a terrain marked by the unequal exercise of power, and it is the product of exclusion and difference.[25] Solidarity is built around points of "resemblance" (phenotypical, experiential, and locational similarities) coupled with experiences of exclusion that are dynamic and create ideational rather than material bonds.[26] It is a bottom-up politics of identity that establishes personal and group power that relies on traditional, contemporary, radical, local, regional, religious, gendered, classed, raced, and ethnic cultures for expression.[27] The sites in which the militant actions of the contemporary Afro-Venezuelan movement take place are modern *cumbes*: communities of survival and resistance.[28] It is in these communities, or modern-day maroon societies, that identity is reappropriated and a particular Afro-Venezuelan identity is constructed.

The struggle for recognition is the struggle to transform a premodern folkloric identity into a contemporary political identity. It has two interrelated fronts: (1)

raising consciousness and self-identification in Afro-descended communities; and
(2) winning legal recognition at the state level. In the first case, creating educational
opportunities for activists in conjunction with their organizing efforts is strategic
to processes of wider self-identification. In the second case, the struggle for legal
recognition by state and local governments is key to opening up access to political,
economic, and social power. The unique configuration of the Bolivarian Revolution, in which the government is an ally of the grassroots movement, makes state
recognition more likely to have an impact on public opinion.[29] Chávez's recognition
of his African ancestry and the high-profile leadership of Afro-Venezuelan cabinet
members such as Aristóbulo Istúriz proved instrumental in opening up national
discourses about race that Afro-Venezuelan activists capitalized on.[30] Recognition
strategies are often criticized as eschewing strategies of confronting racism.[31] However, the Venezuelan case raises the following issue: to what extent can legal recognition translate into political, economic, and social changes?

The experiences of Afro-Venezuelan women activists in the Cumbe de
Mujeres Afrovenezolanas (Afro-Venezuelan Women's Free Community) offer an
example of the complexities involved and creativity employed in raising consciousness and encouraging self-identification. Juana, an Afro-Venezuelan activist in Sucre,
recalled that when she, her sister Ofelia, and their friend Carmen began to organize
families in the region, many Afro-descendants were reluctant to listen.[32] The women
changed their tactic and began to organize over issues of single motherhood, domestic violence, reproductive rights, and a lack of economic opportunities, pointing out
that Afro-Venezuelan women overwhelmingly faced these issues. Juana referred to
this approach as "real social work, from the bottom up," because it prioritized basic
and specific needs while reflecting on how racial formation affected standards of living. She recognized the ease with which the Cumbe de Mujeres formed as opposed
to the Afro-Venezuelan movement in general. She remarked, "There are certain
issues Afro-descendant women face that are better discussed in the Cumbe than
in the national organizations of Afro-Venezuelan men and women." Recent legal
gains for women in Venezuela, including child-support laws, social security credits
for domestic work, and domestic-violence protection owe a great deal to the participation of women from the Cumbe in national forums.[33] Many of these women
participate in the state-funded projects of the National Institute of Women and of
the Women's Development Bank, bringing a strong Afro-Venezuelan presence and
consciousness to the political and legal initiatives of these institutions.

History plays an important role in the process of recognition. As Gustavo, an
Afro-Venezuelan activist in the municipality of Veroes, Yaracuy, explained to me,
gesturing to the hills surrounding his home:

Our struggle is made more difficult by official histories that negate the
contributions of Afro-descendants. If you don't know where you're from, how

are you going to fight? Take, for example, our case here in Yaracuy. There were a lot of maroon settlements, *cumbes*, around here during the colonial times. We revived the history of Andres López de Rosario, we call him Andresote. He was the leader of a slave and freed black rebellion against a Spanish company Guipuzcoana that terrorized black producers and merchants and held a monopoly on agricultural production. He was from right here in these mountains. His struggle was like the Bolivarian Revolution today, anti-imperialist, antimonopoly, and socialist. We have always had a socialist existence. Marx, well that's something different. What is important is that we have contributed politically to Venezuela, not just culturally.[34]

Gustavo explained how other mestizo and Afro-descended Bolivarian revolutionaries questioned his identity as an Afro-Venezuelan:

It is very difficult for many Venezuelans to make the switch from Negro to Afro-descendant. They say that we are segregating ourselves, that *we* are being racist. They say, "forget that stupid thing, the revolution is not about that!" But we are very aware of how exclusion of Afro-descendants and indigenous people in Nicaragua worked against the Sandinista revolution and how in Cuba there is still racism against Afro-Cubans. Here in Venezuela, we can't call this a revolutionary process without the full participation of Afro-descendants.[35]

Gustavo's remarks show how history is important for fostering self-reconceptualization, as well as for the contemporary politics of the Bolivarian Revolution and for participation in the development of twenty-first-century socialism.

During 2003–4, Afro-Venezuelan activists in Veroes revived their own communal history to reclaim lands occupied by cane planters that were subsidized by the government. The planters employed townspeople as cane cutters and to work in the processing plant. Activists succeeded in proving that historically the land was worked and owned communally, not by the state or the planters. Furthermore, in an effort to quell the contestation over the land, absentee planters stalled production and laid off workers after taking government subsidies and simultaneously restricted townspeople from using the land. The community in Veroes was granted the land in a legal decision. Subsequently, they diversified the crops planted, providing a local source of dietary standards that had previously been imported from other regions at high costs. On Earth Day April 2007, activists occupied the processing plant. They have plans to develop an agricultural school on the site.

Democratic participation at the level of constructing and maintaining Afro-Venezuelan organizations is a common goal expressed by activists. Today, activists speak about the importance of the histories of maroon settlements for creating contemporary *cumbes*. They envision the contemporary *cumbes* as spaces that can serve as "laboratories in which ideas and liberation strategies can be worked out democratically."[36] This is understood as requiring a new way of organizing that does not favor hierarchies or representation but rather allows and encourages participation. The Afro-Venezuelan movement has a history of democratic organizing since its inception. Planning and activities take place across the network of more than thirty organizations. The Organización de Mujeres Negras (Organization of Black Women) began preparing participants for national and international forums in the early 1990s. Their goal was to express the gendered and racial marginalization of their community. Leaders from several leftist political parties formed the Information and Documentation Workshop of Afro-Venezuelan Culture, whose objectives were to vindicate Afro-Venezuelan identity by infusing Afro-Venezuelan perspectives into issues of autonomy, social transformation, political and social consciousness, self-reflection, self-esteem, and self-recognition. They held workshops in Afro-Venezuelan communities throughout the country, encouraging and building political participation. The Fundación Afroamérica, founded in 1993 with funding from UNESCO, seeks to conduct systematic research and publish studies relevant to the Afro-Venezuelan communities. Finally, the Network of Afro-Venezuelan Organizations consists of more than thirty diverse organizations across the country. Its primary objectives are to produce educational materials and increase the participation of Afro-Venezuelans in local and national government.

The Afro-Venezuelan movement also seeks to maintain its autonomy from the Venezuelan government. However, this autonomy should be understood as desiring both recognition and a position from which to engage the state. Longtime Afro-Venezuelan activist Jesús "Chucho" García comments: "If groups such as the Network of African-Venezuelan Organizations do not declare themselves to be totally pro-government, the [Bolivarian] process can advance significantly. And then we can truly say that this is a participatory democracy. But if we just wait for Chávez to take the initiative, then we will achieve very little. This is also why we differentiate ourselves from other social movements."[37] Afro-Venezuelan participation in international race-activist networks, mostly with other Afro-Latino organizations, provides the movement with shared and effective discourses to frame issues of race nationally, lends the movement credibility, and legitimates particular organizations as representatives of Afro-Venezuelan civil society.[38] However, as Nirva Camacho, Afro-Venezuelan activist and psychologist, explained to me: "The Afro-Venezuelan movement has its articulations with other Afro-Latino and black movements around the world. However, the movement is based on the specificity of the historical and contemporary experiences of Afro-descendants in Venezuela. This allows us to speak to and include a wider spectrum of Afro-Venezuelans in the movement, who otherwise might be skeptical or unable to identify with a larger movement."[39] Most activists place a high value on the autonomy of the movement, a reflection of the general distaste of the new Venezuelan political class for national institutionalized parties and a wariness of U.S. activist discourses that represent the movement as part of a larger diaspora. Activists routinely comment that diasporic activist identity often obscures the autonomy and historical particularity of the Afro-Venezuelan movement. Coalitional activism is often thought of as hierarchical, placing the Afro-Venezuelan movement under contemporary U.S. black organizing or under the influence of that of the 1960s and 1970s in the United States.

Active marooning is the consolidation of Afro-Venezuelans into a political community that utilizes historical and contemporary Afro-descendant identity, cultures, and politics. It is a strategic process of self-liberation that makes use of a dynamic concept of race that is uplifting for those engaged with it. It involves self-reconceptualization and efforts to win recognition while also supporting democratic participation in collective action. It is the formation of modern *cumbes*. Identity is never unified or singular but rather fragmented, fractured, multiple, and constructed across intersecting and antagonistic discourses, practices, and positions. It is both historical and dynamic.[40] Rather than finding this political community essentialist, constructivist, or exclusionary, I argue that it is strategic. Ethnographic observation shows that the strategic essentialism of the Afro-Venezuelan movement is inclusive by nature of its emergent character.

Conclusion: Afro-Venezuelan Citizenship and Diasporic Identity

On July 6, 2007, at the new Bolivarian University in Caracas, Chucho García opened the exhibit Africa: Perspectives of Ethnic Fragmentation with these words: "Everything with respect to Afro-Venezuelan-ness is in the process of construction and reconstruction."[41] Large portraits of Afro-Venezuelan students, faculty, and staff at the Chaguaramos campus ringed the large exhibit hall—exhibit organizers hoped to draw attention to the Afro-Venezuelan presence on campus.[42] Efforts to exert Afro-Venezuelan visibility were coming to a climax following the debacle over the Mi Negra proposal and the resounding defeat of its sponsor, Rosales. Then, six months later, Afro-Venezuelans lost a bid for inclusion in the constitution. Although support for the amendment was high among National Assembly sponsors and the president, last-minute political wrangling lumped Afro-Venezuelan recognition together with forty-five additional amendments that ranged from lowering the voting age to sixteen to the end of presidential term limits. Voters had to decide yes or no on the forty-six amendments as a group. The president and the National Assembly—mostly Chávez supporters—had been overconfident of voters' unwavering support, but voters decided no. Many Chávez supporters, Bolivarian activists, and Afro-Venezuelans were unable to support all of the reforms and thus had to choose none. The Afro-Venezuelan movement publicly chastised government officials and state institutions for prioritizing the Bolivarian Revolution's general goals over their legal and hopeful social integration into the nation. "Add it to the debt the state owes us," Perdomo exclaimed; "it's just one more instance of denying our existence."[43] He perceived the ideological hegemony or arrogance of the Bolivarian Revolution as burying the latest efforts of activists. While this is an example of the power and racial hierarchies existent in the coalitional politics of the Bolivarian Revolution, it is by no means exclusive to it. Given the proliferation of this dynamic in leftist politics across the Americas, it is easy to understand why race-based activism remains a priority for many groups critical of coalitional politics.

Active marooning involves political action and processes by which Afro-descended Venezuelans position themselves within or with respect to the nation-state. It is in this sense that it enters into debates occurring in scholarship on the African diaspora. The Afro-Venezuelan struggle to transform a premodern folkloric identity into a contemporary political identity rests uneasily within the literature on the African diaspora in at least two ways. First, it does not fit the geographically fluid cultural and political formations that characterize much of African diaspora scholarship, which deemphasize the nation-state in favor of linkages that tie Afro-descendants together according to common histories of domination and consciousness.[44] Afro-Venezuelan activists repeatedly emphasize the movement's particularity rather than its seemingly weak linkages to other movements. Second, the Venezuelan case challenges ideas that diasporic consciousness relies on a practical, edenic existential elsewhere — or on an idyllic homeland in which one does not reside, but perhaps draws inspiration from.[45] The Afro-Venezuelan movement operates within the nation-state by often taking contributions to national history (autochthonous histories) as a focal point for developing an Afro-Venezuelan (nationalist) consciousness. Thus neither of these conceptualizations of the African diaspora fit the Venezuelan situation.

The Venezuelan case raises the question about the relevance of a local Afro-descendant political community to the African diaspora. It also generates questions about how Afro-Latinos fit into dominant notions of the African diaspora. As the social, political, and economic changes of the Bolivarian Revolution deepen into twenty-first-century socialism, it remains to be seen if the Venezuelan case will break with other socialist-inspired revolutions in Latin America. María Josefina Saldaña-Portillo explains that historically Latin American socialist movements have emphasized class — not race — as a marker of difference, which means "leaving behind one's own particularity" including one's gender, race, and culture.[46] At the moment, Afro-Venezuelans continue to struggle against this tendency through a sustained politics of active marooning and by drawing on the lessons of other Afro-descendant communities throughout the Americas. Perhaps it is in this sense — in the struggle for democracy — that linkages to the larger African diaspora can be made.

Notes

Thanks to my committee members, especially to Arlene Torres and Marc Perry. I thank the participants of the Advanced Seminar in Chicano Research and the Chicana/o Latina/o Association for Autonomous Anthropology for continued influence on and support of my perspective and approach to academia. Fieldwork was possible through a grant from the anthropology department at the University of Illinois at Urbana-Champaign. I also thank Fanny Suárez for help with translation.

1. Jesús "Chucho" García, interview by the author, Caracas, January 5, 2007.

2. The Bolivarian Revolution is a plan of participatory, democratic governance and development that prioritizes the poor, nonwhites, women, and children of Venezuela. Chávez supporters participate through direct actions and mobilizations, government-supported social and economic resource programs, local governing organizations, and autonomous mobilizing structures. See Cristóbal Valencia Ramírez, "Venezuela's Bolivarian Revolution: Who Are the Chavistas?" *Latin American Perspectives* 32 (2005): 79–97; and "Venezuela in the Eye of the Hurricane: Landing an Analysis of the Bolivarian Revolution," *Journal of Latin American and Caribbean Anthropology* 11 (2006): 173–86. The Bolivarian Revolution also involves the government's efforts to consolidate a political base from which new social forces can be mobilized and from which a new antineoliberal logic can be developed that is cooperative, participatory in nature, and that stresses solidarity. See Gregory Albo, "The Unexpected Revolution: Venezuela Confronts Neoliberalism" (paper presented at the University of Alberta, www.socialistproject.ca/theory/venezuela_praksis .pdf; accessed February 25, 2008).

3. For example, see Greg Grandin, "Countervailing Powers," *Latin American Studies Association Forum* 38 (2007): 14–17.

4. Luís Perdomo, interview by the author, San José de Barlovento, Miranda, July 20, 2007.

5. Some scholars argue that criollo is an elite ideological construct that refers to biological and culturally mixed peoples who form a homogeneous nationality. See Berta Pérez and Abel Perozo, "Prospects of Mestizaje and Pluricultural Democracy: The Venezuelan Case of an Imagined and Real Venezuelan Society," *Anuário antropológico* 100–101 (2003): 119–46.

6. My use of the term *active marooning* is based on Chucho García's classification of seventeenth- to nineteenth-century Venezuelan national archival data regarding the declarations and discourses of runaway African maroons. García classified the evidence into passive and active marooning categories. The latter indicated a sustained politics and concept of anticolonial liberation. See Jesús García, "Demystifying Africa's Absence in Venezuela History and Culture," *Venezuelanalysis*, January 15, 2004, www.venezuelanalysis .com/print.php?artno=1088.

7. I conducted ethnographic fieldwork in the central coastal states of Yaracuy, Vargas, and Miranda, the eastern coastal state of Sucre, and in Caracas.

8. Michael Hanchard, "Racial Consciousness and Afro-Diasporic Experiences: Antonio Gramsci Reconsidered," *Socialism and Democracy* 7 (1991): 3.

9. Berta Pérez, "Rethinking Venezuelan Anthropology," *Ethnohistory* 47 (2000): 3–4.

10. The InterAmerican Development Bank puts the figure between 10 and 15 percent, the Venezuelan Institute of Scientific Investigation (IVIC) estimates it at 14 percent, and Simon Romero puts it at 30 percent in "Venezuelans Square Off Over Race, Oil, and a Populist Political Slogan," *New York Times*, November 12, 2006. Alejandra Correa and Willie Thompson place it at 60 percent; see "African Venezuelans Fear New U.S. Coup against President Chávez," *Venezuelanalysis*, October 14, 2003, www.venezuelanalysis.com/ analysis/159.

11. Jesús Chucho García, "La deuda del estado Venezolano y los afrodescendientes" ("The Venezuelan State's Debt and Afro-Descendents"), *Journal of Latin American and Caribbean Anthropology* 12 (2007): 223–32.

12. Peter Wade, "Rethinking Mestizaje: Ideology and Lived Experience," *Journal of Latin American Studies* 37 (2005): 243.

13. Antonio Isea, "La narración de lo racial-nacional en 'Pobre Negro' de Rómulo Gallegos" ("The Racial-National Narration in 'Poor Black' by Rómulo Gallegos"), *Afro-Hispanic Review* 20 (2001): 18–22; Marvin Lewis, *Ethnicity and Identity in Contemporary Afro Venezuelan Literature: A Culturist Approach* (Columbia: University of Missouri Press, 1992); Raquel Rivas Rojas, "Cimarronaje, exclusión, mestizaje y blanqueamiento en 'Pobre Negro' de Rómulo Gallegos" ("Maroonage, Exclusion, Miscegenation, and Whitening in Romulo Gallegos' "Poor Black"), *Estudios: Revistas de investigaciones literarias y culturales* 10 (2002): 105–20; Doug Yarrington, "Populist Anxiety: Race and Social Change in the Thought of Rómulo Gallegos," *Americas* 56 (1999): 65–90; García "Demystifying Africa's Absence."

14. Juan Antonio Hernández, "Against the Comedy of Civil Society: Posthegemony, Media, and the 2002 Coup d'Etat in Venezuela," *Journal of Latin American Cultural Studies* 13 (2004): 137–45; Jesús García and Jorge Veloz, *Afrovenezolanidad, racismo e interculturalidad* (*Afro-Venezuelan-ness, Racism, and Interculturality*) (Caracas: Red de Organizaciones Afrovenezolana, 2003).

15. García, "La deuda."

16. Exceptions include Jesús María Herrera Salas, "Ethnicity and Revolution: The Political Economy of Racism in Venezuela," in *Venezuela: Hugo Chávez and the Decline of an "Exceptional Democracy,"* ed. Steve Ellner and Miguel Tinker Salas (Boulder, CO: Rowman and Littlefield, 2007); García, "La deuda"; Pérez and Perozo, "Prospects of Mestizaje and Pluricultural Democracy"; Sujatha Fernandes, "Barrio Women and Popular Politics in Chávez's Venezuela," *Latin American Politics and Society* 49 (2007): 97–127.

17. *Cara de sifrino* means both "white features and arrogant or stuck up." Patricia Márquez, "Vacas flacas y odios gordos: La polarización en Venezuela" ("Hard Times and Intense Hate: Polarization in Venezuela"), in *En esta Venezuela* (*In This Venezuela*), ed. Márquez and Ramón Piñango (Caracas: Ediciones Instituto de Estudios Superiores Administración, 2003), 42.

18. Juliet Hooker, "Indigenous Inclusion/Black Exclusion: Race, Ethnicity, and Multicultural Citizenship in Latin America," *Journal of Latin American Studies* 37 (2005): 285–310.

19. For an in-depth explanation of Afro-Venezuelan invisibility and racism in Venezuelan Creole society, see Berta Pérez, "De invisibilidad à visibilidad: El reto del negro venezolano" ("From Invisibility to Visibility: The Black Venezuelan Challenge"), *Boletín universitario de letras* 2 (1994): 53–68; and Pérez and Perozo, "Prospects of Mestizaje and Pluricultural Democracy."

20. Charles Reavis Price, "Social Change and the Development and Co-optation of a Black Antisystemic Identity: The Case of Rastafarians in Jamaica," *Identity: An International Journal of Theory and Research* 3 (2003): 9–27.

21. Perdomo, author interview, July 20, 2007.

22. Michael Hanchard analyzes this process in the case of Brazil, pointing out that a political community is exclusionary, part imaginary, and fragmented. See his *Orpheus and Power: The Movimento Negro of Rio de Janeiro and São Paulo, Brazil, 1945–1988* (Princeton, NJ: Princeton University Press, 1994). He also argues that culture and politics are not separate

concepts but come together in a political party. See his *Party/Politics: Horizons in Black Political Thought* (New York: Oxford University Press, 2006).

23. Organic activist intellectuals explain Afro-descendant culture as shared: phenotypic resemblance, urban and rural lifestyles, religious and culinary traditions, cultural identity, and agricultural techniques linked through solidarity movements and collective labor. See García "La deuda."

24. Arlene Torres and Norman Whitten, "To Forge the Future in the Fires of the Past: An Interpretive Essay on Racism, Domination, Resistance, and Liberation," in *Blackness in Latin America and the Caribbean: Social Dynamics and Cultural Transformations*, vol. 1, ed. Norman E. Whitten Jr. and Arlene Torres (Bloomington: Indiana University Press, 1998), 3–33.

25. See Stuart Hall, "Introduction: Who Needs Identity," in *Questions of Cultural Identity*, ed. Hall and Paul DuGay (Thousand Oaks, CA: Sage, 1996), 1–17; Alejandro Lugo, "Reflections of Border Theory, Culture, and the Nation," in *Border Theory: The Limits of Cultural Politics*, ed. Scott Michaelsen and David Johnson (Minneapolis: University of Minnesota Press, 1997), 43–67.

26. See Hanchard, "Racial Consciousness and Afro-Diasporic Experiences"; Hall, "Introduction."

27. Jonathan Hill and Thomas Wilson, "Identity Politics and the Politics of Identity," *Identities: Global Studies in Culture and Power* 10 (2003): 1–8.

28. See García, "Demystifying Africa's Absence."

29. See Cristóbal Valencia Ramírez, "Hemos Derrotado el Diablo! Chávez supporters, Anti-neoliberalism, and Twenty-First-Century socialism," *Identities: Global Studies in Culture and Power* 15 (2008): 147–70.

30. See Abigail Elwood, "Teaching Race in Venezuela," *Venezuelanalysis*, May 13, 2005, www.venezuelanalysis.com/php?artno=1447. Also see Correa and Thompson, "African Venezuelans Fear."

31. Hooker, "Indigenous Inclusion/Black Exclusion."

32. Juana Yoco, interview by the author, Sucre, August 4, 2007.

33. Nirva Camacho, interview by the author, Macuto, Vargas, July 18, 2007.

34. Gustavo Farriar, interview by the author, Yaracuy, July 26, 2007.

35. Gustavo Farriar, interview by the author, Yaracuy, July 28, 2007.

36. Perdomo, author interview, January 21, 2004.

37. Gregory Wilpert, "Racism and Racial Divides in Venezuela: An Interview with Jesús 'Chucho' García," *Venezuelanalysis*, January 21, 2004, www.venezuelanalysis.com/articles .php?artno=1091.

38. Jun Ishibashi, "Hacia una apertura del debate sobre el racismo en Venezuela: Exclusión y inclusion estereotipada de personas 'negras' en los medios de comunicación" ("Toward an Opening of the Debate on Racism in Venezuela: Stereotyped Exclusion and Inclusion of 'Black' People in Mass Media"), in *Políticas de identidades y diferencias sociales* (*Identity Politics and Social Differences*), ed. Daniel Mato (Caracas: Facultad de Ciencias Económicas y Sociales, 2003), 33–63.

39. Camacho, interview by the author, July 18, 2007.

40. Hall, "Introduction."

41. Jesús "Chucho" García, presentation at Africa: Perspectives of Ethnic Fragmentation, Bolivarian University, Caracas, July 6, 2007.

42. Flor Márquez, coordinator of African Studies, Bolivarian University Chaguaramos, interview by the author, Caracas, July 6, 2007.

43. Luís Perdomo, personal communication, October 21, 2007.

44. See Tiffany Ruby Patterson and Robin D. G. Kelley, "Unfinished Migrations: Reflections on the African Diaspora and the Making of the Modern World," *African Studies Review* 43 (2000): 11–45. To their credit they consider Afro-Latinos the exception to this characterization. See also Herman L. Bennett, "The Subject in the Plot: National Boundaries and the 'History' of the Black Atlantic," *African Studies Review* 43 (2000): 101–24; and Agustín Lao-Montes, "Decolonial Moves: Trans-locating African Diaspora Spaces," *Cultural Studies* 21 (2007): 309–38.

45. Hanchard, "Racial Consciousness and Afro-Diasporic Experiences."

46. María Josefina Saldaña-Portillo, *The Revolutionary Imagination in the Americas and the Age of Development* (Durham, NC: Duke University Press, 2003), 7. For a Cuban example, see Alejandro de la Fuente, *A Nation for All: Race, Inequality, and Politics in Twentieth-Century Cuba* (Chapel Hill: University of North Carolina Press, 2001); for examples in Nicaragua, see Charles Hale, *Resistance and Contradiction: Miskitu Indians and the Nicaraguan State, 1849–1987* (Stanford, CA: Stanford University Press, 1994); and Edmund T. Gordon, *Disparate Diasporas: Identity and Politics in an African-Nicaraguan Community* (Austin: University of Texas Press, 1998).

Indigenous Acts: Black and Native Performances in Mexico

Anita González

Afro-Mexican Agendas

Even acknowledging the existence of an Afro-diaspora culture in Mexico constitutes a controversial act. While Africans and their descendants are woven into the fabric of Mexico's history, social systems and cultural institutions negate the viability of a dynamic and political black population. In general, *black* is a contested term in Afro–Latin American studies. Throughout the Americas, both Africans and Europeans were newcomers to lands long occupied by diverse Native American civilizations. When Spanish settlers arrived, they divided nonwhite people into *castas* (racial castes) that purposefully defined and then ranked intermixtures, such as black-Indian, black-white, and black-Indian-white. Social policies based on these *castas* reduced the privileges of all non-Spaniards and marked them as outsiders. However, each Native American community in the Americas has interacted with enslaved Africans and/or migrating blacks in different ways. Miscegenation among racial groups created mixtures of peoples that were and are often indistinguishable through phenotypes. Each Latin American country imaginatively re-creates the social implications of these racial intermixtures.

For some nations such as the United States, Brazil, and many Caribbean countries, defining black identity is a political strategy that has effectively mobilized people of African descent. In Mexico, however, there has been no unified struggle for social advancement based on African heritage. Rather, Afro-Mexican culture

Radical History Review

Issue 103 (Winter 2009)   DOI 10.1215/01636545-2008-035

© 2009 by MARHO: The Radical Historians' Organization, Inc.

exists as a nearly indistinguishable subculture in the Mexican nationalist imagination. To publicly attest to black identity is to contradict an ingrained national ideology about what is "Mexican." Many darker-skinned Mexican citizens think of themselves as "indigenous" or native to certain Mexican "homelands" regardless of race.[1] For Afro-Mexicans, or the descendants of Africans in Mexico, these homelands are concentrated in the states of Oaxaca, Guerrero, Veracruz, Tabasco, and Michoacán. And yet, even as these and other communities do not recognize or acknowledge a blood lineage that connects them to Africa, local performance practices re-create mobile histories of ethnic encounters. Intercultural performances of dance dramas in Mexico make visible the presence of African-descended Mexicans, even if minimally, as sites from which multiple populations engage the layered, multiracial history of New World encounters in Mexico.

Although Afro-Mexicans have socially "disappeared" into the political construction of *mestizaje* (mixed-race identity), expressive culture provides multiple examples of the ways in which blackness itself is still a living imaginary in Mexico. Dances based on archetypal images of blackness such as the *negritos* or the *danza del diablo* (devil dance) proliferate at theater and dance festivals throughout the country.[2] The theater historian Joseph Roach has shown that theater and dance performances can uniquely capture histories and memories, providing an alternative way of filling the "vacancies . . . in the network of relationships that constitutes the social fabric."[3] Performance has the capacity to "stand in for an elusive entity that it is not, but that it must vainly aspire both to embody and to replace."[4] Afro-Mexican dance dramas function in this way; they reveal an African presence in Mexico that social systems have disguised.

Political assertions of negritude in Mexico are linked to the most widely accepted watersheds of Mexican history. A series of distinguished scholars such as Gonzalo Aguirre Beltrán, Patrick Carroll, and Ben Vinson III document this presence.[5] There was an African presence in Mexico as early as 1530 when Spanish conquistadores, fresh from the conquest of the Moors, brought African explorers with them on their journeys to the New World.[6] These same voyagers became some of the first settlers of the Americas. Afro-Mexican soldiers participated in the war for independence from Spain and established themselves in the historical archives of the Mexican Revolution. In the early twentieth century, however, Mexican ideologues, inspired by José Vasconcelos, pushed aside discussions about people of African descent in an effort to build nationalist solidarity around Spanish and Indian identities.[7] Racial identities were sublimated to the project of national unification; brown skin, African features, musical innovations, and dance traditions were considered cultural fusion and labeled "indigenous Mexican."

In the new millennium, there is a resurgent interest in unearthing the social and political contributions of Afro-Mexicans. What political agenda does excavating Afro-Mexican expressive cultures fulfill? In part, the interests of international visitors spur these new conceptions of blackness. While some (like the anthropologist Laura Lewis) may argue that this vested interest constitutes yet another act of North American imperialism, for some Mexicans it also forms an important part of the process of self-empowerment.[8] Assuming a politicized "black consciousness" allows disempowered citizens to align with an international community of activists who can provide resources for local community advancement. While Lewis argues that acknowledging black roots or *la tercera raíz* (the third root) gives Afro-Mexicans an inheritance of the past that only "contributes to the perceptions that blacks have about their own marginal status," a contrasting perspective argues that forging alliances with other global organizations to promote black perspectives can propel Afro-Mexicans into a larger movement of black diaspora cultural and economic activities.[9] Historically Afro-Mexicans have attempted to meld into indigenous and/or campesino campaigns. Working with diaspora allies outside Mexico can only create more political options for these communities.

At the same time, excavating Afro-Mexican histories expands on polarized notions of black-white dichotomies in the Americas. It brings into question ideas about how blackness is defined and expressed. Is blackness a skin color, cultural persistence, a sense of marginality or, perhaps, a distance from notions of modernity? Although there is evidence of African continuities in Afro-Mexican dance forms, representations and imagery of local practices illuminate something much more complex—a negotiation of identity within a cultural landscape that minimizes the presence of Afro-Mexicans.[10] Mexico is similar to other Latin American countries in that assessments about blackness are partially based on each individual's understanding of his or her own social status. Blackness is relative and changeable. For example, presumptions about Afro-Mexicans in the eastern provinces (Veracruz, Tabasco, and Mérida), where Cuban influences prevail, are different from understandings about Afro-Mexican identities on the western coast (near Oaxaca and Guerrero).

In Veracruz, the shadow of Cuba with its Santeria, rumba, and other cultural products overlays understandings about local Afro-Mexican practices. Even though Veracruz was the most important entry point for the importation of enslaved African fieldworkers, the Mexican regional culture of *guayabera* shirts, marimba music, dominos, and *café con leche* (coffee with milk) is considered Cuban. Blacks, in the national imagination, *are* Cubans, eternally a part of Mexican culture, but never quite from Mexico. On the Costa Chica on the Pacific Coast, local residents believe that Afro-Mexicans arrived in Mexico by boat from the coast of South America. Statements like these deny Afro-Mexican legitimacy, locate black origins outside Mexico, and perpetuate the myth that Afro-Mexicans hail from "somewhere else."

Layered across local Mexican understandings about African presence are global media representations of African diaspora people that come from television broadcasts. Images of North American sports, African poverty, Caribbean music, island tourism, and hip-hop modernism all permeate the country. These multiple cultural influences sometimes obfuscate origins of racial expressions, leading to peculiar reinventions of ethnic types. One potent example is the Memín Pinguín stamp, circulated by the Mexican government to promote an ostensibly unique Mexican cultural phenomenon.

Within the racialist cultural imagination of Mexico, Memín Pinguín, an uneducated, thick-lipped Cuban boy, was the punch line of a joke that is as old as the *bufos cubanos* (Cuban comedies) of the nineteenth century. *Bufos* were minstrel shows with stock characters that featured mythologized depictions of Afro-Cubans. In these spectacles the typical *negrito* (pejorative expression for "black") was poor, uneducated, subservient, and criminally suspect.[11] *Bufos* were one of the most popular forms of entertainment in Cuba for close to a century. The performance genre quickly migrated to Mesoamerica. Just as the *negrito* was a cultural icon of colonial Cuba, so too, did the *negrito* become ingrained in the Mexican psyche. Indigenous as well as mestizo communities developed local interpretations of *negrito* culture, and cartoon characters like Memín Pinguín replicated popular beliefs about "real" black attributes. By the time the Memín Pinguín stamp was released, the *negrito* icon seemed so familiar that most Mexicans could not understand why African American leaders and activists felt the image was offensive.

Jesse Jackson and other African American civil rights activists greeted the stamp's issue with an outcry. Jackson declared, "Comedy masks tragedy . . . in this instance, it's comedy with a demeaning punch line, and we hope that President Fox will take it off the market."[12] Mexicans pointed to similarly racist images in North America (like Speedy González or Aunt Jemima) to justify their own cultural blindness. For Mexicans the black Cuban Memín Pinguín was both naturalized and nationalized. Despite Jackson's protests, the Mexican government, and indeed most Mexicans, continued to support the stamp.

The controversy surrounding the Memín Pinguín stamp underscores how important performance and representation are in constructing Afro-Mexican identities. Performance is a place where "improvised narratives of authenticity and priority may congeal into full-blown myths of legitimacy and origin."[13] It involves iterations and responses; the artist circulates a representative image and observers respond. Audience response becomes a mirror that helps the artist situate him- or herself within a social arena. Black identity is a part of the social performance of self, which articulates itself within a global call-and-response of images.

Afro-Mexican Dances: An Overview

Today, the largest visible communities of Afro-Mexicans are concentrated on the eastern coast of Mexico and near the border of Oaxaca and Guerrero (although there are settlements in twenty of the thirty-two Mexican states).[14] It is within these two coastal regions that the most typical Afro-Mexican dances and songs emerge.

Some dances like the *jarocho* or the *chilena* are folkloric dances in which women wear long, full dresses with ruffles and adornments while the men wear variations on peasant attire—long pants and simple cotton shirts.

Contrasting with these folkloric styles, however, is masked Afro-Mexican dances like the devil dance, the turtle dance, and the *toro de petate* or straw bull dance. In these performances dancers do not appear human; instead, they wear the faces of animal-like deities and emerge in public to frighten bystanders. Masking creates a sense of anonymity for the performer while metaphysically transporting both performers and audience members into the realm of archetypal myth. Masked dances subvert societal norms because the disguise allows the dancer to perform outrageous actions under the guise of character. Two characters in particular, the Pancho and the Minga—the devil and his wife—appear in almost every dance. The Pancho is a fearsome character, while his wife, the Minga, is lascivious and rambunctious. Collectively, the archetypal masked dances push mythologies about African diaspora people to their limits. Public, in-your-face performances of black stereotypes seem both to reify and to contradict expectations about who and what blacks are.

In contrast, indigenous village dancers act out inversions of blackness in masked ceremonial rituals called *negritos*. These dances are almost always performed by Native American or mestizo performers who wear jet-black wooden masks with exaggerated features: red lips, wild wooly hair, and chiseled features (see figure 1). *Negrito* dance performances capture fears and alliances between

Figure 1. Pescaditos dance: Coaxtlahuacan Guerrero. Photograph by George O. Jackson

blacks and Natives in surprising ways. Unlike the cartoonlike Memín Pinguín, the *negrito* character in dance can appear in various guises. Sometimes the personage is a tall and distinguished cowboy, sometimes a skilled fisherman, and sometimes a violent and angry gangster who invades the village. Always the character is masked and represents the not-from-here. Each appearance of the *negrito* in indigenous dances marks a history of relationships between neighboring black and Native communities. Masked dances, folkloric dances, and indigenous dances together utilize performance imagery to articulate an ongoing conversation about the role that Afro-Mexicans play in Mexican society. The devil dance, however, speaks the most eloquently to the circulation of racial myths within the country.

Devil Dances of the Costa Chica

The devil dance of the Costa Chica in many ways exemplifies the exotic and violent archetype of the Afro-Mexican. The dance is said to have originated as a ritual to honor the god Rua who represents all "bad" things. *Tenangos* (runaway day laborers) prayed to Rua to liberate them from the conditions of hard labor. The mountains of the west coast harbored renegades who fled to escape the cruelties of the slave system. In historical context it is easy to see how Afro–Mexicans, after enduring the injustices of the Spanish slavery system, might have chosen to embrace the devil—the figure that symbolically represents the opposite of Spanish "charity." Devil dances challenge authority, frighten observers, and empower their performers through acts of impropriety.

In devil dance performance, a double file of masked dancers—usually between sixteen and twenty of them—moves through the streets. The lead devil, who is called the Pancho or Tenango, carries a whip. His wife, the Minga, a sexual and dangerous *mulata* (mixed-race woman), accompanies him. All of the dancers wear horned masks covered with animal fur. The dancers stop the processional at intervals and perform a cloglike step with their boots pounding on the earth. Sometimes they lie down on the ground while the lead devil beats them to demonstrate his power. Then the dancers rise and continue their journey through the performance square. At times they may stop to repeat a chant or to directly threaten other dancers or street observers. Elements of the devil dance might be compared to trick-or-treat Halloween rituals played in the United States because the chant asks the audience members to give money, drinks, or treats on behalf of Rua, or they will be hurt. The crowd, in response, passes token gifts to the performers.

The chorus of devil dancers represents a rebellious spirit that needs to be tamed. They demonstrate rebellion as they step out of line to cavort with the masses, but they also represent subservience when they lie down in the street to allow the Pancho to whip them. When Afro-Mexicans impersonate devils, they temporarily escape into a world of corporal expression where they take charge of their physical and social surroundings. Citizens use the dances to create fantastical order and to reenact a sense of power. An important element of the devil dances is the presence of the Minga. A man always plays this woman because men are the primary enactors of Mexican traditional village performance. The transgender nature of the role makes it one of the most challenging parts for the male dancer. There is a broad spectrum of physical representations of the Minga, from an innocent childlike figure to a miniskirt-wearing vamp, and the character has unique symbolic connotations. Because she is a *mulata*, she is by definition an embodiment of racial mixing. Her constant flirtations in the dances mark her as a sexualized vamp who seems always ready to promiscuously copulate. She is also aggressive; the more ferocious Mingas do not hesitate to engage in confrontational warrior-like behavior with both their "husbands" and with men who refuse their sexual solicitations.

Not only is there a huge variety in types of Mingas, but the figure also appears in most of the masked dances of the Costa Chica. Usually she brings her child—a white baby—with her as evidence of inappropriate copulations. The Minga represents the uncontrollable aspects of racial mixing—the copulations and alliances that happen outside the boundaries of official mandates and institutional regulations. Her dance appearances embody a national fear of the darker side of *mestizaje*. Because she is truly black, the Minga shape shifts into nightmarish representations of the Mexican woman. Like La Malinche, Hernán Cortés's concubine, she is the inevitable result of racial mixing in the Americas, but this more-black-than-Native woman is unpredictable, uncontainable, and irrepressible.

The devil dance intervenes in the social status quo of Mexico because behind the mask of the devil, Afro-Mexicans are able to restructure—albeit briefly—the social hierarchies that circumscribe their daily lives. Performing the devil dance does not change local politics. It does, however, temporarily invert power in favor of Afro-Mexicans, and it simultaneously provides a chance for villages to unite around a culturally unique ritual event.[15]

Indigenous Performances of Blackness: Negritos Dances in Huamelula

The perceptions of Afro-Mexican identities articulated by Native American and mestizo communities serve as counterpoints to these self-expressions of Afro-Mexican identity. These groups have developed complex dance theater scenarios to explain the presence and persistence of their darker-skinned neighbors. Enacting these confrontations helps alleviate seething tensions between Native American and Afro-Mexican communities. One example of this complex theatricality is the *negrito* dance performed by the Chontal Indians in the village of Huamelula, Oaxaca, during the Fiesta de San Pedro (June 24). The feast is known for its lengthy evocation of cultural histories.[16] While ostensibly a patron saint day festival, the event encapsulates local belief systems about the region. Festivities last for several days and include feasting, processionals, dances, and religious ceremonies. The performances include archetypal characters of Turks, *negritos*, and Chontal leaders, as well as

Figure 2. *Negritos* dancers from Huamelula. Photograph by George O. Jackson

animal characters. Each year there are slight variations on the presentation. Afro-Mexicans, represented by black-faced characters, are considered part of a larger panorama of inside and outside influences that affect the Chontales.

The mask play begins when characters wearing yellow masks (known as "Turks") enter the town square in a rolling float decorated to look like a boat. In this ethnic history, they represent wealthy outsiders who control the village residents. As dramatic characters the Turks meet with one another to discuss "important affairs" while they enjoy the amenities of the village. Next, the black men, or *negritos*, arrive. These characters represent disorder. Wearing urban street clothing with red bandanas wrapped around their heads, they disturb community peace by blocking the road with sticks and carrying pornographic pictures which they insist on showing to the innocent townspeople (see figure 2). Like unruly children, the *negritos* steal from the Turks in multiple acts of subversion as they try to appropriate/share their wealth.

The Turks, in response, appeal to the mayor and ask him to allow them to punish the *negritos* for their conduct. The ethnic dialogue continues when the mayor agrees. What follows is a symbolic murder. The Turks gather up the black men and bring them to the town square, where they hang them individually upside down from a tall pole. This act alludes to collusions between colonizers and indigenous leaders. The mayor covertly agrees to the destruction of the blacks by calling for a punishment that is interpreted by the Turks as a license to kill.[17] The reenactment continues when a group of *negritos* complain to the mayor and ask for the right to punish the Turks for their cruelty. The mayor responds by giving the *negritos* permission to retaliate. With the mayor's consent, the *negritos* gather up the Turks and throw them into the town jail. Capricious "play" between law and order is at the heart of the performed exchanges in Huamelula. Each ethnic constituent participates in a power struggle enacted through make-believe. Because the event is improvisatory and changes from year to year, the dramatic actions account for shifting political consciousnesses. The ritual allows the community to reinvestigate its relationship with external and internal histories. Through masked play and reenactment, the actors renegotiate their positions in the material and metaphysical worlds. The Chontal Native American village sits in close proximity to Afro-Mexican coastal areas, and thus *negritos* are included in the village's imagination of itself. The performed commentary combines historical experiences, global stereotypes, and metaphysical understandings of blackness.

Village performances such as the above demonstrate the importance of local responses to the African diaspora. Too often, diaspora studies are framed as dialogues between European and African constituencies. Indigenous performance in Mexico provides an alternative analytical frame for rethinking the impact of Africans in the Americas. Both Native Americans and Afro-Mexicans are indigenous to Mexico, and their dialogic exchanges encapsulate a wealth of social and historical experiences. Discussions of American histories that neglect these types of conversations articulate an incomplete narrative.[18]

Conclusion

These examples of Native American and Afro-Mexican performances highlight the multiple dialogues that surround African presence in Mexico. In general, mainstream Spanish and mestizo communities envision Afro-Mexicans as extensions of Cuban or Caribbean blackness. Cultural icons like Memín Pinguín or cultural expressions like mambo or Santeria — both Cuban — signify black identity in the Mexican national consciousness. If Afro-Mexicans are Cuban, however, they are eternal outsiders, never really a part of Mexico's mainstream cultural consciousness. Indigenous Afro-Mexicans — African diaspora people living in Mexico since the conquest — are thus relegated to a position of uneasy invisibility. Native American communities, however, respond to Afro-Mexicans through vivid performances that enact local histories. Even as they adopt the diminutive phrase *negritos* to describe dances that include black figures, these dances depict Afro-Mexicans as influential compatriots in national struggles. Indigenous dances (both Native American and Afro-Mexican) attest to an ongoing and evolving relationship between Afro-Mexicans and their Mexican homeland. Recent publications, conferences, and exhibitions on both sides of the Mexican-U.S. border have taken up the legacy of the African-descended in Mexico.[19] African diaspora communities in Mexico struggle to articulate their presence in a way that situates Afro-Mexican citizens within historical and contemporary culture. Acknowledging Afro-Mexican contributions to ongoing social and political movements in the country will enable local citizens to appeal for a share of valuable national resources. Dance, with its gestured codes and musical accompaniments, persists as evidence of a distinctive diaspora presence in a country where African people run the risk of invisibility. Devil dances, indigenous *negritos* performances, and even racist Cuban cartoons are all performance markers that allude to a historical reality of Afro-Mexicans that cannot be erased.

Notes

Versions of this article have been presented at the Center for African and African American Studies and the Center for Mexican Studies at the University of Texas, Austin. Special thanks to the photographers, George O. Jackson and José Manuel Pellicer, for documenting these dance events. Joni Jones and Ted Gordon of the Center for African and African American Studies at the University of Texas, Austin, have provided research funding for this project.

1. Here the word *homeland* describes the affiliation that various sectors of the Mexican population have with certain geographic areas of the country. When Mexico institutionalized cultural nationalism after the Mexican Revolution, residents were encouraged to embrace the customs and cultures of specific geographical locales. When asked about their identity, many Mexicans would say they are Oaxacan or Veracruzano or "de la Costa Chica," rather than referring to their indigenous or ethnic identity.

2. In most Latin American contexts, *negrito* is a pejorative term referring to the African-descended. The word has a range of meanings and translates imprecisely and variously into North American English—depending on context and intent—as "nigger," "little black," "little black boy," "my dear black," and so on.

3. Joseph Roach, *Cities of the Dead: Circum-Atlantic Performance* (New York: Columbia University Press, 1996), 2.

4. Ibid., 3.

5. Gonzalo Aguirre Beltrán, ed., *La población negra de México: Estudio etnohistórico* (*The Black Population of Mexico: Ethnohistoric Study*), 3rd ed. (Veracruz, Mexico: Universidad Veracruzana Instituto Nacional Indigenista Gobierno del Estado de Veracruz Fondo de Cultura Económico, 1989); Patrick J. Carroll, *Blacks in Colonial Veracruz: Race, Ethnicity, and Regional Development* (Austin: University of Texas Press, 1991); Ben Vinson III and Bobby Vaughn, *Afroméxico: El pulso de la población negra en México; Una historia recordada, olvidada, y vuelta a recordar* (*Afro-Mexico: The Pulse of the Black Population in Mexico; A History Remembered, Forgotten, and Returned to Memory*) (Mexico City: Centro de Investigación y Docencia Económicas/Fondo de Cultura Económica, 2004).

6. Ben Vinson III, "Fading from Memory: Historiographical Reflections on the Afro-Mexican Presence," *Review of Black Political Economy* 33 (2005): 59.

7. Colin M. Maclachlan and Jaime Rodriguez, *The Forging of the Cosmic Race: A Reinterpretation of Colonial Mexico* (Berkeley: University of California Press, 1990).

8. Laura A. Lewis, "Negros, Negros-Indios, Afromexicanos: Raza, nación e identidad en una comunidad mexicana morena (Guerrero)" ("Negros, Negros-Indios, and Afro-Mexicans: Race, Nation, and Identity in a Brown Mexican Community [Guerrero]"), *Guaraguao* 9 (2005): 49–73.

9. Ibid., 62. The original Spanish text reads, "contribuye á las percepciones que los morenos tienen de su propia marginalidad."

10. Some of these continuities include polyrhythm, articulated torsos, and West African foot patterns. See Brenda Dixon Gottschild, *Digging the Africanist Presence in American Performance* (Westport, CT: Greenwood, 1996).

11. There were variations on the form; for example, the *negro catedrático* was a pretentious buffoon and the *negro bozal* (a newly arrived African laborer) was wild and uncivilized. See Jill Lane, *Blackface Cuba, 1840–1895* (Philadelphia: University of Pennsylvania Press, 2005); and Robin D. Moore, *Nationalizing Blackness: Afrocubanismo and Artistic Revolution in Havana, 1920–1940* (Pittsburgh: University of Pittsburgh Press, 1997).

12. James C. McKinley Jr., "Mexican Stamp Sets Off a New Racial Fracas," *New York Times*, June 30, 2005.

13. Roach, *Cities of the Dead*, 3.

14. These regions include the Costa Chica of Guerrero, the Tierra Caliente of Michoacán, the Costa Grande region of Oaxaca, and parts of Los Altos on the coast of the Isthmus of Tehuantepec. There are also communities in Chiapas, Quintana Roo, and the Gulf region of the State of Veracruz. Benigno Jarquin Javier, "¿Continuidad o ruptura cultural africano en el México actual?" ("Continuity or African Cultural Rupture in Present-Day Mexico?"), in *Congrés Internacional d'Estudies Africans del Món Ibéric* (Barcelona, 2004).

15. There are other unmasked dances performed by Afro-Mexicans of the western coast, most notably the *artesa* couple dances and the *chilena* dances with their accompanying *sones* or musical poetry. These forms are said to have arrived on the Costa Chica in 1822 when a boatload of sailors from Chile landed in Acapulco, bringing a unique style of song and dance with them. Afro-Mexicans adopted the *chilena* music and dance forms, transforming them into cultural products representative of the region.

16. Alicia M. González, *The Edge of Enchantment: Sovereignty and Ceremony in Huatulco, Mexico* (Washington, DC: National Museum of the American Indian, Smithsonian Institution, 2002).

17. This information comes from the photographer George O. Jackson who has attended the Huamelula festival for several years.

18. *American* refers to "of the Americas" in this sentence.

19. The 2007 Chicago exhibition The African Presence in Mexico at the Mexican Fine Arts Center was an important site for symposiums and discussions of Afro-Mexican history and culture. The project emerged in collaboration with the Museo de Historia Mexicana. In addition, there have been ongoing conferences on the topic at the Universidad Veracruzana. The most recent Mexican publication on the topic is Juan de Dios González Ibarra, *La negritude: Terecra raíz mexicana (Negritude: The Third Mexican Root)* (Mexico City: Universidad Autónoma del Estado de Morelos, 2007).

Sovereignty, Neoliberalism, and the Postdiasporic Politics of Globalization: A Conversation about South Africa with Patrick Bond, Ashwin Desai, and Molefi Mafereka ka Ndlovu

Christopher J. Lee

In a recent essay titled "A New Cosmopolitanism," Paul Gilroy has argued for the centrality of South Africa in defining a contemporary politics of global cosmopolitanism and democratic humanism. "Critical consideration of South Africa's democratic transition can inspire new responses to the current geo-political situation," he insists in his opening paragraph. More specifically, South Africa's transition to democracy in 1994 "can be used to challenge the idea that civilizations are closed and finished cultural units which must be preserved at all costs. . . . [its] blend of diversity and solidarity yields a special lesson for a world where we are increasingly told that diversity and solidarity cannot mix."[1] Yet despite this sense of opportunity, South Africa has "dropped out of debates" regarding the linkages between multiculturalism, democracy, and cosmopolitan governance.[2] This "disappearance," in Gilroy's view, can be attributed to an ongoing failure on the part of political leaders and intellectuals to address the connections between racism and sovereignty in a persistent, nuanced fashion. Although South Africa once represented the apex of such connections—with a global antiapartheid movement marking this

Radical History Review
Issue 103 (Winter 2009)   DOI 10.1215/01636545-2008-036
© 2009 by MARHO: The Radical Historians' Organization, Inc.

recognition—its political revolution has not generated a sufficient level of inquiry or reflection to reshape global conversations over race, citizenship, and their meanings in the present.

Gilroy's remarks are significant for this issue of *Radical History Review* in that they evince a new set of questions regarding the interchange between the Black Atlantic paradigm and more recent discussions of cosmopolitanism as a new global ethic.[3] Furthermore, they suggest the need for a new configuration of diasporic politics vis-à-vis contemporary dilemmas of postcolonial sovereignty and neoliberal globalization.[4] Indeed, the following interview implicitly interrogates the possibilities of an emergent postdiasporic political order in this rapidly evolving present. The invocation of "postdiasporic" must be understood in a specific *political* sense given the foundational and ongoing roles diasporas have played in prefiguring and constituting current patterns of global migration and cultural change. Furthermore, as with cases elsewhere, the prefix *post-* suggests as much a dialectic with the past as it is forward-looking.[5] What is intentionally observed here is a gradual shift from an early to mid-twentieth-century politics of transcontinental black social movements to a new set of politics based on the achievement of postcolonial independence across sub-Saharan Africa, beginning with Ghana in 1957 and culminating with the end of apartheid in 1994. To what extent does African sovereignty change the dynamics and qualitative meaning of diasporic politics? Does it represent a decisive end point, one that fundamentally relocates political concern away from the Black Atlantic metropoles of Kingston, Fort-de-France, New York, and Paris to capitals like Pretoria, Accra, and Nairobi? To what degree are conventionally understood uses of "the diaspora" fixed to a twentieth-century political project—encompassing pan-Africanism, Négritude, and other forms of black internationalism—whose time and goals have largely been surpassed and are now to be replaced by a new, twenty-first-century political agenda as identified in part by Gilroy, but also including such challenges as the HIV/AIDS pandemic, neoliberal globalization, and ethnic violence that have preoccupied Africa's sovereign states?[6]

Further dialogue is consequently needed to explore the interplay between postcoloniality as a political condition and the chronology of the Black Atlantic to determine if the rubric "postdiaspora" may be politically or analytically useful for understanding current political concerns and engagements found on the continent. Postdiaspora therefore does not signal an end to the Black Atlantic paradigm as such, but instead seeks to articulate its temporal and geographic boundaries by historicizing specific discursive and political shifts within it. Some initial distinctions can be readily drawn. For example, although questions of sovereignty can be traced to figures such as Edward Blyden and C. L. R. James, postcolonial African intellectuals ranging from A. M. Babu and Mahmood Mamdani to Ruth First and Ngũgĩ wa Thiong'o have tackled more forcefully its acute lived predicaments, often based on personal experiences of political marginalization, imprisonment, and exile.[7] In a separate vein, the pan-Africanism embodied in the African Union today and its identification of the diaspora as a "Sixth Region" within its structure must be viewed as vital changes, reflecting a practice of autonomy and a regional hierarchy that emphasize the centrality of the continent.[8] The post-1957 political order that has unfolded across sub-Saharan Africa accordingly marks a tentative disjuncture in the worlds of the Black Atlantic, a relocation of meaning that remains to be fully explored.[9] David Scott's timely engagements in *Refashioning Futures: Criticism after Postcoloniality* (1999), which follow the earlier concerns of Walter Rodney, are a crucial, connective intervention in this regard, offering a set of considerations for rethinking the value and exchange between postcolonial and Black Atlantic criticism.[10] *The Black Atlantic* (1993) itself has been widely critiqued for the absence of Africa—serving more as a geographic backdrop than an active location of history—and Gilroy's more recent intervention can be viewed as an attempt at making amends within this new political sphere.[11]

However, the mere inclusion of Africa presents its own issues. Gilroy's observations can be balanced with the parallel predicament of African modes of self-writing as identified by Achille Mbembe, a scholar based at the Wits Institute for Social and Economic Research (WISER) at the University of the Witwatersrand in Johannesburg.[12] Mbembe provides an internal perspective on the dilemmas of politics and academic knowledge in postapartheid South Africa, though his thoughts also transcend this context. His critique addresses what he has discerned as the prevalent practices for constituting African identities, namely, Afro-radicalism and nativism. Afro-radicalism is limited by its instrumentality and subsequent political opportunism. In Mbembe's words, this approach has "used Marxist and nationalist categories to develop an imaginaire of culture and politics in which a manipulation of the rhetoric of autonomy, resistance, and emancipation serves as the sole criterion for determining the legitimacy of an authentic African discourse" (240–41). On the other hand, the prose of nativism has "promoted the idea of a unique African identity founded on membership of the black race" (241). Mbembe finds the reduction of African identities to "blood, race, or geography" problematic (272). In both cases, the histories of slavery, colonization, and apartheid in South Africa proved pivotal, not only denying more diverse and holistic senses of African selfhood from taking hold, but also disabling the very perspective for acknowledging such possibilities. "Not only is the [African] self no longer recognized by the Other," Mbembe writes, but "the self no longer recognizes itself" (241). With the end of apartheid, a renewed opportunity to move beyond these two approaches and their intrinsic limits has been presented. Mbembe consequently advocates a repositioning beyond the practice of equating identity with geography and race—what might be perceived as a diasporic determinism—to unlock what he calls the possibility of a wider range of African self-styling.

This interview is situated amid these political and conceptual perspectives.

Following Gilroy, it is concerned with South Africa's new global role, politically and intellectually, and with the manner in which such recent political shifts provide a new research valence beyond more culturally fixated definitions of the African diaspora. Like Mbembe, it also seeks to locate the formation of new political subjectivities in Africa beyond those previously identified. However, it has equally sought to unearth a pragmatic perspective: the day-to-day views, experiences, and outlooks of activist-intellectuals currently teaching, administrating, and conducting critical research in the South African academy today. If the politics of the antiapartheid struggle were easy to identify with given the transparent racial dynamics involved, the current political ferment has been far more complex to interpret and engage. South Africa's postapartheid civil society is still very much in the making, with many members of the academy and beyond being forced to negotiate the multifaceted legacies of apartheid—racism, poverty, class inequality, limited social services, and the claims and meaning of citizenship prominently among them. Intersecting with these enduring concerns are new developments connected to global capital and neoliberal policies embraced by the African National Congress (ANC) government, which mark a sharp contrast with its socialist principles held during the antiapartheid struggle. Such issues have undermined the romance of what former president Thabo Mbeki once referred to as the "African Renaissance."[13]

Yet despite persistent problems with the slow growth of student and staff diversity, the university landscape of postapartheid South Africa has witnessed a remarkable expansion in certain quarters, creating a new horizon for collaborative intellectual ventures. WISER in Johannesburg and the Mayibuye Centre at the University of the Western Cape have provided novel intersections for a range of issues including citizenship, HIV/AIDS, contemporary urban life, South African cultural theory, public memory, and the practice and meanings of heritage. The Centre for Civil Society (CCS) at the University of KwaZulu-Natal (UKZN), Durban, is situated amid this intellectual ferment and is arguably the most politically driven. Headed by Patrick Bond—a political economist trained by David Harvey at Johns Hopkins University—the center has provided a forum and base of activity for scholars and activists from around South Africa and Africa generally. Ashwin Desai, author of the acclaimed *We Are the Poors: Community Struggles in Post-apartheid South Africa* (2002), is perhaps the best-known activist to have been affiliated with CCS.[14] However, residents have also included Dennis Brutus—the antiapartheid activist, poet, and former inmate on Robben Island—Joel Kovel, editor of the journal *Capitalism Nature Socialism*, and a host of other scholars. I spoke with Bond, Desai, and Molefi Mafereka ka Ndlovu, a student and activist, about their various projects and how grassroots politics of the apartheid years have since transformed into new social movements addressing national, regional, and global issues urgent in the present.

Christopher J. Lee (CJL):   *Let's start with you, Patrick. How long have you been at the Centre for Civil Society, and what is your vision for it within UKZN and South Africa generally?*

Patrick Bond (PB):   CCS was founded by Adam Habib, a political scientist, in 2001. Since then, aside from following the interests of staff and associates—for me, personally, those would be in political economy and political ecology—we have mainly been strengthening an existing trajectory. From the early 2000s, work at CCS has reflected the rise of oppositional civil society activity in South Africa in relation to state and capital, to patriarchy and durable racism, and to ecological destruction. With ten thousand protests a year according to the police, South Africa has possibly the highest per capita protest rate in the world—organized labor produced a record 13 million strike days (more than 650,000 workers striking approximately twenty days each) in 2007, for example. CCS has therefore reflected upon this society's huge class, gender, race, and environmental contradictions. Overall the center's objective, decided in 2005, is "to advance *socio-economic and environmental justice* by developing critical knowledge about, for, and in dialogue with civil society through teaching, research, and publishing."

My sense is that we have achieved a critical mass of research about the kinds of struggles for justice engaged in by South Africans, and we should be turning our attention more to the continent and world. We have begun that through the World Social Forum and its various affiliates—locally, the closest is the Social Movements Indaba, albeit without the direct input of labor, church, and health care activists as of yet. With Eunice Sahle of the University of North Carolina, Chapel Hill, we are working on a book about contemporary African social movements. Within UKZN itself, we have a quadruple function of, first, relating intellectual work on social justice to the broader community through several dozen public events each year, including major lectures as well as tailored courses for activists, all of which are free of charge. Second, we do broad-based dissemination of our research in creative ways such as a DVD set with three dozen video documentaries thus far, as well as our Web-based library. Third, we offer rigorous postgraduate courses—one on civil society and the other on the political economy of the welfare state. And fourth, by publishing up a storm, to ensure the research is considered viable in peer-reviewed periodicals and in books. In the process, what we hope we are contributing to is an epistemological commitment to *praxis*. We think we are demonstrating to fellow intellectuals that *knowledge is produced at sites of social conflict*, as struggle teaches us about the give-and-take of structure and agency in a way you simply cannot learn by sitting in the academic armchair.

CJL: *What is your take, Ashwin? How would you describe its balance between activism versus producing academic knowledge, if one can make that distinction?*

Ashwin Desai (AD):   I think you are getting to the heart of an important debate because there has been a burst of writing on social movements by activist academics who have squabbled among themselves about who has the right to write about struggles and who has the mandate of this or that organization. What they have *not* questioned is their authority to be the people to write on movements and the relationship between knowledge production and political commitments. Because of their need to keep close to the movements to ensure access, what is written and passed off as serious ethnographic research must be carefully scrutinized, for much of it is really a romanticization of what the movements are really about. We need to take seriously the issue of establishing evidence and justifying interpretations, constantly interrogating the relationship between activism and producing academic knowledge. At the moment, the quality of research is generally superficial, impressionistic, and provides very few clues to what drives movements, what are their future trajectories, and how they could link into a broader radical challenge to neoliberal South Africa. Generally, those of a more Marxist bent and those with more Fanonian and autonomist leanings have vied for influence in social movements. There is an overlap of these approaches—all put their own twist on developments to fit their ideological dispositions and vie to outpublish each other in staid academic journals, while purporting to want the poor to represent themselves.

I expect the academic machine needs to be oiled, while forms of gatekeeping are unfortunately allowing research territories to be carved up and monopolized. A localized version of the scramble for Africa made all the more stark by the fact that almost all these academics happen to be white.

CJL: *So, you are suggesting that a current need exists for critical self-reflection regarding the relationship between these two practices.*

AD: Yes. Broadly two positions have emerged. One sees the poor as the embodiment of "truth," and therefore the poor do not need any theory or any forms of knowledge from the outside. The role of the "involved" academic is to record "voices" and to tell the world the necessary story to be told. Meanwhile, their own authenticity and authority ostensibly come from the fact that they are members of the movement, even though they continue to be ensconced in middle-class neighborhoods and in the academy. There is little self-reflection of the contradictory locations they occupy, and what this means for knowledge production.

A second approach at the center has been to situate contemporary struggles within an a priori framework of Marxist categories and reading contemporary political struggles found in South Africa as more globally oriented, like "IMF riots," when in reality they are often more locally based and inward looking. This approach says nothing to the lived experience of those protesting, but such work is littered with the necessary code words of *accumulation* through *dispossession* and the like.

Both approaches and *their* poors have their own form of pigeonholing and duplicity. While there is a commitment to be involved in organic struggles, the form and nature of those interventions and commitments is in itself a highly contested terrain.

CJL: *Molefi, your personal trajectory speaks to these issues. Can you discuss your intellectual and activist background?*

Molefi Mafereka ka Ndlovu (MN): I was born in 1982 in Soweto, Johannesburg, and raised by a single parent and my extended family on my mother's side. I completed my high school education in 1999 with a distinction in economics and got involved in student politics since finishing. I originally registered at the Pretoria College of Engineering in 2000, where I studied engineering and was the branch secretary of the South African Students' Congress. However, at the beginning of 2001, I registered at the University of the Witwatersrand for a degree in constitutional law and African literature. While at Wits, I got involved with the Anti-Privatisation Forum (APF) and joined comrades for a march at the UN World Conference Against Racism that took place in Durban in 2001. That is where I got interested in alternative media and activist journalism. From 2001 to the present, I have remained an active member of the Independent Media Center. In 2002, I also joined Research, Education, and Development, where I worked on popular community workshops to build the media capacities of mostly APF-affiliated organizations as well as other groups such as the Landless People's Movement. For example, I have participated in building RASA FM, a radio project intended to instigate community control and access to low-power radio as a means of democratizing media production and dissemination. We ran the station from February 2005, involving youth activists and unemployed neighborhood youth from around Soweto. Through this project, we were able to build links with similar groups in Tanzania and Zimbabwe, along with a network all over the globe, particularly in the United States.

My research has primarily focused on assessing major problems faced by township schools. I've worked with comrades to develop research questions and set up focus group discussions on aspects of the research process for primary and secondary schools in Soweto and the Sebokeng Township in the Sedibeng area of Gauteng. Currently, I am registered at UKZN, where I am completing a degree in community development, media, and comparative literature. CCS has been a natural base given the work it does in the area of civil society. I am also presently involved in the energy project at CCS. Some key points of interest are developing a strategy to integrate existing research on community responses to the commercialization of energy sources (mainly electricity), and how this has affected poor communities' access to these resources. The idea is to find linkages between problems of access and the environmental impact of climate change, along with the consequent implications of adaptation strategies on the cost of these basic utilities, especially to poor communities.

CJL: *How would you describe the current intellectual climate in South Africa today, and how would you characterize the pace of institutional change from a racial perspective? Are black intellectuals finding new spaces within the South African academy?*

MN: It has been thirteen long years of waiting in anticipation for a revolution that never happened. The South African political climate is caught in a time warp. The transition deal from apartheid to democracy happened largely above the heads of the primary protagonists — the people. A liberal democratic state was sanctioned, and the people were told the climax to struggle was to put a cross on a piece of paper and expect "delivery." On reflection thirteen years later, it seems all spheres of power — including the academy — were at best complacent, at worst active perpetrators of building a myth of the "Rainbow Nation" and superficial reconciliation. The current intellectual climate of the country needs to be read in light of the role that centers of the production and reproduction of social knowledge — that is, academic institutions like universities and the agents of these institutions, academic intellectuals — have played in producing the knowledge and legitimating arguments that have resulted in these neoliberal conditions of postcolonial South Africa.

My point is that there is a need to reflect on intellectual agency rather than leave this to the phrase of "climate." Southern Africa is potentially gearing itself for a serious meltdown: the instability in Lesotho, the Zimbabwe insurgence, Swaziland . . . the list is extensive. For me these tensions are just the tip of the iceberg, a signal of what is yet to take shape in this country. Within the boundaries of the republic, the picture is somewhat more disconcerting. The ruling black elite has finally taken their gloves off, each cabal sabotaging its rivals using the media, the law, the church, the mall, and just about any circus act of socialism, nationalism, and/or modernity. The whole situation is very sad indeed. On the other hand, 2007 has seen the revival of mass protest comparable to the P. W. Botha regime of the 1980s.

CJL: *Do you think the concerns and predicaments of black intellectuals in South Africa are the same, then, as those among black intellectuals in the diaspora? Or do you find that the set of politics found on the continent is fundamentally different?*

MN: I think the concerns of Africans on the mainland and those of their descendents outside of the continent are connected in profound ways. I cannot speak for intellectuals as a group, but certainly those who use the academy not as an end in and of itself, but rather those that use the academic idiom as part of a broader emancipatory project to free our world from servitude and exploitation: I can identify with that. Africans share a proud history of resistance against white supremacy, and hegemony bonds our blood ties and spiritual oneness. However, for as long as the academy remains an important leg on which capitalist hegemony stands, then these institutions remain not ours. Thus it would be ridiculous for a black progressive to demarcate their subject position as tied only to the academy, since to do that would reduce that individual to an energetic tool for the further perpetuation of blaxploitation. Such a strata of subjects does exist; indeed this remains the dominant layer of the black bodies that occupy academic posts.

My interactions with black intellectuals from the U.S. have not been with university professors as much as it has been with conscious souls actively building networks throughout the diaspora highlighting common conditions that face the black subject: poverty, dependency, hopelessness, incarceration, and a loss of identity. These intellectuals occupy a space beyond the academy. To be fair to purely academic intellectuals, we have them to thank for the mainstreaming of African/black studies in university faculties and departments.

CJL: *Building upon this, can you all elaborate on the status of CCS amidst the Left in South Africa? How would you characterize and situate the Left in South Africa's political landscape today?*

PB: In what we might term the "independent Left" within South Africa—in other words, outside the center-left Tripartite Alliance of the African National Congress (ANC), the Congress of South African Trade Unions (COSATU), and the Communist Party (SACP)—CCS sits as possibly the one place, aside from a couple of sociology departments, where a critical mass of formal academics devote themselves to social change. Most universities here will not give space to more than one or two such scholar-activists, so we are fortunate that our milieu has an exciting buzz and enough resources—though these are dwindling as donor fashions shift—to hold events and generate ideas that profile and justify social justice advocacy. In this regard, we fit well into a network of organic intellectuals of the independent Left, with their small NGOs, the struggling alternative media, the Listservs, the various writing projects, and the devotion to these new movements that have arisen to take the antiapartheid spirit further and deeper. It is not just through understanding the grievances that lead to protest, but also having critical intellectual engagements with the mass-based and community-based activists whom we admire but also regularly challenge.

Within Africa, we are just beginning to explore the ways an academic site can prove useful. Our staff and students include people from nearly every southern African country, so this work will proceed much more durably in coming years, we hope, in alliance with like-minded centers and academics on the continent. South Africa's subimperialist posture on many fronts—especially economic—makes this a profound responsibility.

Globally, our networks include the leading progressive think tanks in every part of the world, and we have developed a small reputation for analysis, strategy, and alliances that are relevant to global justice movements. Like-minded institutions whose leading staff we have hosted recently include Focus on the Global South, the Brazilian Institute for Social and Economic Research, the Transnational Institute, the Dag Hammarskjöld Foundation, and the Institute for Policy Studies, and we're also working with the Institute for Social Science at Gyeongsang National University in South Korea on political economic analysis.

AD: There is a Left tendency in the ANC-led alliance that centers on the South African Communist Party and the Congress of South African Trade Unions. The dominant tendency here has put a lot of energy into getting Jacob Zuma elected president of the ANC. However, this has also led to a residue of SACP branches criticizing this move, and their position is now very difficult. Where do they go and what constituency can they carry with them is still to be seen.

The really interesting developments on the Left have taken place outside the alliance. And these have revolved around community movements who have challenged electricity disconnections, evictions, land redistribution programs, and so on. There is no central ideology that runs through these movements, and some have celebrated this, while others have pointed to a need for a clear anticapitalist program. The debate continues.

In terms of CCS, a debate has emerged around the relationship of the academy and movements. As I mentioned before, we need to problematize the relationship between knowledge production and resistance and keep asking how is knowledge developed, how is it disseminated, and what are the relations of power that steer and trespass on its journey. This is important because history is replete with how those with academic capital have used this to try and control movements, thus compounding problems rather than alleviating them. Now more than ever, given the experiences of CCS in their involvement with community movements, we need to inspire a conversation between academic activists and community movements around the practical implications of how and to what ends knowledge is produced and how theory forms a part of political practice.

CJL: *So, given this context, are there continuities or differences in being an intellectual today vis-à-vis the apartheid period?*

PB: A good question worthy of deep reflection, which I will leave to those who spent more time in struggles then. Except, at the risk of being flippant, let me make the point about loyalties. In 1997, a special issue of the journal *Debate* entitled "Intellectuals in Retreat" tackled the *lack* of continuity in a particular generation during the transition from racial apartheid to class apartheid. Ashwin and Heinrich Bohmke were especially scathing in their article "Death of the Intellectual,

Birth of the Salesman."[15] Quite a few antiapartheid intellectuals' groundings came a bit loose.

AD: When I wrote *We Are the Poors*, I was intensely aware that we were caught up in the Mandela mania and so on, and I wanted to show the other side of the Mandela period: the deepening poverty, the crony capitalism, and the genuflection to organizations and ideas of the World Bank. But as I began to think through the underside of the transition, I saw a developing militant response from community movements. In wanting to develop a countermania, I suspended a critical eye. Given the way these movements rise and fall, their tendency to be parochial and even be co-opted, I think we need to bring to bear a more critical response. It does the movements a disservice not to open debate on the strengths and weaknesses of these movements by referring to other times and places where movements have arisen and why they failed. The conversations we are having with activist-intellectuals outside of South Africa have been a tremendous asset in this regard.

We are at a particular postapartheid moment, and how we read this conjuncture is crucial. If you asked me what the objectives of "the struggle" during the apartheid period were, it was easy: defeat the apartheid state. And maybe in the easy answer lies the heart of the problem—an intellectual and political laziness among antiapartheid intellectuals revolving around the overlooked possibility of a nonracial capitalism consolidating itself. We have to learn the lessons of the fight against apartheid and why things went so horribly wrong.

Today the liberators are in power, nationalism continues to be a powerful mobilizer, while at the same time there is a realization that the ability to wield the state and even nationalism as a weapon of redistribution contends with a globalized capitalist world and is often found wanting. The tensions between sovereignty and global free markets are pretty stark. It is not a time for intellectual and political laziness or for simply espousing the usual mantras of left programs like nationalization without interrogating the effect of the revenge of credit agencies and the like on the local economy. Often left programs read like revamped versions of "socialism in one country," and history has shown us the perils of that journey.

The conjuncture has changed. The social forces let loose globally are different, the locations where power and counterpower lie, the possibilities of new radical subjectivities, the experiments with new forms of organizing: these factors must influence where we research, what we research, and where we throw our activism. Various intellectuals and activists are saying we must settle scores with our own bourgeoisie, but already our bourgeoisie is integrated into the global rhythms of capital with headquarters in London and New York. It is a mobile force. At least we are debating the broader issues of state power and how it can be used as a progressive force and not simply seeing it as an inevitable poisoned chalice or an inevitable good.

Through struggle we have destroyed the idea of the "Rainbow Nation," which, in truth, actually naturalized and legitimized apartheid categories for the postapartheid era. A new radical subjectivity of "the poors" that transcends such apartheid racial designations is still struggling to grow, spread its wings, and capture the imagination. South Africa is still revolting, and people are once again realizing that it is them that can make history, even if it is against their own leaders who come with liberation credentials. For me, that is the most significant development—the ability of the poor to see the betrayal of the ideals of the liberation struggle and to be increasingly prepared to take to the streets to challenge the new ruling class. I love the way the ruling class at marches is mocked and often put on the run.

The coming to power of Mandela and Mbeki was not, then, the end of extraparliamentary politics—it was the beginning of a new phase that is reimagining new forms of struggle and identities. The exciting thing is that while there is always the danger of a lurch back into parochialism and insularity, there is also an impulse to cross national borders and make global linkages.

MN: In my view, the "intellectual" needs to be problematized. It is my contention that the neoliberal agenda is not just an economic matter: it finds its conceptualization and refinement in the desks and seminar rooms of academic conferences. Over fourteen years, we have seen the disappearance of critical discourse in the academy. Due to the imperatives of "world class citizenry," universities have unilaterally adopted a market orientation in terms of their priorities. Most institutions, including UKZN, were subject to mergers that saw schools and departments being reconfigured for market viability and commercial conformity. Many subjects in the humanities were trashed because they were not desirable in the open market and industry. The number of black students able to complete their degrees continues to dwindle, and the emphasis on commerce and industry has meant that even fewer black students engage in humanities or the social sciences, opting for more secure degrees in the natural sciences and finance. The academy is seen as the terminal for a prosperous future on the job market. It has ceased to be the site for contesting ideas and producing perspectives that would inform radical social change. But perhaps the white academy has always played this role, and the above expectations I express are a reflection of my own ignorance and blind idealism.

CJL: *To bring together several points of discussion, then, what is to be done, intellectually and politically? How do we position ourselves in a context that is shaped by the obvious legacies of the past that in turn are being reinforced by a neoliberal present?*

AD: At the moment South African intellectual life is sterile with many old neo-Marxists espousing neoliberalism, many younger intellectuals espousing a kind of social history that simply wants to record the voices of the poor devoid of any theory, and Marxists, while waiting for the next global economic crisis to defeat capitalism, who are caught in the quagmire of their global anticapitalist commitments and their fascination with capturing state power. It is only when the minor skirmishes that characterize the challenge of movements in South Africa become generalized that I think we will see a development of new ideas and the emergence of a stratum of radical intellectuals whose theory will form a part of political practice. In the interim, we must return to the intellectual craft of serious research with the express purpose of getting a sense of cracks in the ruling class and the potential of new radical subjectivities to exacerbate and take advantage of those cracks. This entails at one level an understanding of the wave of violent upsurges in communities across the country and at another the researching and debating of the organizational forms and languages that can unite labor and community struggles.

I think one of the directions that this research will take us is the debunking of the idea of civil society as a radical space, and perhaps the idea that a *center* for civil society can only lend itself to an emasculation of struggle and its channeling into constitutionalism. What we need to build, I think, is the idea of an "uncivil" society that challenges ideas of human rights, rule of law, and multiculturalism. It is my belief that to build an effective radical challenge to capitalist globalization that is sustainable locally and reaches globally, we need—rather than using these code words—to build movements to confront them.

We must also put race more firmly on the agenda. It was quite stark during the antiapartheid struggle that antiapartheid intellectuals occupying the academy were overwhelmingly white. Besides the privilege enjoyed at white universities and by northern contacts in the academy, white intellectuals—unlike black intellectuals, because of where they lived—enjoyed a relative autonomy from the everyday organizing and action of the struggle. One only needs to look at university knowledge production to see this dominance, and this continuing dominance needs a concerted challenge. It must be done in a way, though, that learns lessons from that period of the late 1970s and 1980s when white left intellectuals espoused an unimaginative structuralist neo-Marxism and with embarrassing haste became ideologues of neoliberalism, cashing in their antiapartheid kudos to wield significant influence in the policy-making organs of the liberation movement. Black intellectuals are not immune to those same slides.

It is also important to take cognizance that with the opening up of South Africa, a clutch of northern academics have since zoomed into the country, in what I have called the "three-day phenomenon," to "study" social movements and then publish in journals back home in the North and quickly set themselves up as "experts." They contribute little to the debates within South Africa and in the building of a black radical intelligentsia. Although there are political and analytic risks in essentializing the expressions "North" and "South," we do need to debate the relationship between northern and southern scholar-activists, for there seems to be an unequal exchange so far that smacks of intellectual imperialism.

PB: The independent Left has been very active, producing more than a dozen major books — Martin Legassick's new tome, *Towards Socialist Democracy* (2007), is exemplary — devoted to critique.[16] The center-left of the Tripartite Alliance has fewer than half a dozen, so the main disappointment is the lack of ongoing engagement by intellectuals *within* the power structures. The critique of the old Left in academia is that too many took up consultancy careers — or academic careerism — from the early 1990s as more opportunities emerged. They went from the grassroots to their class roots, as the saying goes, especially those in the generation now in their fifties.

One of the major projects we have embarked on at CCS is a rereading of the traditions in South Africa and Africa which once inspired radical intellectual work, especially the "articulation of modes of production" debate with Harold Wolpe, who died in 1996, and the regional problems associated with dependency theory, which Malawian economist Guy Mhone worked on so fruitfully to solve through the theory of "enclavity" until his death in 2005. Another great theorist who has helped us consolidate theories of capitalist crisis, superexploitation, and imperialism is Rosa Luxemburg, because of her concern about capitalist/noncapitalist systemic expropriation. Frantz Fanon is obviously a very inspiring figure, along with many other African scholars who have tackled neocolonial power relations. Another influential intellectual current comes from the dialectical way that Michael Buroway has played off the ideas of [Antonio] Gramsci and [Karl] Polanyi: one stressing the slow, gradual building of counterhegemony in the trenches of civil society; the other providing inspiration that a double movement of social activists can counter excessively intrusive market forces.

All of this has generated a sense that where neoliberal capitalism has commodified everything under the sun — including the air, through the new carbon-trading mechanisms of the Kyoto Protocol — we are seeing vigorous contestations from below. A huge challenge is to work with the excellent organic intellectual critiques of capitalism that have emerged, *issue by issue*, and assist in their linkage, not from above in an overarching theoretical sense (though we keep track of efforts such as David Harvey's "accumulation by dispossession"), but from below via interlocking, overlapping struggles. In most of these struggles — for example, access to AIDS medicines, antiprivatization on the water and electricity fronts, landlessness and homelessness, free education, rights to employment, domestic violence, and so on — we have superb intellectuals allied to social movements. But there is not enough work across the silos. You find the same problem in the World Social Forum. So, we probably will devote more resources in coming years to getting these bottom-up linkages more clearly articulated so as to establish genuine programmatic work that's well grounded in campaigns for justice.

CJL: *What, then, are your summary views of the Mbeki era? What are the future prospects for the ANC and South Africa generally?*

MN: The closing of the Mbeki era marks a new phase in the development of radical alternatives. All the noise about a "renaissance" has revealed itself for what it is. Mbeki himself boasts the knighthood of the British Empire. Truly, this facade that has been trumpeted as liberation has shown itself for what it is. The ANC power alliance will not endure the next ten years, and this is to be generous. Already it is obvious to even the blindest of observers that this ANC-negotiated settlement was nothing more than a handful of the black and ambitious agreeing to run the Boer republic essentially unchanged. Democracy and a progressive constitution written in collaboration with our exploiters were bound to hit a solid wall in time — both could not guarantee liberation from the site of exploitation, namely, white-owned companies and factories. Neither could they set the majority of the black population on the path to self-reliance and true realization. The heat has only just begun: either the state will reveal its true oppressive nature by unleashing violence, or a population tired of being spectators will take new, dramatic steps in the shaping of their own destiny.

PB: Mbeki-ism, as Ashwin calls it, mixes straightforwardly pro-business public policy with nationalist rhetoric, so that we often witness the problem of "talk left, walk right." The latest major collection of political economy articles we've gathered — for the journal *Africanus* in the November 2007 edition, but free for download on our Web site [www.ukzn.ac.za/ccs] — is devoted to the question of how "two economies," the "developmental state," and the "national democratic revolution" are deployed as ideas to confuse the broad public. So, you'll often hear middle-of-the-road intellectuals lulled into satisfied tributes to South African social democracy under construction, with AIDS medicines finally available, free basic water and electricity, higher welfare payments, and a renewed state commitment to industrial policy. Our efforts seek out the devil in the details, with a view to exploring the grievances so many still have in all these areas of public policy.

Our overall view is that a harsh neoliberal project remains, though the expansion of existing welfare payments may disguise some of the most virulent poverty and a bubbling consumer-credit market lets some of the working class enjoy higher levels of consumption. Most of the free basic service delivery is sabotaged by bureaucrats whose first recourse is disconnection, followed by evictions. The commitment to AIDS treatment is obviously not yet solid, given Mbeki's firing of deputy health minister Nozizwe Madlala-Routledge in August 2007. Industrial policy is erratic and oriented to corporate welfare. As Mbeki himself once told journalists as he unveiled the Growth, Employment, and Redistribution (GEAR) macroeconomic policy in 1996, "Just call me a Thatcherite." GEAR's replacement, the Accelerated and Shared Growth Initiative for South Africa (ASGISA) established in 2004, is not fundamentally different. If Jacob Zuma, former deputy president of South Africa and current president of the ANC, has influence post-Mbeki, we would not expect any changes, as he has already advised. The business community's candidates, Cyril Ramaphosa and Tokyo Sexwale, would not likely change course either. It seems that only protest of the sort the Treatment Action Campaign, COSATU, and independent left groups engage in so often is the only language the politicians will understand.

CJL: *Building upon your last comments, how does South Africa then fit into the politics of antiglobalization today? Are there specific social movements that you feel are particularly significant?*

PB: South Africa is a leading site for people to contest the globalization of capital. The most powerful example, the Treatment Action Campaign, achieved what none of us thought possible: decommodification and deglobalization of AIDS medicine production. To get that the activists defeated Big Pharma, as well as a government whose policies have been called genocidal by leading medical authorities. The key drugs are now produced in South Africa on a generic, not branded, basis and are sufficiently affordable that more than 450,000 people now have access when only a few hundred did a decade ago.

   In the field of water, the big, Paris-based private firm Suez has been kicked out of Johannesburg and Nkonkobe, where the University of Fort Hare is, and others are afraid to enter. The Jubilee Movement to cancel "third world" debt, prior to a major split, was strong enough to force Mbeki into declaring the South African state's allegiance to U.S. capital during a 2003 court case—a move prompted by then U.S. Secretary of State Colin Powell's intervention, which showed clearly which side of the globalization divide Mbeki comes down on. There are countless other cases of trade unions, social movements, and NGOs using anticapitalist networks and internationalist strategies to build new kinds of power. The most spectacular protests associated with our local chapter of the global justice movement, if you will, were here in Durban in 2001 at the World Conference Against Racism and a year later at the Johannesburg World Summit on Sustainable Development (WSSD).

CJL: *You just mentioned water as an issue, and your most recent work has turned directly to the environment. How has this concern intersected with more familiar issues of unemployment, housing, and so forth?*

PB: From around 1995, it was apparent that the major battles of the urban social movements—and I used to work with the South African National Civic Organisation—would no longer be on housing. Civic demands in the Reconstruction and Development Programme were decisively rejected by then-minister Joe Slovo, who took World Bank advice instead. So from 1997 onwards, municipal services like water and electricity were the main sites of social movement struggles, with riots breaking out across Gauteng, the Eastern Cape, and many other places. Soon enough these turned into major social movement mobilizations, featuring a new, independent Left emergence in 1999 in Chatsworth, a township in Durban, followed by Soweto and Cape Town.

Around then it was increasingly important for activists and allied researchers to trace why the costs of water were so high in townships, and, of course, the answer was Lesotho's dams, the largest in Africa. They had just come on line and, ironically, that huge overdose of supply with its vast and adverse ecological implications led to dramatic increases in disconnections for poor people forced to shoulder an extremely high proportion of the bill. We found the same process at work within Eskom, South Africa's leading electricity provider, as the government pushed it toward commercialization and cost-reflective pricing. The end of excess capacity meant higher disconnection rates for poor people, while large commercial smelters got ridiculously cheap electricity because they argued the marginal cost of supply was much lower as they bought in bulk. That of course helps explain South Africa's contribution to CO_2 emissions, which is currently at a level twenty times that of the United States per person per unit of economic output.

So, what we found, soon enough, was that it would be fruitful to blend red and green politics and establish higher levels of consciousness — especially for those of us who are frequent-flyer petit bourgeois internationalists! — regarding the links between environment and development. Then all of this came to a head at the WSSD, which represented the global and local elites' best effort to "privatize nature." That in turn allowed tremendous struggles to surface and link across borders, such as the international Water Warriors network and the Durban Group for Climate Justice, which opposes carbon trading. It turns out that Durban is one of the world's leading sites of eco-injustice, especially with respect to respiratory problems associated with the petro-chemical works near the airport, as well as a methane-electricity project the World Bank wanted to fund. In both cases, courageous activists have pushed and pulled, so that the commodification of the environment has not gone according to plan.

These are also gendered struggles and fights against environmental racism so that, to return where we started, the processes of accumulation by dispossession that link class, race, gender, and ecology all come together. There are plenty of hurdles and shows of disunity, but the most important elements of a radical politics are moving into place. One day these forces will unite the South African Left across the single-issue divides and generate more durable links between organized labor and communities. Perhaps this will occur, as activist and intellectual Fatima Meer advocates, via a "South African Social Forum," and maybe as well, after the 2009 presidential election, in a new left political party.

Notes

I thank Sean Jacobs, Eunice Sahle, Emily Burrill, and Lisa Lindsay for comments and encouragement. This interview was originally recorded in June 2007.

1. Paul Gilroy, "A New Cosmopolitanism," *interventions* 7 (2005): 287, 288.
2. Ibid., 291.
3. For a select reading on cosmopolitanism, see Walter D. Mignolo, "The Many Faces of Cosmo-polis: Border Thinking and Critical Cosmopolitanism," *Public Culture* 12 (2000): 721–48; Craig Calhoun, "The Class Consciousness of Frequent Travelers: Toward a Critique of Actually Existing Cosmopolitanism," *South Atlantic Quarterly* 101 (2002): 869–97; Kwame Anthony Appiah, *Cosmopolitanism: Ethics in a World of Strangers* (New York: Norton, 2006).
4. My thoughts here draw in part from James Ferguson, *Global Shadows: Africa in the Neoliberal World Order* (Durham, NC: Duke University Press, 2006).
5. On the uses of *post-*, see Kwame Anthony Appiah, *In My Father's House: Africa in the Philosophy of Culture* (New York: Oxford University Press, 1992), chap. 7.
6. Gilroy's deepening engagement with imperialism, decolonization, and their political legacies in the present can be found in Paul Gilroy, *Postcolonial Melancholia* (New York: Columbia University Press, 2004).
7. The cases of Haiti, Liberia, Sierra Leone, and Ethiopia, of course, inspired the longevity of such discourse. This list of intellectuals is much abbreviated, given the well-known writings of such figures as Kwame Nkrumah, Julius Nyerere, and other leaders. See Abdul Rahman Mohamed Babu, *The Future That Works: Selected Writings of A. M. Babu*, ed. Salma Babu and Amrit Wilson (Trenton, NJ: Africa World Press, 2002); Mahmood Mamdani, *Citizen and Subject: Contemporary Africa and the Legacy of Late Colonialism* (Princeton, NJ: Princeton University Press, 1996); Ruth First, *The Barrel of a Gun: Political Power in Africa and the Coup d'État* (London: Allen Lane, 1970); Ngũgĩ wa Thiong'o, *Petals of Blood* (London: Heinemann, 1977).
8. The other five regions are East, West, Central, North, and Southern Africa. It should be noted as well that this recent inclusion of the diaspora within the African Union is motivated not only by historical connections with the Western hemisphere and elsewhere but also by contemporary patterns of migration and new diasporas in the making. The potential financial benefits of this sixth region have been a key incentive. See African Union, *Statutes of the Economic, Social, and Cultural Council of the African Union* (Addis Ababa, 2004); African Union, *Report of the African Civil Society Organizations' Consultation on AU/EU Joint Strategy for Africa's Development* (Accra, 2007).
9. For one examination of this relocation of meaning with its continuities and discontinuities with the diaspora, see Kevin Gaines, *American Africans in Ghana: Black Expatriates and the Civil Rights Era* (Chapel Hill: University of North Carolina Press, 2006).
10. David Scott, *Refashioning Futures: Criticism after Postcoloniality* (Princeton, NJ: Princeton University Press, 1999). Walter Rodney, like Scott a Caribbean intellectual, addressed the limitations of postcolonial autonomy most vividly in his political economic study, *How Europe Underdeveloped Africa* (Washington, DC: Howard University Press, 1974). Other scholars, such as Appiah and Laura Chrisman, have also worked at the intersection of Black Atlantic and postcolonial criticism. However, Scott, like other postcolonial critics who have recently turned to address globalization rather than past imperialism, has focused primarily on the challenges of the political present.
11. See, for example, Ntongela Masilela, "The 'Black Atlantic' and African Modernity in South

Africa," *Research in African Literatures* 27 (1996): 88–96; Laura Chrisman, *Postcolonial Contraventions: Cultural Readings of Race, Imperialism, and Transnationalism* (Manchester: Manchester University Press, 2003).

12. Achille Mbembe, "African Modes of Self-Writing," *Public Culture* 14 (2002): 239–73.

13. Thabo Mbeki, "The African Renaissance, South Africa and the World," in *Africa—The Time Has Come: Selected Speeches* (Cape Town: Tafelberg, 1998), 239–51. Thabo Mbeki was President of South Africa when the interview was conducted. Mbeki served in that position from June 14, 1999 to September 24, 2008. He formally announced his resignation on September 21, 2008, after the African National Congress' National Executive Committee decided to withdraw their parliamentary support of him.

14. It is important to note that after the publication of *We Are the Poors: Community Struggles in Post-apartheid South Africa* (New York: Monthly Review Press, 2002), Desai was forced out of the Centre for political reasons by university authorities, and despite petitions and protests by faculty and students, the ban is still in place.

15. Ashwin Desai and Heinrich Bohmke, "Death of the Intellectual, Birth of the Salesman," *Debate* 3 (1997): 10–34.

16. Martin Legassick, *Towards Socialist Democracy* (Scottsville, South Africa: University of KwaZulu-Natal Press, 2007).

Transnationalism and the Construction of Black Political Identities

Prudence D. Cumberbatch

In addressing the absence of discussions of people of color in the classroom, black studies curricula have been defined historically by geographically specific courses based in traditional disciplines. This curriculum structure remains essential to the education of well-rounded students, but more recently, there has been an important trend toward creating courses that reflect an interrelated, transnational, and diasporic perspective on the experiences of Africans and their descendents. Transnational studies has increased the wealth of scholarship on the global black experience and has generated new models for interdisciplinary studies of the African diaspora. And yet, while scholars are now paying considerable theoretical attention to global perspectives in black studies, there are fewer examples of this outlook translating into course design.

As an African American with one set of grandparents from the Caribbean raised to be conscious of the contributions of black immigrants to the United States, I find these new models to be particularly resonant. They offer an opportunity to refashion perspectives that center the students' experiences and identities within exclusively national boundaries. Alongside the personal sense of the complexity of my own background and multiple heritages, as a faculty member in an Africana studies department that focuses its attention equally on Africa, the Caribbean, and North America, I have been keenly aware of the vast reservoir of differences among our black students. Earlier generations of immigrants from the African diaspora

Radical History Review

Issue 103 (Winter 2009)   DOI 10.1215/01636545-2008-037

© 2009 by MARHO: The Radical Historians' Organization, Inc.

often downplayed their country of origin or their status as first-generation Americans. Now, partly due to the emergence of various ethnic studies and interdisciplinary programs—Africana studies, women's studies, Puerto Rican and Latino studies, Judaic studies, and gay and lesbian studies—it is more and more the case that students feel no need to separate or subsume the different heritages, histories, and politics that shape their more multivalent sense of race or nationality.

The growing numbers of African and Caribbean populations in New York City and elsewhere have also enhanced the sense of the importance of these heritages both in identity formations and in urban politics.[1] On the one hand, New York's large black immigrant population is unique because there are enough members of each national group to sustain individual heritages. Even when students are born in the United States, they often identify with their parents' and grandparents' country of origin. The increasing representation of Africans and Caribbeans in American popular culture and the recent migrations of these populations to other areas of the United States are changing the discourse of what it means to be black in the United States. As such, traditional nationalist-based courses often fail to address the historical and lived experiences of this diverse black student population as they inhabit a space that exists both within and between specific national and cultural zones in the black world.

My own growing awareness of changes in the ethnic identification of my students, and a developing sense of the lack of understanding on American college campuses of the evolving nature of the black population in this country, motivated me to create a course that would explore—for the campus and with our students—part of the historical dialogue between Africans, African Americans, and Caribbeans. In a workshop on pedagogy I became keenly aware of how few of my peers were conscious of the differences among their black students. In the midst of a discussion on vernacular "African American English," a colleague informed the group that a significant number, maybe even a majority, of our black students were immigrants from various African and Caribbean nations and had received a substantial portion of their schooling in systems outside the United States. Many of my colleagues were surprised by this information, which was apparent to me the first day that I walked into a Brooklyn College classroom. Additionally, the common assumption that those students who attended urban public institutions tend to be first-generation college students from working-class backgrounds often disguises the educational and economic complexities of a diverse black student population. Research studies have found, for example, that black immigrants to the United States have higher rates of college education than the native-born population.[2]

While scholars have long studied the differences between black immigrant and native-born communities, more recently they have devoted their attention to the rates of representation of these groups in American colleges and universities.[3] Harvard University law professor Lani Guinier points out that "many colleges rely on private networks that disproportionately benefit the children of African and West Indian immigrants who come from majority black countries and who arrived in the United States after 1965."[4] She argues that these students of color often "enjoy material and cultural advantages" that undermine the purpose of a policy designed to redress the historical inequities of race. Guinier contends that currently, "racial affirmative action mimics the elitist nature of admissions generally when it rewards high-stakes test-takers to the detriment of democratic values."[5] Moving away from private education to the world of public colleges, the black immigrant population is also disproportionately represented in the black student populations of public institutions.[6] These changes reflect the movement or ambitions of an international educated middle class to the United States. Thus the stereotypes revealed among my colleagues, in which race is the marker of economic and educational disadvantages, are quickly becoming obsolete.

The driving question in the development of this course is how to speak to the current diversity of the black student population by illuminating the historical international political conversation among Africans, African Americans, and Caribbeans. In my traditional African American history courses, students, rather than view history in isolation, examine the development of transnational perspectives among black Americans as a way to understand the construction of politically engaged black communities. Prior to the nineteenth century, people of African descent in the New World (specifically in the American colonies/United States) incorporated a transnational understanding of themselves into their political outlook as they strove to carve out a place in communities that were hostile to blacks and black socioeconomic advancement. The inclusion of the word *African* as a term to identify black schools, benevolent societies, and religious institutions spoke to the desires of the transplanted to gain freedom and self-determination by forming symbolic ties to a place with both a name and a history. In my traditional twentieth-century African American history courses, in addition to provoking discussions of Marcus Garvey, I point to the contributions of noted Caribbeans and first-generation Americans such as Stokely Carmichael, Shirley Chisholm, and Richard B. Moore. Additionally, I tell my students about African leaders, such as Nnamdi Azikiwe and Kwame Nkrumah, who both studied at Lincoln University and the University of Pennsylvania. Azikiwe and Thurgood Marshall were classmates at Lincoln; both men went on to become prominent leaders — Azikiwe as the first president of Nigeria and Marshall as a United States Supreme Court justice.

All too often, the significance of Africans and Caribbeans in their relationships to African American history is obscured. Indeed, most students in my traditional African American history courses are attracted to the "American" experiences of these activists, rather than to exploring how their African and Caribbean heritages framed their political activities. As such, I believe that it is important to broaden the focal points of my African American history classes, not only to go beyond discussions of the contributions of those not necessarily born in the United States but also to point out that struggles for racial justice took place within a worldwide movement of people of African descent. Additionally, I believe that by highlighting the role of conversations between Africans, African Americans, and Caribbeans in the context of a traditional African American history class I can open up new paths of engagement for students of African and Caribbean heritages, encouraging them to think about their historical stake in the struggles of African Americans. While the changes in my African American history courses reflect the needs of my students, there is also a need for new courses that engage diasporic history more directly.

The goal of the course "Transnationalism and the Construction of Black Political Identities" is to examine the political intersections of black people in the United States, the Caribbean, and on the continent of Africa. While black studies has always promoted a global consciousness, it has done so from an American standpoint rather than from a transnational perspective that examines internationalism from a range of national experiences. By reorienting the course to reflect multiple perspectives, students examine differing points of view based on local and international conditions and link these differences into a broader and potentially unifying discourse. I often find that students desire a unified and meaningful black struggle that will impact their lives, but are unable to imagine what one would look like. By examining the political discourses of Africans, African Americans, and Caribbeans as they existed in dialogue with each other, students will be able to understand the historical and intellectual points of overlap—and that their own interest in imagining and promoting an internationalist black movement has historical antecedents. In light of the redefinition of blackness on today's college campuses, the course highlights the multiple identities of black activists of the past as they participated, both through physical migration and intellectual conversation, in a transatlantic exchange of ideas on the future of the global black community.

The class begins with a discussion of black colonization movements in the early 1800s and concludes with an examination of the international black struggle to end apartheid in South Africa. Beginning with a discussion of migration and colonization allows for an examination of historical connections based more on class, national independence, and political struggles than on the shared experience of slavery in the Americas that excises Africa from the conversation. This framework also offers an alternative picture of Africa as more than the point of origin of the Middle Passage; rather, the continent now emerges as a place that figured into the development of an international political consciousness among African Americans.

The focus of the course hews closer to the black studies tradition than to the cultural studies paradigm. As such, it is still grounded at its foundation in location; but instead of being constrained by older comparative or area studies paradigms, the model this course offers is one that aims to reflect the true fluidity of these political dialogues as they occurred in history.[7] Rather than focus on identities or subjectivities in general, the course focuses on the development of political identities in their own historical contexts and explores how the emergent transnational subjects might serve as a paradigm for political engagement. Thus this course continues the black studies tradition of promoting a global consciousness but lays the groundwork for new discussions that can incorporate the realities of a changing black student population that now includes a higher proportion of post-1960s black immigrants. The course is structured to avoid notions of linear influence—usually African American influence on the rest of the world—in favor of a more coequal dialogue among regions.

Alongside an examination of the evolution of transnational black political identities, this course will also address how individuals worked in both traditional and radical political movements in their freedom struggles, exploring the convergences and divergences among emerging black political consciousnesses. By looking back at historical conversations about race and identity in a transnational context, students will learn that these were often parallel and interconnected discussions, regardless of location. The course also reflects my hope that students will find new ways to engage in the dialogue, moving away from constructions of black ethnic essentialism to consider what all groups bring to the intellectual table. The syllabus is still a work in progress, pending further reading and continuing discussions.

Brief Course Description

This seminar examines the interrelationships of struggles for liberation, self-determination, and political autonomy led by people of African descent from the early nineteenth century through the twentieth. Beginning with the black colonization movement in the United States and the Caribbean, this course will explore the evolution of relationships among African American, Afro-Caribbean, and African political traditions that emphasized the need for people of color to live free of restrictive racial biases and economic exploitation. The course concludes with an examination of the international movement to end apartheid in South Africa, providing an opportunity to explore, in microcosm, the historical interconnections of the African diaspora and its expressions in both a political and economic global consciousness. An important component of the course is to examine the creation of international and transnational dialogues focused on the liberation of peoples throughout Africa and the diaspora. Beginning in the nineteenth century, these conversations were marked by challenges to Western ideals that both labeled and positioned "black" or "African" peoples as outsiders within the places of their birth. By connecting the struggles of Africans, Caribbeans, and African Americans, intellectuals and activists were able to forge, on a number of key occasions—pan-Africanism, decolonization, civil rights, and black power—worldwide black movements for social, political, and economic liberation.

Using multidisciplinary and interdisciplinary models, this course highlights the ways in which Africans on the continent and throughout the diaspora resisted state-supported and state-imposed oppression and created new social and political movements. It also examines how they reshaped both their individual national heritages and an international political heritage based in common struggles. The first five weeks of the course move from the construction of the idea of Africa by African Americans to the very real engagements by African Americans and Caribbeans with the political struggles on the continent. It then shifts to focus on the construction of a pan-Caribbean identity as Caribbean intellectuals began to explore their shared economic and political concerns and moved throughout the diaspora. The course then examines the anticolonial struggles in Africa and the historically overlapping development of a "Third World" consciousness among a new generation of black activists involved in the civil rights and black power movements. After World War II, blacks throughout the diaspora used a variety of strategies—labor organizing, political activism, and social movements—in a struggle to eliminate the instruments of state-based racial oppression. Exploring overlapping movements in Africa, the Caribbean, and the United States, students can examine the seismic shifts in the interrelated local and global power structure as activists at the time experienced them. By ending the discussion of anticolonial struggles with the antiapartheid movement, the course combines discussions of both local and global struggles, describing a moment in which Africans, African Americans, and Caribbeans worked together in a concerted, focused campaign to challenge the racial hierarchy of a specific location. This case provides an example of how blacks throughout the diaspora employed economic, moral, and political pressure to force an end to a system of race-based oppression. Finally, to counter the overwhelmingly masculinist constructions of transnational dialogues, this course incorporates discussions by and about women activists whose participation in these conversations has often been overlooked in the historical record.

Course Outline
Week 1   Introduction to Transnationalism; or, The African Diaspora Defined: Understanding Transnationalism in the Context of Political Identities
Readings:

Kim D. Butler, "Defining Diaspora, Refining a Discourse," *Diaspora: A Journal of Transnational Studies* 10 (2001): 189–219.

Robin D. G. Kelley, "'But a Local Phase of a World Problem': Black History's Global Vision, 1883–1950," *Journal of American History* 86 (1999): 1045–77.

Tiffany Ruby Patterson and Robin D. G. Kelley, "Unfinished Migrations: Reflections on the African Diaspora and the Making of the Modern World," *African Studies Review* 43/1 (2000): 11–45.

Week 2   The African Imaginary: Back to Africa

Readings:

Alexander Crummell, *The Future of Africa: Being Addresses, Sermons, etc., etc., Delivered in the Republic of Liberia*, reprint of 1862 ed. (New York: Negro Universities Press, 1969), selections from chap. 8.

Martin R. Delany, *The Condition, Elevation, Emigration, and Destiny of the Colored People of the United States and Official Report of the Niger Valley Exploring Party* (Amherst, NY: Humanity Books, 2004), chaps. 17–18, 22.

Henry Highland Garnet, *The Past and Present Condition, and the Destiny, of the Colored Race* (1848), ed. Paul Royster, digitalcommons.unl.edu.

Edwin S. Redkey, "Bishop Turner's African Dream," *Journal of American History* 54 (1967): 271–90.

Maria W. Stewart, "An Address Delivered at the African Masonic Hall," in *Maria W. Stewart: America's First Black Woman Political Writer: Essays and Speeches*, ed. Marilyn Richardson (Bloomington: Indiana University Press, 1987), 56–64.

Rosalind Cobb Wiggins, ed., *Captain Paul Cuffe's Logs and Letters, 1808–1817: A Black Quaker's "Voice from Within the Veil"* (Washington, DC: Howard University Press, 1996), selections.

Week 3   The African/American Reality

Readings:

Martin R. Delany, *A Documentary Reader*, ed. Robert S. Levine (Chapel Hill: University of North Carolina Press, 2003), selections.

W. E. B. Du Bois, *The Souls of Black Folk* (New York: Vintage, 1990), chap. 3.

W. E. B. Du Bois, *Writings* (New York: Library of America, 1986), 625–51.

Louis R. Harlan, "Booker T. Washington and the White Man's Burden," *American Historical Review* 71 (1966): 441–67.

Sylvia M. Jacobs, "Afro-American Women Missionaries Confront the African Way of Life," in *Women in Africa and the African Diaspora*, ed. Rosalyn Terborg-Penn, Sharon Harley, and Andrea Benton Rushing (Washington, DC: Howard University Press, 1987), 121–32.

W. Manning Marable, "Booker T. Washington and African Nationalism," *Phylon* 35 (1974): 398–406.

I. K. Sundiata, "The On to Africa Congress," *Journal of Negro History* 61 (1976): 393–400.

Booker T. Washington, *1904–6*, vol. 8 of *The Booker T. Washington Papers*, ed. Louis R. Harlan (Urbana: University of Illinois Press, 1989), 548–52.

Booker T. Washington, *Up from Slavery*, ed. William Andrews (New York: Norton, 1996), chap. 14.

Week 4   Defining Pan-Africanism

Readings:

Kate Dossett, *Bridging Race Divides: Black Nationalism, Feminism, and Integration in the United States, 1896–1935* (Gainesville: University Press of Florida, 2008), chap. 4.

W. E. B. Du Bois, *Darkwater: Voices from within the Veil* (Mineola, NY: Dover, 1999), chap. 3.

Amy Jacques-Garvey, ed., *Philosophy and Opinions of Marcus Garvey* (New York: Atheneum, 1992), selections.

Alexandre Mboukou, "The Pan African Movement, 1900–1945: A Study in Leadership
    Conflicts among the Disciples of Pan Africanism," *Journal of Black Studies* 13 (1983):
    275–88.
"Pan-African Congress Resolution (1919)," in *African Intellectual Heritage: A Book of Sources*,
    ed. Molefi Kete Asante and Abu S. Abarry (Philadelphia: Temple University Press, 1996),
    517.
Walter Rucker, "'A Negro Nation within the Nation': W. E. B. Du Bois and the Creation of a
    Revolutionary Pan-Africanist Tradition, 1903–1947," *Black Scholar* 32 no. 3/4 (2002):
    37–46.
Michelle A. Stephens, *Black Empire: The Masculine Global Imaginary of Caribbean
    Intellectuals in the United States, 1914–1962* (Durham, NC: Duke University Press, 2005),
    chaps. 3–4.
William L. Van Deburg, ed., *Modern Black Nationalism: From Marcus Garvey to Louis
    Farrakhan* (New York: New York University Press, 1997), chap. 4.

Week 5   French- and Spanish-Speaking Caribbeans in the Transnational Dialogue
Readings:
Anténor Firmin, *The Equality of the Human Races*, trans. Asselin Charles (New York:
    Garland, 2000), selections.
Winston James, *Holding Aloft the Banner of Ethiopia: Caribbean Radicalism in Early
    Twentieth-Century America* (New York: Verso, 1998), selections.
Gérarde Magloire-Danton, "Anténor Firmin and Jean Price-Mars: Revolution, Memory,
    Humanism," *Small Axe*, 18 (2005): 150–70.
Jean Price-Mars, *So Spoke the Uncle*, trans. Magdaline W. Shannon (1928; Washington, DC:
    Three Continents, 1990), selections.

Week 6   Women's Voices and Transnational Identities
Readings:
Natasha Barnes, "Reluctant Matriarch: Sylvia Wynter and the Problematics of Caribbean
    Feminism," *Small Axe* 5 (1999): 34–47.
Veronica Marie Gregg, "'How with this rage shall beauty hold a plea': The Writings of Miss Amy
    Beckford Bailey as Moral Education in the Era of Jamaican Nation Building," *Small Axe* 23
    (2007): 16–33.
Louis J. Parascandola, ed., *"Look for Me All Around You": Anglophone Caribbean Immigrants
    in the Harlem Renaissance* (Detroit: Wayne State University Press, 2005), 107–28.
Rhoda Reddock, "Feminism, Nationalism, and the Early Women's Movement in the English-
    Speaking Caribbean (with Special Reference to Jamaica and Trinidad and Tobago)," in
    Caribbean Women Writers: Essays from the First International Conference, ed. Selwyn R.
    Cudjoe (Wellesley, MA: Calaloux, 1990), 61–81.

Week 7   The Pan-Caribbean Movement
Readings:
Tony Martin, "Eric Williams and the Anglo-American Caribbean Commission: Trinidad's
    Future Nationalist Leader as Aspiring Imperial Bureaucrat, 1942–1944," *Journal of
    African American History* 88 (2003): 274–90.
W. Burghardt Turner and Joyce Moore Turner, eds., *Richard B. Moore, Caribbean Militant in
    Harlem: Collected Writings, 1920–1972* (Bloomington: Indiana University Press, 1992),
    chap. 6.

Eric Williams, "The Impact of the International Crisis upon the Negro in the Caribbean," *Journal of Negro Education* 10 (1941): 536–44.

Week 8   The Post–World War II Pan-Caribbean Movement
Readings:

C. L. R. James, *At the Rendezvous of Victory: Selected Writings* (London: Allison and Busby, 1984), chap. 10.

Jason Parker, "'Capital of the Caribbean': The African American–West Indian 'Harlem Nexus' and the Transnational Drive for Black Freedom, 1940–1948," *Journal of African American History* 89 (2004): 98–117.

Turner and Turner, *Richard B. Moore*, chap. 11.

Week 9   Pan-Africanisms: From the West to Africa
Readings:

Aimé Césaire, *Discourse on Colonialism*, trans. Joan Pinkham (New York: Monthly Review Press, 2000), 31–46.

James H. Meriwether, *Proudly We Can Be Africans: Black Americans and Africa, 1935–1961* (Chapel Hill: University of North Carolina Press, 2002), chaps. 1–2.

"Pan-African Congress Resolution (1945)," in Asante and Abarry, *African Intellectual Heritage*, 518–21.

Haile Selassie, "Address to the League of Nations" (1936), in Asante and Abarry, *African Intellectual Heritage*, 664–70.

Ula Y. Taylor, *The Veiled Garvey: The Life and Times of Amy Jacques Garvey* (Chapel Hill: University of North Carolina Press, 2002), chap. 9–10.

Week 10   Transnational Labor Activism
Readings:

Carole Boyce Davies, *Left of Karl Marx: The Political Life of Black Communist Claudia Jones* (Durham, NC: Duke University Press, 2007), selections.

George Padmore, *The Life and Struggles of Negro Toilers* (1931), www.marxists.org/archive/padmore/index.htm.

Yevette Richards, *Maida Springer: Pan Africanist and International Labor Leader* (Pittsburgh: University of Pittsburgh Press, 2004), selections.

Week 11   Understanding an Independent Africa
Readings:

W. E. B. Du Bois, "I Never Dreamed I Would See This Miracle" (1960), reprinted in *New Crisis* 105, no. 3 (1998): 71–72.

Kevin K. Gaines, *African Americans in Ghana: Black Expatriates and the Civil Rights Era* (Chapel Hill: University of North Carolina Press, 2006), selections.

Russell Warren Howe, "Did Nkrumah Favor Pan-Africanism?" *Transition*, 75–76 (1997): 128–34.

C. L. R. James, "The Rise and Fall of Nkrumah," in Asante and Abarry, *African Intellectual Heritage*, 573–79.

Meriwether, *Proudly We Can Be Africans*, chap. 5.

Kwame Nkrumah, "The Need for a Union Government for Africa," in Asante and Abarry, *African Intellectual Heritage*, 559–72.

Week 12   Imagining Radical Political Alternatives

Readings:

Amilcar Cabral, "Identity and Dignity in the Context of Struggle," in Asante and Abarry, *African Intellectual Heritage*, 243–47.

Frantz Fanon, *The Wretched of the Earth* (1961), trans. Richard Philcox (New York: Grove, 2005), selections.

David Hillard and Donald Weise, eds., *The Huey P. Newton Reader* (New York: Seven Stories Press, 2002), 181–99.

Ali A. Mazrui, "On the Concept of 'We Are All Africans,'" *American Political Science Review* 57 (1963): 88–97.

Kwame Nantambu, "Pan-Africanism Versus Pan-African Nationalism: An Afrocentric Analysis," *Journal of Black Studies* 28 (1998): 561–74.

Julius K. Nyerere, "One-Party Government," in Asante and Abarry, *African Intellectual Heritage*, 555–58.

Léopold Sédar Senghor, "African Socialism," in Asante and Abarry, *African Intellectual Heritage*, 342–53.

Week 13   Black Power in the Diaspora

Readings:

Stokely Carmichael, *Stokely Speaks: From Black Power to Pan-Africanism* (Chicago: Lawrence Hill, 2007), chaps. 7, 14–15.

Kathleen Neal Cleaver, "Back to Africa: The Evolution of the International Section of the Black Panther Party (1969–1972)," in *The Black Panther Party Reconsidered*, ed. Charles E. Jones (Baltimore: Black Classic Press, 1998), 211–54.

William R. Lux, "Black Power in the Caribbean," *Journal of Black Studies* 3 (1972): 207–25.

Nikhil Pal Singh, "The Black Panthers and the 'Undeveloped Country' of the Left," in Jones, *Black Panther Party Reconsidered*, 57–105.

Simboonath Singh, "Resistance, Essentialism, and Empowerment in Black Nationalist Discourse in the African Diaspora: A Comparison of the Back to Africa, Black Power, and Rastafari Movements," *Journal of African American Studies* 8, no. 3 (2004): 18–36.

Week 14   Black Liberation and International Consciousness

Readings:

Walter Rodney, "Towards the Sixth Pan African Congress: Aspects of the International Class Struggle in Africa, the Caribbean, and America" (1974), in Asante and Abarry, *African Intellectual Heritage*, 729–39.

Walter Rodney, "African History in the Service of the Black Liberation," *Small Axe* 10 (2001): 66–80.

Cynthia Young, *Soul Power: Culture, Radicalism, and the Making of a U.S. Third World Left* (Durham, NC: Duke University Press, 2006), chaps. 1, 5.

Week 15   Understanding Apartheid and the Antiapartheid Movement in South Africa

Readings:

Alan Gregor Cobley, "'Far from Home': The Origins and Significance of the Afro-Caribbean Community in South Africa to 1930," *Journal of Southern African Studies* 18 (1992): 349–70.

Alan Gregor Cobley and Alvin Thompson, eds., *The African-Caribbean Connection: Historical and Cultural Perspectives* (Bridgetown, Barbados: Dept. of History, University of the West Indies; National Cultural Foundation, 1990), selections.

Sheridan Johns and R. Hunt Davis, eds., *Mandela, Tambo, and the African National Congress: The Struggle against Apartheid, 1948–1990; A Documentary Survey* (New York: Oxford University Press, 1991), selections.

Amanda D. Kemp and Robert Trent Vinson, "'Poking Holes in the Sky': Professor James Thaele, American Negroes, and Modernity in 1920s Segregationist South Africa," *African Studies Review* 43 (2000): 141–59.

Meriwether, *Proudly We Can Be Africans*, chap. 3.

Christopher Saunders, "From Trinidad to Cape Town: The First Black Lawyer at the Cape," *Quarterly Bulletin of the National Library of South Africa* 55 (2001): 146–61.

Have You Heard from Johannesburg? Apartheid and the Club of the West, dir. Connie Field, DVD (2006; San Francisco: California Newsreel, 2007).

Notes

I thank the editors of *RHR* 103, George P. Cunningham, Régine Latortue, Karen Miller, Sonya Ramsey, Grace P. Willis, and the students of Africana Studies 14.3 (spring 2006) for their comments and suggestions.

1. According to a 2004 *New York Times* article, data from the 2000 census revealed that of the total black population in New York City, 30 percent was born outside the United States. Rachel L. Swarns, "'African-American' Becomes a Term for Debate," *New York Times*, August 29, 2004.

2. Kristin F. Butcher, "Black Immigrants in the United States: A Comparison with Native Blacks and Other Immigrants," *Industrial and Labor Relations Review* 47 (1994): 267–68.

3. Douglas S. Massey et al., "Black Immigrants and Black Natives Attending Selective Colleges and Universities in the United States," *American Journal of Education* 113 (2007): 243–71; see also Butcher, "Black Immigrants in the United States," 265–84. Butcher's study does not focus on education, but it does contain some valuable information on the subject.

4. Lani Guinier, "Our Preference for the Privileged," *Boston Globe*, July 9, 2004. See also Jason B. Johnson, "Shades of Gray in Black Enrollment: Immigrants' Rising Numbers a Concern to Some Activists," *San Francisco Chronicle*, February 22, 2005; Cara Anna, "More Immigrants among Blacks at Colleges," *Associated Press Online*, April 30, 2007; Joanna Walters, "Education: 'Any Black Student Will Do'; A Disturbing Report Shows Some African Americans Are Being Squeezed Out of the US University Population," *Guardian*, May 29, 2007.

5. Guinier, "Our Preference for the Privileged"; for a counterargument to the ideas of black immigrant privilege in higher education, see Belinda Edmondson, "The Myth of Black Immigrant Privilege," *Anthurium: A Caribbean Studies Journal* 4 (2006), anthurium.miami .edu/volume_4/issue_1/edmondson-themyth.html.

6. Massey et al., "Black Immigrants," 248, table 1. The percentage of undergraduate students who identify themselves as African- or Caribbean-born is higher at Brooklyn College than was found among public institutions in the Massey et al. study. These students at Brooklyn College comprised 40.8 percent in the fall of 2005 and 36.9 percent of the black student population in the fall of 2006. It is also interesting to note that among the native-born and Caribbean student groups, the population is overwhelmingly female, while the majority

of African-born students are male (Office of the AVP for Finance, Budget and Planning, "Brooklyn College Enrollment Trends: Student Enrollment by Ethnicity and Gender, Fall 2005 / Fall 2006" [updated, 2007]).

7. Area and comparative studies still view regions and nations as static entities governed by their own dynamics, whereas I am proposing that we look at the mutual influence that these regions and nations have on each other.

Black Global Metropolis: Sexual History

Kevin Mumford

I recently taught this course on the role of sexuality in the African diaspora entitled "Black Global Metropolis: Sexual History." It was to serve as the capstone seminar for the Sexuality Studies Program (SSP) at the University of Iowa, one of several requirements for the certificate. Because of my joint appointment, we cross-listed it in the Department of History and in the African American Studies Program (with nine students from sexuality studies, three from history, and three from African American studies). The course attracted more women than men, and a variety of gay, lesbian, African American, and white students. Although SSP offers courses under the rubric "diverse sexual communities," mine was one of the first to center race to such a degree and to examine sexuality, reproduction, and erotic cultures across the multiple locations and periods of the black diaspora.

Given the novelty of the topic, and its potential to stimulate heightened sensitivities, I began the course by asking students to describe a significant experience they had had with racism. We talked about the hardships faced by our families, lovers, friends, and neighbors and considered how these related to larger historical trends in racial discrimination or definition, including the construction of the category of whiteness. An African American man, for whom this was his first course on sexual history, recounted an incident in a nightclub where a white woman called him a racial epithet. Another participant (a white woman) described how her white neighbors had attempted to run an Asian family out of their neighborhood for no apparent reason other than racism. By the end of this somewhat wrenching discussion, I decided not to pursue the question of gay or lesbian identity, homophobia,

Radical History Review

Issue 103 (Winter 2009)   DOI 10.1215/01636545-2008-038

or individual experiences of coming out in part because the course schedule began with slavery and race, not with the category of identity. It was not that sexism and homophobia were unrelated or incomparable to racism, but rather that it felt anachronistic to lead off with a major discussion of queerness when the first lectures and readings began with the seventeenth-century slave trade.

One of the challenges of the course concerned the length of the reading assignments of more than one hundred pages per week. As such, students paired up, created lists of discussion questions, and cofacilitated the class meetings to get a handle on the material. I posted their questions on the Web site several days before the meeting and gave 25 percent of the grade for facilitating one session, and another 25 percent for overall attendance and participation. Another problem with the reading was that much of the best work focuses on race and sexuality in the United States and far less on the topic in Africa or the other destinations of the diaspora. In researching the course I learned that many scholars of the slave trade and colonialism tend to work less on sexuality per se than on gender and family relations, such as the female reproduction of slavery and "miscegenation" relations in the empire. This raised methodological and logistical questions about the application of sexuality frameworks (with their focus on erotic ideas, acts, regulation) to the study of non-Western social arrangements, especially about relating discursive or cultural studies in the field of sexuality with the more materialist social analysis in African and Caribbean studies. On the other hand, when new research on the African diaspora looked at constructions of sexuality in South African work camps, in colonial Caribbean or Latin American prostitution, within postemancipation marriage and codes of respectability, we could draw comparisons between various race/sex systems in ways that demonstrated the importance of race relations in the organization of erotic experience.

Along those lines, our first key question was: Why did the sexual imagery of the seventeenth century distort the representation of the bodies of African and indigenous women or obsess over the size of the sexual organs of African and indigenous men? In this part we examined documents and secondary literature on the slave trade to give us a sense of background and as a way to prepare for an analysis of subsequent processes of urbanization and sexuality formation. I suspect that specialists in African studies or cultural anthropology would spend more time working with indigenous sources, rather than with the white travelers' accounts that we used. Although some course participants had a limited background in history, I felt that we benefited from the understanding that these stereotypes (for want of a better term) reached far back and had both changed and persisted and that the circulation of African figurations offered the continuing possibility for a diaspora of recuperation and reconnection. In the span of three to four weeks, the class moved from sharing stories of racism to talking about sexuality in changing temporal and national or geographical contexts to considering its dependency on both racialized labor supplies and visual economies.

There was a high level of discussion on the topic of race and rape and, later, on the sexual dimension of hip-hop culture. A number of students engaged the historical scholarship on the rape of black women during the era of slavery, though they sometimes did so from the perspective of contemporary social science findings that have come to conceive of rape as a crime of violence. To that extent, some students passed over questions of consent or trauma as obvious and inevitable and were not prepared to consider how historians locate the rape of black women on a continuum of coercion in the system of slavery. They seemed to think of the story of Harriet Jacobs, the runaway and author, in much the same way that contemporary feminist theorists do—that rape was a kind of ritualized enforcement of patriarchy. And yet many students were still concerned with the question of how slavery limited women's resistance—how it was embedded in its own historical context in which whites defined black women's relationship to men, work, respectability, and other issues such as physical assault. One thing that I tried to introduce was the question of how the forces at work in the African diaspora—the context of the transatlantic slave trade and ongoing white domination—required that we address the nature of intersections. Along those lines, I asked participants to consider if a strong gender perspective adequately recognized the extent to which enslaved black men or emancipated black men were vulnerable to sexual violence. What happens to theories of rape as a tool of patriarchy when black men become victims of comparable sexual violence in the history of lynching? Another challenge was teaching students more familiar with the history of sexuality to consider the impact of the social forces caused by the African diaspora. What happens when instead of examining a nineteenth century punctuated by the rise of the middle-class family and the idea of separate spheres, we study the rise of emancipation and the migration of ex-slaves away from masters toward the cities? Rather than asking how market capitalism constructed bourgeois sexual roles, we asked how the end of slavery not only reconstructed black-white relations in an intensely conflicted public sphere but also infused sexuality with racial power dynamics in Trinidad, Barbados, Cuba, New Orleans, and Memphis.

One of the more interesting sections of the course concerned our study of the history of queers of color. When we came to the subject of transgender and transsexuals in the African diaspora, I discovered common ground as well as points of theoretical disagreement. By the end of this section, I was arguing that the key readings on transsexual prostitutes in Brazil had displaced the fact that they were dark skinned and lived in racially defined ghettos and that black transgender sex workers were probably overrepresented in U.S. vice districts. It seemed that transgender studies had failed to incorporate new theories of the diaspora, neglecting the ways in which blackness shaped the economic status, safety, and culture of transgender populations. If some of the students with a gender studies background seemed to valorize transsexuals as transgressors of biological sex norms, my approach focused on the political economy of race. We were interested in possible connections between transgender people of color through racial networks and other modes of cross-identification.

One of the successes and pleasures of the course was that many students adeptly utilized popular media to illustrate themes of sexuality in the African diaspora, bringing in film clips, music, and images from the Internet. We thus benefited from a greater sense of visuality and therefore of the "embodiment" of our black sexual subjects. In the process, our analysis dropped some of the historical depth we had achieved on the modern city and postwar black family structure, and again the scholarship on the United States overshadowed the few writings on queers in the Caribbean, Africa, or Europe. Many students found the discussion of the "down-low," in which black men both disidentify with gay men and are sexually attracted to other (usually black) men, to be problematic. But I feel that we also gained from a diaspora perspective because of our insight into the extent of continuity with submerged definitions of queer sexuality in the Harlem Renaissance or in segregated, poor urban neighborhoods or in migratory work camps. It was clear that black queerness was frequently seen as ambiguous and varying in its expression, but that it was not exclusive to Western situations or recent times. In the final part of the course, I tried to encourage students to apply these constructions of queer black sexuality to an examination of AIDS and to theorize about diverse understandings of transmission, responsibility, disclosure, and mobilization, compared to earlier attachments of deviance, disease, and disfigurement to black sexuality.

In the end, this course on the black sexual metropolis provided a space in which to test variables and trends in a global historical perspective. By comparing the response of black subjects to emancipation, the course helped show that black women were consistently subordinated in sexual relations even after their reproductive capacity was supposedly freed. The comparison of state policies toward poverty and dependent families highlighted how modernization and advanced capitalism impact black diaspora sexualities, such as in work camps and ghettoes, through migration and immigration, as well as through reproductive technologies. These and other comparisons uncovered the effects of the government's deployment of deviance and surveillance technologies on marginalized, displaced subjects. At the same time, with the formation of diaspora spaces, black subjects and black-white interactions created a complex erotic imaginary through such forms as the blues and jazz, dance and youth culture, and a variety of media. Comparing and contrasting the role of homosexuality across sites of the diaspora highlighted the emergent outlines of what might be termed a shared patterning of black queer identity. Finally, the course presented the chronological and structural forces at play in the history of black sexuality, which included an analysis both of white oppression and of spaces in which people of the diaspora expressed and felt sexual desire.

SYLLABUS

Black Global Metropolis: Sexual History

The purpose of this course is to introduce students to themes and conceptual problems in the transnational history of the construction of race and sexuality from the opening of the slave trade to the rise of the black global metropolis. The major sites or nations are the United States, England, France, Brazil, Cuba, Puerto Rico, South Africa, Zimbabwe, Jamaica, Trinidad, and Barbados, focusing on their major cities. Additional theoretical readings complement this tracing of the global urbanization process by considering dynamics of sexual racism, psychological domination, and colonial identification—how erotic cultures secure structural relations of inequality, as well as how subalterns assert sexual desires and identities that challenge their terms. The course examines the rise of modernity and the cultures of modernism opened up by new metropolitan (formally) capitalist economies. This modernization of sex was defined by flows of citizens and desires across both urban and national borders, as well as new styles of urbanism and consumption. The course concentrates on new racial masculinities, black and black-white prostitution, and queer identities. The final section is set in the context of the rising hegemony of Western definitions of the particular sex/gender system and status orders throughout areas of globalization. In particular, the course seeks to place the AIDS pandemic in the long historical process of the racialization of sexuality.

The course requires three writing assignments, consistent and significant participation in the discussions, and the submission of brief reviews of the readings or films to demonstrate your engagement in the course. The conduct of the course generally follows the guidelines prescribed by the College of Liberal Arts and Sciences, the Department of History, and the Sexuality Studies Program. Participants are expected to respect the diversity of students and of opinion and to express their ideas in such a way as to open the broadest discussion.

Writing Assignments:

1. *Review Essay*: This paper examines the readings assigned in one seminar session in a fresh light by locating them in the historical framework under way in the course and by drawing from facilitation of the discussion. The essay is to serve as the basis for one or more participants' facilitation of the particular class in which we discuss the readings, and then facilitators submit their review essay to the instructor (5–8 pp.).

2. *Film Review*: Thinking critically about the films is crucial to a successful conceptualization of the historical problems of race, sexuality, and the metropolis. The second review essay involves watching one or more of the films, or a film outside the course that is selected in consultation with the instructor, and composing a summary of the plot, an analysis of its racialization of sexuality processes, and the relationship of the film to the readings. Again, every writer is expected to present his or her written work to the class before submitting it for evaluation.

3. *Final Essay*: This is a longer review essay that gives students the opportunity to delve into a variety of disciplines, not only history—to look at documents, sociology, urban planning, fiction, and visual culture (from pornography to maps). This assignment

requires a critical summary that incorporates the topic and the readings of one or more of the seminars, but then it goes on to ask a new historical question and to provide some kind of preliminary response. The preparation of the research and the outline of the essay will be done in consultation with the instructor. This essay is ten to fifteen pages and is due on the last week of the course (instead of a final exam).

The final grade consists of the following percentages:
First review essay: 25 percent
Film essay: 25 percent
Final paper: 25 percent
Discussion (including summaries of reading): 25 percent

Books
The bulk of the reading has been made available in the course reader (CR), which is on sale at the Iowa Bookstore. A copy of the CR is on two-hour reserve in Reserve Readings at the Main Library, and the citations on the syllabus also give the titles of various books and journals, which are shelved at the Main Library.

Syllabus
All assignments, topics, and readings are listed on the syllabus. Also, the discussion questions point to lines of inquiry, and sometimes to a conceptual challenge, but they are not meant to exhaust the various subjects related to the black global metropolis.

Seminar #1: January 16, 2007: Introduction to the Course
The requirements of the course, assignment of the first set of essays, and explanation of the terms of evaluation

Seminar #2: January 23, 2007: The Construction of Difference and Theorizing the Black Metropolis
Readings: Robert Staples, *Exploring Black Sexuality* (Lanham, MD: Rowman and Littlefield, 2006), 1–35, 157–74; Horace Cayton and St. Clair Drake, *Black Metropolis*, vol. 2 (New York: Harper and Row, 1962), 565–99; John D'Emilio, "Capitalism and Gay Identity," in *Making Trouble: Essays on Gay History, Politics, and the University* (New York: Routledge, 1992), 3–16.

Discussion: What are the larger historical processes that contribute to the social construction of sexuality? Why would different racial groups experience sexuality in different ways? How has the rise of the modern urban system in turn shaped both sexuality and race? What are leading modes of critical intervention or protest of sexual racism and objectification in colonization by the subaltern?

Film: Isaac Julien, *Frantz Fanon: Black Skin, White Mask* (1996)

Seminar #3: January 30, 2007: Europeans and Africans in the Black Atlantic

Readings: Winthrop Jordan, *White Over Black: American Attitudes toward the Negro, 1550–1812* (Chapel Hill: University of North Carolina Press, 1968), 3–43, 136–78; Jennifer Morgan, " 'Some Could Suckle Over Their Shoulders': Male Travelers, Female Bodies, and the Gendering of Racial Ideology," *William and Mary Quarterly* 54 (1997): 167–92; Frantz Fanon, *Black Skin, White Masks*, trans. Charles Lam (1967; New York: Grove Weidenfeld, 1982), 41–82; Linden Lewis, introduction to *The Culture of Gender and Sexuality in the Caribbean*, ed. Lewis (Gainesville: University Press of Florida, 2003), 1–21; Owen White, *Children of the French Empire: Miscegenation and Colonial Society in French West Africa, 1896–1960* (New York: Oxford University Press, 1999).

Discussion: What are the historical time frames of the Black Atlantic? What is the role of European culture or white "vision" in the making of black sexualities? How does one explain the content and/or variations in the "black image in the white mind"? In this vein, consider not only sexual images that were circulating but the difference between attributes assigned to black men and to black women. What is the role of the black viewpoint in this racialization of sexuality?

Film: Zola Maseko, *The Life and Times of Sara Baartman* (1998)

Seminar #4: February 6, 2007: The Rise of the Interzone: Colonial Port Cities

Readings: Thelma Willis Foote, *Black and White Manhattan: Racial Formation in Colonial New York* (New York: Oxford, 2006), 124–59; Philip Morgan, "Interracial Sex in the Chesapeake and the Caribbean," in *Sally Hemings and Thomas Jefferson: History, Memory, and Civic Culture*, ed. Jan Lewis (Charlottesville: University of Virginia, 1999), 52–84; Gretchen Holbrook Gerzina, *Black London: Life before Emancipation* (New Brunswick, NJ: Rutgers University Press, 1995), 133–65; Leslie M. Harris, "From Abolitionist Amalgamators to 'Rulers of the Five Points': The Discourse of Interracial Sex and Reform in the Antebellum New York City," in *Love, Sex, Race: Crossing Boundaries in North American History*, ed. Martha Hodes (New York: New York University Press, 1999), 191–212; Herbert Asbury, *The Gangs of New York: An Informal History of the Underworld* (New York: Capricorn, 1970), 174–202.

Discussion: How does the "landing" or "settlement" of black people in the New World affect the older model or conception of black/primitive sexuality? To what extent are gender, class, labor and status systems shaping these New World sexualities? What are some of the dominant stereotypes of black sexuality? If we turn these against a mirror, what are some of the characteristics of white sexuality?

Films: James Ivory, *Jefferson in Paris* (1995); Martin Scorsese, *Gangs of New York* (2002)

**Seminar #5: February 13, 2007: The Problem of Consent and the Construction
of Enslaved Black Female Sexuality**

Readings: Sharon Block, "Lines of Color, Sex, and Service: Comparative Sexual Coercion
in Early America," in Hodes, *Sex, Love, Race*, 141–63; Harriet Jacobs, *Incidents in the
Life of a Slave Girl* (New York: Norton, 2001), 25–105; Jean Fagan Yellin, *Harriet Jacobs:
A Life* (New York: Basic Books, 2004), 17–43; Joseph Dorsey, "It Hurt Very Much at the
Time," in Lewis, *Culture of Gender and Sexuality*, 294–322; Jacqui Alexander, " 'Not Just
(Any)Body Can be a Citizen': The Politics of Law," in *Cultures of Empire: A Reader*, ed.
Catherine Hall (New York: Routledge, 2000), 359–75; Patricia Hill Collins, "Assume the
Position: The Changing Contours of Sexual Violence," in *Black Sexual Politics: African
Americans, Gender, and the New Racism* (New York: Routledge, 2004), 215–45.

Discussion: What is the nature of settlement and commodity production under slavery?
How does it feel to be a slave, do you imagine? How does slavery operate as a hegemonic
institution (and how does sexuality shape and reflect such discussions of consent and
domination)? If one is enslaved, is sexual consent possible? Is there a difference in the level
of sexual domination for enslaved black men and enslaved black women?

Film: Richard Fleischer, *Mandingo* (1975)

**Seminar #6: February 20, 2007: Reconstructing Sexuality and Race in New Orleans,
Memphis, Trinidad, Cuba**

Readings: Hanah Rosen, "Sexual Violence against Black Women in the Memphis Riots,
1866," in Hodes, *Race, Sex, and Love*, 267–93; Alecia P. Long, "It's Because You Are a
Colored Woman: Sex, Race, and Concubinage after the Civil War," in *Great Southern
Babylon: Sex, Race, and Respectability in New Orleans, 1865–1920* (Baton Rouge:
Louisiana State University Press, 2004), 10–59; Sheena Boa, "Young Ladies and Dissolute
Women: Conflicting Views of Culture and Gender in Public Entertainment, Kingstown,
St. Vincent, 1838–1888," in *Gender and Slave Emancipation in the Atlantic World*, ed.
Pamela Scully and Diana Paton (Durham, NC: Duke University Press, 2005), 247–66;
Darlene Clark Hine, "Culture of Dissemblance," in *Hine Sight: Black Women and the
Re-construction of American History* (Bloomington: Indiana University Press, 1997),
37–47; Verena Martínez-Alier, *Marriage, Class, and Color in Nineteenth-Century Cuba*
(1974; Ann Arbor: University of Michigan Press, 1989), 82–99, 103–19.

Discussion: What are some of the variations of caste and citizenship in Memphis, New
Orleans, Havana, and Trinidad? Now that the coercion of black female sexuality is no
longer reinforced by a regime of enslaved labor, what are the new sources and dynamics
that provide gradations of relative sexual autonomy—from rape and concubinage to
seduction and elopement? In what ways does emancipation serve as a new starting point for
black sexual politics?

Films: D. W. Griffith, *Birth of a Nation* (1915); Mya B., *Silence: In Search of Black Female
Sexuality in America* (2004) (first half)

Seminar #7: February 27, 2007: White Sexual Purity and Black Masculinity
Readings: Linden Lewis, "Caribbean Masculinity: Unpacking the Narrative," in Lewis, *Culture of Gender and Sexuality*, 94–125; Jacqueline Dowd Hall, "The Mind That Burns in Each Body: The Southern Lynching Complex," in *The Politics of Desire*, ed. Ann Snitow (New York: Monthly Review Press, 1983), 23–36; Ida B. Wells, "Southern Horrors: Lynched for an Attempted Assault," in *Southern Horrors and Other Writings* (Boston: Bedford, 1997), 113–17; Marlon Bryan Ross, *Manning the Race: Reforming Black Men in the Age of Jim Crow* (New York: New York University Press, 2004), 120–66 ; Brian Donovan, *White Slave Crusades: Race, Gender, and Anti-vice Activism, 1887–1917* (Urbana: University of Illinois Press, 2006), 1–4, 89–109.

Discussion: To what extent, and in which particular ways, has sexual violence against women spilled over into the making of black manhood? What is the relationship between the assertion of black manhood in the city and the taboo against miscegenation? In what ways did sexual reform movements intersect with black social and sexual reform? How does a politics of sexual purity impact a racialized space or cityscape?

Film: Ken Burns, *Unforgivable Blackness: The Life of Jack Johnson* (2004); "Without Sanctuary: Postcards and Photography of Lynching in America" (Web site)

Seminar #8: March 6, 2007: The Black Sexual Metropolis in Chicago, New York, Johannesburg, and New Orleans
Readings: Eric Lott, *Love and Theft: Blackface Minstrelsy and the American Working-Class* (New York: Oxford, 1993), 63–168; Asbury, *Gangs of New York*, 174–202; Kevin J. Mumford, *Interzones: Black/White Sex Districts in Chicago and New York in the Early Twentieth Century* (New York: Columbia University Press, 1997), 52–117; Alecia P. Long, "Notorious Attraction: Sex and Tourism in New Orleans, 1897–1917," in *Southern Journeys: Tourism, History, and Culture in the Modern South*, ed. Richard D. Starnes (Tuscaloosa: University of Alabama Press, 2003), 15–41; Glen S. Elder, *Malevolent Geographies: Hostels, Sexuality, and Apartheid Legacy* (Athens: Ohio State University Press, 2003), 41–92.

Discussion: How was the popular conception of vice redefined in the modern city? In what ways and why have racial spaces changed, and what was their impact on black-white relations? How does the concept of race and space, or geography, in turn define sexuality?

Films: Oscar Micheaux, *Within Our Gates* (1920); Burns, *Unforgivable Blackness* (scenes from disk 2).

Seminar #9: March 13, 2007: The Culture of Black Urban Sexual Modernism
Readings: Sander Gilman, "Black Bodies, White Bodies: Towards an Iconography of Female Sexuality in Late Nineteenth-Century Art, Medicine, and Literature," in *Race, Culture, and Difference*, ed. James Donald and Ali Rattansi (Thousand Oaks, CA: Sage, 1992); Brett A. Berliner, *Ambivalent Desire: The Exotic Black Other in Jazz Age France*

(Amherst: University of Massachusetts Press, 2002), 189–233; Angela Davis, *The Blues Legacies and Black Feminism: Gertrude "Ma" Rainey, Bessie Smith, and Billie Holiday* (New York: Pantheon, 1998), 181–97; Siobahn Somerville, *Queering the Color Line: Race and the Invention of Homosexuality* (Durham, NC: Duke University Press, 2000), 39–110.

Discussion: In what ways and why has the representation or discussion of black female sexuality changed over the past half century? In what ways did the assertion of the black female self and identity in turn shape the construction of a new modern culture? What are the constraints on the "memory" of black gay and lesbian contributions to the Harlem Renaissance? Was Langston Hughes gay?

Films: Isaac Julien, *Looking for Langston* (1988); Sidney Furie, *The Lady Sings the Blues* (1972)

Seminar #10: March 27, 2007: Postwar Race, Sexuality, Reproduction, and the Black Urban Family

Readings: Laura Briggs, *Reproducing Empire: Race, Sex, Science, and U.S. Imperialism* (Berkeley: University of California Press, 2002), 162–92; Lee Rainwater, "Moynihan Report," in *The Moynihan Report and the Politics of Controversy* (Cambridge, MA: MIT, 1967), 47–94; Elizabeth Herzog, "Is There A 'Breakdown' of the Negro Family?" in *Moynihan Report*, 344–64; Charles Carolle, "Popular Imageries of Gender and Sexuality: Poor and Working Class," in Lewis, *Culture of Gender and Sexuality*, 169–89.

Discussion: How have the contours of sexual respectability changed since the late nineteenth century? Similarly, in what ways did black female sexuality respond to changing historical contexts, that is, family structures, economies, and social reform policies? To what extent have migration and the rise of the modern state impacted the processes of racialization of sexuality?

Film: Mya B., *Silence* (all)

Seminar #11: April 3, 2007: Crossing the Nation, Sex, and Color Lines

Readings: Sonya O. Rose, "Sex, Citizenship, and the Nation in World War II Britain," in *Cultures of Empire: Colonizers in Britain and the Empire in the Nineteenth and Twentieth Centuries; A Reader*, ed. Catherine Hall (New York: Routledge, 2000), 246–77; Don Kulick, *Travesti: Sex, Gender, and Culture among Brazilian Transgendered Prostitutes* (Chicago: University of Chicago Press, 1998), 29–45, 191–238; Charlotte A. Suthrell, *Unzipping Gender: Sex, Cross Dressing, and Culture* (New York: Berg, 2004), 147–62; Rochella Thorpe, "'A House Where Queers Go': African-American Lesbian Night Life in Detroit, 1940–1975," in *Inventing Lesbian Cultures in America*, ed. Ellen Lewin (Boston: Beacon, 1996), 40–61.

Discussion: In the context of the global racializations of sexuality, how have sexual subcultures and subjectivities proliferated and responded? How has the sexual margin changed since the days of port cities? What does the global metropolitan landscape now reveal about the end of modernity and about breaks with the past, including the transition from modern identity to postmodernism?

Film: Jennie Livingston, *Paris Is Burning* (1990)

Seminar #12: April 10, 2007: Rise of Black Queer Identity in Chicago, Philadelphia, Rio de Janeiro, and Johannesburg

Readings: Allen Drexel, "Race, Class, and Male Homosexuality on the Chicago South Side," in *Creating a Place for Ourselves: Lesbian, Gay, and Bisexual Community Histories*, ed. Brett Beemyn (New York: Routledge, 1997), 119–39; Joseph Beam, *In the Life: A Black Gay Anthology* (Boston: Allyson, 1986), 13–18, 224–42; Huey Newton, "The Women's Liberation and the Gay Liberation Movements," in *Black Men on Race, Gender, and Sexuality: A Critical Reader*, ed. Devon Carbado (New York: New York University Press, 1998), 387–89; Marc Epprecht, *Hungochani: The History of a Dissident Sexuality in Southern Africa* (Montreal: McGill-Queen's University Press, 2004), 50–82; Richard Parker, *Beneath the Equator: Cultures of Desire, Male Homosexuality, and Emerging Gay Communities* (New York: Routledge, 1999), 53–97.

Discussion: What are the origins of black gay identity? To what extent do they constitute an urban formation? To what extent is there a continuing influence of racism and segregation on the emergence of queer identities? What are the origins of homophobia in the black community? What are those origins in the Caribbean and the black diaspora? What are the effects of key social movements and nationalism in yet again reconstructing queer identities?

Film: Marlon Riggs, *Tongues Untied* (1990)

Seminar #13: April 17, 2007: The Global AIDS Crisis

Readings: Cathy J. Cohen, *Boundaries of Blackness: AIDS and the Breakdown of Black Politics* (Chicago: University of Chicago Press, 1999), 33–77, Keith Boykin, *Beyond the Down Low: Sex, Lies, and Denial in Black America* (New York: Carroll and Graf, 2005), 75–132.

Discussion: In what ways have the original European conceptions of the racial other or of the colonial gaze shaped the AIDS pandemic? How do we understand nationalist and ethnocentric defenses of black masculinity and of homophobia in the context of this and other crises?

Film: *Frontline Series: The Age of AIDS* (2006); Jonathan Demme, *Philadelphia* (1993); Karen Boswell, *Dancing on the Edge: Steps for the Future* (2002)

Seminar #14: April 24, 2007: The Global Sexual Politics of Hip Hop

Readings: Joshua Gamson, *The Famous Sylvester: The Legend, the Music, and the 70s in San Francisco* (New York: Holt, 2005), 134–220; Tod Swedenburg, "Homies in the 'Hood': Rap's Commodification of Insubordination," in *That's the Joint! The Hip-Hop Studies Reader*, ed. Murray Forman and Mark Anthony Neal (New York: Routledge, 2004), 579–91; Johnnetta Betsch Cole and Beverly Guy-Sheftall, "No Respect: Gender Politics and Hip-Hop," in *Gender Talk: The Struggle for Women's Equality in African American Communities*, ed. Johnnetta Betsch Cole and Beverly Guy-Sheftall (New York: Ballantine, 2003), 182–215.

Discussion: In what ways has the construction of a sexualized black masculinity in rap displaced both black gay disco and black female blues singers in the postmodern metropolis? In what ways is hip hip a reaction against, or expression of anxieties about, the state of black sexuality in the metropolis?

Seminar #15: May 1, 2007: Project Presentations

May 8, 2007: All Papers and Reviews Due

Introduction

For this issue of *Radical History Review*, Curated Spaces presents an extended focus on the role of visual culture in the African diaspora. The featured articles by Leon Wainwright and Jacqueline Francis look in depth at the issues that impact African diaspora artists and provide an expanded context for understanding the presentation and framing of such work. Wainwright interrogates the work of diaspora artists and recent curatorial practices in Britain and the United States; he challenges the centralizing dominance of approaches to curating in both countries. Francis examines the work of key artists who were instrumental in defining what it meant to be "black" in the United Kingdom from the 1970s to the 1990s. She also focuses on two contemporary artists from the United States, Rasheed Araeen and Roshini Kempadoo, whose work expands existing definitions of blackness as a way to visually reactivate its socially transformative potential. Like Wainwright, Francis also explores the politics of curatorial practice, in this case three exhibitions on representations of blackness at the Charles H. Wright Museum of African American History in Detroit.

—Conor McGrady

Radical History Review
Issue 103 (Winter 2009)
© 2009 by MARHO: The Radical Historians' Organization, Inc.

To Be Real: Figuring Blackness
in Modern and Contemporary African
Diaspora Visual Cultures

Jacqueline Francis

In a 1994 essay titled "Identity, Authenticity, Survival: Multicultural Societies and Social Reproduction," the philosopher K. Anthony Appiah examines the limits of "the politics of recognition," which his Canadian counterpart, Charles Taylor, has described as a multicultural procedure of naming and celebrating diversity.[1] Yet while multiculturalism has mitigated some of the resolutely exclusionary operations of the distant and recent past, it also tends to regulate artistic bodies and classify creative expression in ways that do not decidedly move Western societies toward the pluralist ideal. Our poorly conceived multicultural policies merely encourage us to look for the recognizable markers of minority difference, to parrot the rhetoric that advances essentialist ideas about nonwhite subjects, and to create demand for the ethnic and racial particularity that is valued as authentic, natural, and real.[2]

This essay explores figuration in artistic and museum exhibiting practices of the late twentieth century and the early twenty-first that undermine the authority of authentic blackness as a primary tenet of African diasporic identification. It takes its cue from the cultural theorist Stuart Hall's keen assessment: "The fact is that 'black' has never been just there. It has always been an unstable identity, psychically, culturally, and politically."[3] The essay's first section provides an analysis of art by Rasheed Araeen and Roshini Kempadoo created in the 1970s and 1990s, an era

Radical History Review
Issue 103 (Winter 2009)   DOI 10.1215/01636545-2008-040
© 2009 by MARHO: The Radical Historians' Organization, Inc.

during which they and other progressives of African, Asian, and Caribbean descent in the United Kingdom claimed the political and cultural position "black." In the work and words of Araeen and Kempadoo, diaspora constitutes an active, polemical site from which they challenge prescriptions for black identity. The essay's second section considers the representation of blackness in three exhibitions from 1997 to 2007 at the Charles H. Wright Museum of African American History. During these years, the shifts in curatorial strategies for displaying and defining blackness illuminate the broad, dialogic character of identity, a quality necessarily interrogated by the museum's visitors. The essay's final section examines the cartoonlike paintings of the African American artists Laylah Ali and Kojo Griffin. Their comic-serious images offer stark departures from the heroic and naturalistic portrayals of black figures that are the standard representational approaches taken by many other African American artists who seek to protest and overwhelm racist stereotypes in visual culture. As evident in Araeen's and Kempadoo's art and the Wright displays, Ali's and Griffin's choices for figuration put pressure on overdetermined notions of blackness in our time by questioning the presumed stability of racial categories. In each instance, the figure is a creative provocation (rather than an illustration) befitting the dynamism of diaspora. Figuring is the conceptual thread uniting these African diasporic moments, which, though not causally related, similarly transgress limiting definitions of blackness to privilege its productive, transforming visibilities.

U.K. Blak: 1978, 1990

In 1978, the artist and critic Rasheed Araeen (born 1935) published "Preliminary Notes for a Black Manifesto" in the inaugural issue of *Black Phoenix: Journal of Contemporary Art and Culture in the Third World*, a London journal he coedited with the poet Mahmood Jamal. "Preliminary Notes for a Black Manifesto" epitomizes Araeen's lifetime work of battling art-world exclusionism and, ultimately, its palliative approach to multicultural integration. "Black," the Pakistan-born Araeen writes, denotes those in the underdeveloped nations of Africa, Asia, the Caribbean, and Latin America, and includes "all those non-European peoples (whom we shall call 'blacks' or 'black people') who now live in various Western countries and find themselves in a similar predicament to that of the actual Third World."[4] Araeen's definition of black extends beyond the gesture of solidarity or the announcement of affiliation among British colonial and postcolonial subjects, for it boldly states an experiential connection. In the same year that Edward W. Said published *Orientalism* and a quarter century after the publication of Frantz Fanon's *Peau noire, masques blanc* (*Black Skin, White Masks*, 1952), Araeen, who has often cited these works, proffered the radically unifying rubric "black" for the British cultural and political arena.[5]

From the time of his 1959 arrival in Britain, Araeen has worked conceptually, producing painting, mixed-media construction, graphic art, and performance that dialogue with Western art history while simultaneously struggling against its hegemonic force. In "Preliminary Notes for a Black Manifesto," he argues:

Let us take the example of American Pop Art. What international significance is there in the images of Coca-Cola, Marilyn Monroe, Pin-ups, the American Flag, Hamburgers, etc.? These images, of course, are the *ethnic* images of American culture and there is no reason why they should not play a role in the development of her art. But when these very images are *universalized* through an international projection, their very function changes. . . .

The question of how to resist and confront domination, and the values/ forms which perpetuate it, becomes central here. . . .This cannot be achieved, however, by ignoring 20th century developments (in the West) and looking exclusively to our own past tradition for the solutions to our contemporary problems. . . . Modern knowledge now belongs to all humanity.[6]

His hopes for historically grounded, critical debates and oppositional visual culture are furthered by the article's illustrations (which, incidentally, he does not reference in the text): Benin bronze plaques held in the British Museum, the white American painter Jasper Johns's *Flag* (1954), a black-and-white photograph of an indigenous Australian artist sitting by a ceremonial ground painting, and two early mixed-media works by Araeen himself. *For Oluwale* (1971–73) accompanies the "Blacks in Britain" section of the essay; it is a collage of posters and pamphlets proposing action against institutionalized racism, pointedly named for a Nigerian immigrant killed by Leeds policemen in 1969. A subsequent section, "Towards Third World Art Movements," includes a cropped reproduction of Araeen's *Fire!* (1975) in which the U.S. flag is transformed by graffiti, flames, and bomber plane icons that symbolize the American militarist program in Southeast Asia (figure 1).[7] Modestly reproduced in black and white, these images constitute a primer for the pluralist discourse Araeen has sought for a global art history and an internationally engaged criticism.

If *For Oluwale* and *Fire!* stand at an antiracist, anti-imperialist, postcolonial nexus, "Preliminary Notes for a Black Manifesto" nonetheless steers clear of a prescriptive "black aesthetic," an idea frequently raised and never entirely defined in political, nationalist, and cultural movements throughout the African diaspora. Indeed, Araeen never used the phrase "black art" in the 1970s and 1980s, and after the ethnocultural and racial alliances formed in these decades collapsed in the 1990s, he found it necessary to restate the aim of institutional reform. In "A New Beginning: Beyond Postcolonial Cultural Theory and Identity Politics" (2002), Araeen embraces the widening critique that multiculturalism is "an attempt by neoliberalism to contain and displace the struggle of the deprived and oppressed," adding: "The struggle now is not just against what some 'black' artists in Britain used to call 'white institutions,' but with the system which now also includes black, brown,

Figure 1. Rasheed Araeen, *Fire!*, 1977. Photomontage. Courtesy of the artist

and yellow faces. It should therefore be clear that we cannot build solidarity only on the basis of race, culture, ethnicity or nation. Our new alliance should be with those who are committed to a genuine change and are prepared to enter into dialogue with us."[8]

Araeen also questions the exoticizing tendencies of multiculturalism, noting that critical responses to nonwhite artists' practices rarely address styles or creative influences, but instead focus on "Otherness . . . invoked both culturally and racially."[9] It is significant that in "Identity, Authenticity, Survival," Appiah raises a related question, asking, "If what matters about me is my individual and authentic self, why is so much contemporary talk of identity about large categories—gender, ethnicity, race, sexuality—that seem so far from individual?"[10] Appiah argues that identities—including those that precede the ones we fashion today—have always been shaped into unified narratives that facilitate individuals' identification with one or more collectives. The problem, he concludes, is that some "tightly scripted" identities undermine individual autonomy, for they expect each subject to perform a single way of being. Rejecting the confines of multiculturalism and its reliance on authentic blackness, Appiah and Araeen demand a recognition of the diversity of identities within difference, something that Hall has characterized as a hallmark of diasporas.[11]

As a work with four parts, Roshini Kempadoo's 1990 photo project *Presence* physically resists singularity and questions stable readings of modern, black female identities. Kempadoo (born 1959) appropriates the layout of the New York–based black women's monthly *Essence*, a magazine she read as a young woman growing up in the United Kingdom and in Trinidad and that she admired for its affirming images and its articles intended to inspire their audience with models for personal and professional success. Yet in the large-scale poster format of *Presence*, Kempadoo critiques the narrow, bourgeois ideal of black femininity marketed to women of the African diaspora around the world. In panel one of *Presence*, she destabilizes the "positive" tone of *Essence* and of women's magazines in general by presenting a color portrait of herself in which her expression is forlorn. Instead of the usual cover text that publicizes a magazine's articles, this first panel of *Presence* offers excerpts from an array of diasporic, feminist writings: poetry and prose by Maya Angelou, Debjani Chatterjee, Audre Lorde, Grace Nichols, and Sonia Sánchez. Kempadoo deploys the same parodic tactic in the other three panels of *Presence*, which look like the inner pages of *Essence* and feature a cheery ad, health and beauty advice, and a brief news item that celebrates women's workplace advancements (figure 2).

Although there are two other women of color photographed in *Presence*, Kempadoo's larger, reiterated form forms part of all four panels; even if viewers are unaware that she is the project's maker, she clearly emerges as its focal point.[12] Perhaps indebted to the white American artist Cindy Sherman's use of her own body in the theatrical Film Stills series of photographs of the 1970s, Kempadoo nonetheless

Figure 2. Roshini Kempadoo, *Presence* (panel 4), 1990. Color photograph, 48 × 34 inches.
Courtesy of the artist

pursues a different kind of iconicity in *Presence*. The embodiments that Sherman (born 1954) and Kempadoo create critique the confining gender and racialized roles propagated in popular media. The difference is that Sherman's body appears perfectly simulacral, for it references a popular cultural catalog of white, middle-class American female images of the mid-twentieth century, while Kempadoo's costume and changing form (clad in a mud-cloth print shawl in one panel and a white-collar businesswoman's jacket and skirt suit in another) do not. Kempadoo presents different versions of her body too: in the first and third panels of *Presence*, she appears with a mole above her left eyebrow; pictured again in the fourth panel, the artist sports the mole above her right eyebrow. Whether or not the fourth panel is an inverse print of the photographic negative—for Kempadoo has been photographed elsewhere with moles on one or the other eyebrow—her apparent goal is to draw attention to the manifest construction of images in art and life. She makes clear that, as Hall has put it, identity is production that is "constituted within, not outside, representation."[13]

In 1990, Kempadoo explained about *Presence*:

By centering myself as the black subject visually, it contributes to my constant redefining of the self or selves. Self-articulation still forms an integral part of my work but [it is] not the only strategy in use here. It links closely to the wider post-modern notion of identities that seems to be in use with most of the magazines on our shelves at the moment. The "self" is experienced as more fragmented and incomplete, composed of multiple selves or identities in relation to the different social worlds.[14]

In the same statement, Kempadoo also describes her ambition in *Presence*: to problematize and decode the societally produced and accepted models of black female respectability and identity that circulate across the African diaspora. In the fourth panel of *Presence*, Kempadoo sends up the widely marketed hair product Dark and Lovely with "before" and "after" pictures of herself and with text borrowed from Lorde: "Is Your Hair Still Political? / Tell Me When It Starts To Burn."[15] Confronted with the acid substance of Dark and Lovely and Lorde's acidic tone, viewers are compelled to ponder the placement of an ad for a painful and popular hair-straightening treatment in a magazine exalting black womanhood. Kempadoo's intention does not seem to be to bring down *Essence*, a formative influence on her and millions of black women, but rather, to draw attention to its participation in the transnational market economies of beauty culture focused on narrow notions of physical perfection. *Presence* problematizes identities and identifications, for its view of *Essence*'s paradigms of modern black womanhood is ambivalent. As an artist—that is, as one who produces representation—Kempadoo is likely aware of, if not empathetic toward, the magazine's authority to constitute a source and a site of authentic blackness.

Exhibiting Race: 1997, 2004, 2007

Museums, too, speak to and with institutional authority, and yet their products—exhibitions—often betray the difficulty of neatly framing complex, overlapping narratives in singularly articulated terms of identity and identification. Opened in Detroit's Midtown neighborhood in 1997, the Wright Museum of African American History has since mounted two core exhibitions that have proven contested sites for the representation of blackness.[16] The response to these shows—Of the People: The African American Experience and And Still We Rise: Our Journey through African American History and Culture—reveal much about the way the public expects the black experience and the African diaspora to be represented.

Of the People, the museum's first permanent exhibit, featured myriad things including dramatic *chi wara* (also known as *tyi wara*) headdresses that Bamana peoples have traditionally used to celebrate planting and harvest seasons, placards with capsule versions of African American slave narratives, and twentieth-century Ku Klux Klan hoods that document racist, Southern terror. But the first major object encountered on entering Of the People was a sculptural installation representing the seventy-seven-foot outline of a slave ship hold and its bent-over African captives rendered in gray plaster. These fifty figures were designed to put a human face on the Middle Passage and start off the narrative of diaspora. The exhibition designers clearly hoped that, flanked by these bodies and the facade hulls of the ship, the museum visitor—whether black or nonblack—would be emotionally and experientially thrust into the maw of history.[17] Yet neither visitors nor critics reacted favorably to this installation, and the slave ship re-creation became the most derided aspect of the Of the People exhibit. Polled museum audiences and focus groups mercilessly laid into it, finding the figures too healthy-looking to be slaves and their pallid forms insufficiently "black." Departing from the accepted convention of depicting all people of African descent as brown-skinned, "the gray boys," as they were called, were deemed inauthentic. Such responses speak volumes about the expectations for an agreed-on truth in representation and reaffirmations of reality, about the languages that we inherit and sustain, and about the images (conscious and unconscious) that we carry in our heads.

In 2003 the slave ship installation and the entire Of the People core exhibition was taken down. It was replaced the following year by And Still We Rise, a show that has been popular with audiences since its opening.[18] The "journey" is told over twenty-two thousand square feet of displays: maps of Africa; animated silicone sculptures of Harriet Tubman and Frederick Douglass; photos and illustrations of Detroit heroes, among them the city's first black mayor, Coleman A. Young, and the mid-twentieth-century white union leader Walter P. Reuther; and installations designed to replicate historical monuments and symbolic locales, such as the fifteenth-century Benin kingdom in West Africa, the Maryland harbor where the enslaved disembarked, and the mid-twentieth-century African American Detroit neighborhood called Black Bottom. Like the Of the People exhibition, And Still We Rise also offers a slave ship hold display. Visitors descend into this dimly lit space and discover chained, life-size, uniformly brown-colored sculptures lying on cargo tiers and the simulated sounds of a creaking vessel crossing the Atlantic with its suffering captives. This section of And Still We Rise, much like the exhibition as whole, offers a multisensory encounter with the familiar significations of the African diaspora and its narrative of sub-Saharan beginnings and American destinations. Its historical realism is, of course, a move away from the abstracted rendering of enslaved Africans as gray figures in Of the People. Yet as the cultural studies scholar Brent Hayes Edwards has argued, the term *African diaspora* befits studies of two related phenomena: "A complex past of forced migrations and racialization." In Edwards's view "the use of the term diaspora . . . is not that it offers the comfort of abstraction, an easy recourse to origins, but that it forces us to consider discourses of cultural and political linkage only through and across difference."[19]

In 2007, the Wright invited new questions about the meanings and consequences of racialization by hosting the traveling exhibition Race: Are We So Different? First mounted at the Science Museum of Minnesota in St. Paul, Race is undeniably a science show, replete with interactive computer programs and long audio and video presentations that situate the subject as a historical and ideological phenomenon. The exhibit complicated the U.S.-specific operations of and assumptions about race evident in And Still We Rise by broadly exploring its constructions. Fitting the exhibition's advertising tag line — "One piece doesn't tell the whole story. Come see the bigger picture" — race is variably explained by anthropologists, geneticists, and historians and represented by "everyday people" from Australia, Canada, the United Kingdom, and the United States who discuss their ethno-racial identifications and the ways they acquired them. Even whiteness, an understudied and normalized racial formation, is broached as a topic. The Wright's decision to host Race is a critically important one, for it investigates the foundations on which the museum was built, offering its visitors, as this exhibition's ad copy quoted above promises, more complex ways to conceptualize race both as symbolic knowledge and as lived experience.

Tired: The Colored Body (Now)

Although the essentialist formulation of blackness and the reductive rhetoric of "the black experience" remain stubborn obstacles that prevent the broad, political contemplation of race and racism in the United States, a number of artists are doing so by departing from more typical means of representing "colored" bodies in contemporary painting and drawing. While the body was an oft-visited site for postmodernist intervention in the 1980s and 1990s, Laylah Ali (born 1968) and Kojo Griffin (born 1971) are two African American artists who have turned away from this trend, treating the naturalized and idealized human form as an exhausted motif. Ali and Griffin embrace the cartoon's popular cultural status; each mimics its bright, decorative palette and static panel format. Ali's and Griffin's figures gesture and posture as humans do, but far from resembling everyday people, they look like aliens, animals, and stuffed toys. Simply put, Ali and Griffin do not "do" black bodies the way many artists of color have done in the past and presently, that is, naturalistically and mimetically. Furthermore, Ali's and Griffin's figures are neither legibly raced nor resolutely positive repudiations of racist stereotypes. At the same time, Ali and Griffin determinedly produce scenes of tension, psychic violence, and raised anxieties in individuals and groups where power is unevenly distributed and leveraged.

Ali and Griffin certainly are not the first artists to disrupt the grand narrative of race in modern, Western iconography. One predecessor is David Hammons (born 1944), whose silkscreen print *Rabbi* (early 1960s) confronts the phenotypical and social contexts that make race legible (see figure 3). Hammons used his own body to stamp the rabbi silhouette. The print is hazy, yet the visual signs are clear synecdoches for a Jewish stereotype: the implied texture of a beard, an index finger in a pointing gesture, and the outline of a skullcap. That is, these parts of the body in the printed image stand in for the corporeal and collective Jewish whole. Like Hammons's mixed-media print *Spade* (1974), Rabbi indicts us for our assumptions about and quick recognition of the supposedly Jewish form. Unlike *Spade*, which might be collapsed with Hammons's African American body, *Rabbi* provokes questions about the trustworthiness of racial appearances and the descriptive thinness of our ethno-racial lexicon.

Ali's and Griffin's ambitions also follow those of the white American artist Art Spiegelman (born 1948), who narrated family and Jewish Holocaust history in his graphic novels *Maus* (1986) and *Maus 2* (1991). The metaphoric intentions of Ali and Griffin, however, are more oblique than those created by Spiegelman, for there are no parallels to the Jewish mice and Nazi cats of the *Maus* books in these younger artists' works. Still they, like Spiegelman, often produce troubling images of exploitation. Strikingly, there is no particularity to the environments in which Ali's and Griffin's figures exist, which seems to indicate that they could be anywhere and within any nation's borders. In a small, untitled gouache on paper painting of 1999 by Ali, backdrops are empty and monochromatic, drawing extra attention to the foreground figures and their interactions (see figure 4). These figures—called "Greenheads" by Ali and blacks by others—are certainly forms with darkly shaded skins and cue-ball heads that resemble the racist Golliwog character. And because the Greenheads usually look panicked, fearful, and engaged in conflict, it is easy to see them as black people, as people of color in racist struggle against white domination and oppression. Ali's figures move us to think about blackness in two ways: as a universal sign that is both iconic and as a representational form that symbolizes domination, struggle,

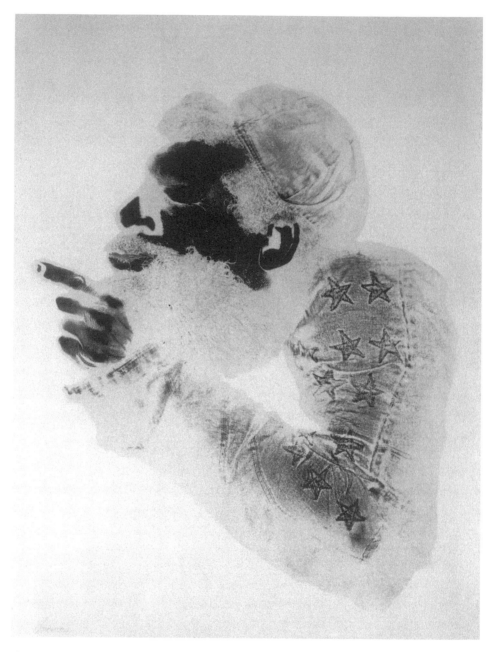

Figure 3. David Hammons. *Rabbi*, early 1960s. Mixed-media print, 28 × 22 inches. Formerly in the collection of La Monte and Dr. Martina Westmoreland. No longer extant

Figure 4. Laylah Ali. Untitled (Greenheads), 1999. Gouache on paper, 9 3/16 × 14 5/16 inches. Collection Museum of Contemporary Art, Chicago. The William B. Cook Memorial Fund 1999. Photo copyright Museum of Contemporary Art, Chicago

and resistance. Furthermore, Ali uses black and brown hues and greens that will not fit within the black-white dichotomy, hence displacing whiteness from the niche of universality that it has held throughout the modern period.

Expressive hue is also put to serious use in Griffin's art, where local color is not literally tied to raced bodies and his varied palette choices — painted purples, oranges, soiled beiges — exceed our present terms of racial description. Aware of the formulaic approaches to interpreting African American artists' production, Griffin, like Ali, provides no figures that could be readily read as black (or white or Asian or Native American), thus avoiding the search for and appraisal of racial content always presumed in nonwhite U.S. artists' work and rarely perceived in that of their white counterparts. Even more obvious is that Griffin's figures are animals or animalistic. Here, animals are not the romantic symbols of purity that they are, say, in the German expressionist art of Franz Marc (1880–1916). In Griffin's compositions, animals are neither higher nor lower than human beings, and of course, humans are not their masters. The take-away message is that we humans are not even masters of ourselves, of our desires, or of our fates. In the untitled collage painting of 2001 reproduced here, an adult-sized figure with an elephant head tempts a smaller form that is a bear in knee pants (see figure 5). It is an eerie mock-up of a pedophile approaching two children, and Griffin leaves the scene open-ended and without a comforting denouement.

Figure 5. Kojo Griffin. Untitled (Man Handing Candy to Girl), 2001. Mixed media wood on panel, 95 3/4 × 119 5/8 inches. Courtesy Mitchell-Inness and Nash Gallery, New York

Eschewing extended narrative, Ali and Griffin invite audiences to enter the brief incidents that they imbue with graphic immediacy. Their quirky figures earn our empathy in tragicomic vignettes of dominion, moral bankruptcy, and degeneracy, the acts of imperfect, frail beings. In sum, there is something leveling about their depictions, a quality they share with the superreal scene paintings of the 1990s by Kerry James Marshall (born 1955) and the silhouette wall tableaux that brought Kara Walker (born 1969) notoriety in the same decade. But different from Marshall's and Walker's embodied dramas that are tied to historical bodies, eras, places, and human subjects, Ali and Griffin move away from these specificities and try to picture transcendent realities. Actions communicate what Ali's and Griffin's characters—types, really—are about, requiring that we look beneath the surface of things for meanings that are more than skin deep.

To examine the structures of race and racialization, and in doing so, the insufficiency of authentic blackness, is not a retreat from black identification, embraced by Ali, Araeen, Griffin, and Kempadoo, and institutionally in name and mission by the Wright Museum. Nor do their interpellations of the essential black figure signal the postblack consciousness ventured by the African American curator Thelma

Golden in a 2001 essay.[20] Instead, figuration, variably conceived and deployed in the practices discussed in this essay, broadens and widens the discourse of identity, beyond the closures and restrictions that threaten to reify it.

Notes

1. K. Anthony Appiah, "Identity, Authenticity, Survival: Multicultural Societies and Social Reproduction," in *Multiculturalism: Examining the Politics of Recognition,* ed. Amy Gutmann (Princeton, NJ: Princeton University Press, 1994), 153; and Charles Taylor, "The Politics of Recognition," in Gutmann, *Multiculturalism,* 25–75.

2. This essay's title is inspired by the hit disco single "Got to Be Real," recorded by African American singer Cheryl Lynn in 1978. Music also inspired the title of this essay's first section, "U.K. Blak: 1978, 1990." Here the reference is to British singer Caron Wheeler's "U.K. Blak," a 1990 Top 40 single from the R&B album of the same name.

3. Stuart Hall, "Minimal Selves," in *Black British Cultural Studies: A Reader,* ed. Houston A. Baker Jr. et al. (Chicago: University of Chicago Press, 1996), 116.

4. Rasheed Araeen, "Preliminary Notes for a Black Manifesto," *Black Phoenix: Journal of Contemporary Art and Culture in the Third World* 1 (1978): 3.

5. Edward W. Said, *Orientalism* (New York: Pantheon, 1978); Frantz Fanon, *Peau noire, masques blancs* (*Black Skin, White Masks*) (Paris: Seuil, 1952).

6. Araeen, "Preliminary Notes for a Black Manifesto," 6, 10. Although they did not cite Araeen, the U.S. art historians Kellie Jones and Thomas W. Sokolowski were among the first to reveal black British politics to an American audience in their 1991–92 traveling exhibition Interrogating Identity, which included the art of Araeen and Kempadoo. The exhibition's catalog is titled *Interrogating Identity* (New York: Grey Art Gallery and Study Center, New York University, 1991).

7. In addition, the article reproduces a composed graphic from the British *Sunday Times* of January 23, 1977: a photo of the Egyptian president Anwar Al Sadat is juxtaposed to a chant heard in Cairo protests against his authoritarian rule: "Sadat, oh Sadat / You dress in the latest fashion / While we sleep 12 to a room" (Araeen, "Preliminary Notes for a Black Manifesto," 5).

8. Araeen, "A New Beginning: Beyond Postcolonial Cultural Theory and Identity Politics," in *The Third Text Reader,* ed. Araeen et al. (London: Continuum, 2002), 343, 342.

9. Ibid., 336.

10. Appiah, "Identity, Authenticity, Survival," 159.

11. "The diaspora experience as I intend it here is defined, not by an essence or purity, but by the recognition of a necessary heterogeneity and diversity; by a conception of 'identity' which lives through, not despite difference; by *hybridity.* Diaspora identities are those which are constantly producing and reproducing themselves anew, through transformation and difference" (Stuart Hall, "Cultural Identity and Diaspora," in *Identity, Culture, Difference,* ed. Jonathan Rutherford [London: Lawrence and Wishart, 1990], 235; emphasis original).

12. Kempadoo's contemporaries, the painter Gurminder Sikand and the choreographer Hilary Carty, are pictured in panel three of *Presence* and could be recognized by those familiar with London's black cultural scene in the 1980s and 1990s.

13. Hall, "Cultural Identity and Diaspora," 222.

14. Qtd. in "The Artists: Roshini Kempadoo," in *Interrogating Identity,* 118.

15. These lines conclude Lorde's poem "A Question of Essence," which was published in her collection *Our Dead behind Us* (New York: Norton, 1986) and has been republished in *The Collected Poems of Audre Lorde* (New York: Norton, 1997), 410. Lorde mentions "A Question of *Essence*" in an autobiographical essay, "Is Your Hair Still Political?" *Essence*, September 1990, 40, 110.

16. The museum's origins date back to the post–World War II era, when its founder, Charles H. Wright, began collecting African American and African visual and material culture. In 1965 Wright opened the International Afro-American Museum, operating out of his home and then out of a mobile home. Later, in 1985, Wright partnered with the city of Detroit to establish the Museum of African American History, which opened in 1987. A new structure was built on its current site in 1997 and was rededicated to bear Wright's name the following year.

17. Of the People: The African American Experience was designed by Ralph Appelbaum Associates of New York.

18. And Still We Rise was designed by Display Dynamics of Clayton, Ohio. The exhibition's seven animated sculptures—of Douglass, Tubman, and other historical figures—were made by Life Formations of Bowling Green, Ohio.

19. Brent Hayes Edwards, "The Uses of Diaspora," *Social Text* 19 (2001): 64.

20. Thelma Golden, "Introduction: Post. . .," in *Freestyle*, by Golden with Christine Y. Kim et al. (New York: Studio Museum in Harlem, 2001), 14–15. Often misinterpreted as a naive pronouncement of American racism's demise, Golden's imperfect phrase *postblack* sincerely attempts to characterize a number of African diaspora artists' investment in "complex notions of blackness" (14) in the late 1990s and a recognition of it.

New Provincialisms:
Curating Art of the African Diaspora

Leon Wainwright

Over the past decade there have been various curatorial attempts to assemble and understand the art of the African diaspora and to offer a more global sense of the histories from which such works emerge. The diaspora concept once promised fresh possibilities for imagining community beyond the nation; however, its internationalist emphasis has given way to a provincializing attitude grounded in United States–centered experiences. When art exhibitions are designed to mobilize the African diaspora and to reverse its traditional exclusion from art history and public memory, it is less clear whether such designs also prove capable of reversing the direction of this new provincialism. And yet, while the otherwise international relevance of the diaspora analytic has become susceptible to political and social priorities with a locus in the United States, much can be gained from interrogating the ways in which this locus generates new "margins" and "centers" in the world of art and blackness.

In Britain and the Caribbean such practices of provincializing can be seen with particular clarity. These Anglophone settings of the African diaspora stand apart from other European or South American ones, such as France or Brazil, because they are implicated in a shared language of curatorial practice and historical scholarship in relation to the United States. When United States–based attempts to increase the visibility of the African diaspora extend abroad, they penetrate these locations first and most freely. This is a pattern of influence that mirrors the Carib-

Radical History Review

Issue 103 (Winter 2009)   DOI 10.1215/01636545-2008-041

© 2009 by MARHO: The Radical Historians' Organization, Inc.

bean's long-standing status as an American leisure resort and a convenient laboratory for U.S. studies of culture and ethnicity.[1] In Britain, curatorial practices insti-
tutionalize the British-American "special relationship" in the field of the visual arts.
They also draw on the defining conditions and struggles of the North American
black experience. One example is the effort to "blacken Europe" by "making the
African American experience primary" in European history, a concern with foregrounding the presence of North American ideas and practices—namely, in the
areas of literature, social studies, politics, film, dance, and music—tracing how they
have traveled to Europe and changed some of the latter's traditional structures.[2] But
if this shares anything with what Paul Gilroy has described as an "Americo-centric
discourse" animated by "its extreme attachments to a reified notion of race," then
the prospect of historicizing an expanded, circum-Atlantic geography of the African
diaspora—traced out in the field of art—is slipping from view.[3]

The curatorial turn toward diaspora has not delivered a fresh framework for
thinking about art and blackness in any specifically international or transnational
way. This is not without the efforts and legacies of those who have shown the cour-
age to challenge the wider art history community for its weak participation in asking
how blackness is to be thought about and remembered. There was a moment when
attention to black popular culture and subsequently black visual culture seemed
to offer perspectives on the African diaspora that bore relevance beyond national
borders.[4] These concepts' impact on art history and museum practice opened up
entirely new critical areas, a discursive intervention of its time that reversed the
critical gaze onto curators and art historians through sustained institutional critique.
Yet this has been superseded by a more bounded, far less transgressive sense of the
significance of the African diaspora in the context of art and visual culture. In the
desire to seek out a definite break between diaspora and nationalism, sometimes,
as Aihwa Ong has warned, the "complicated accommodations, alliances, and creative tensions" that exist between them can be overlooked.[5] The most widely visible
frameworks for historicizing diaspora have been unable to maintain the separation
from the national necessary to ensure their analytical and strategic usefulness, and
spaces of curating are as much in danger of provincializing the African diaspora's
diverse geography.

As we attempt to bring to light the growing global influence of the United
States' domestic script on race, we can also recognize attempts by artists and curators
to turn this orientation around. Even as the display and historiography of art found
in the Caribbean and Britain share a familial proximity with those in the United
States, this hegemonic arrangement also elicits some dynamic tensions, and the project of reconceptualizing a creative (visual) community is taking some novel shapes.
Through curating and its concomitant practices of documentation there is the promise of dismantling and disavowing the hegemonic uses to which race and the diaspora
concept have been put as founding categories of art historiography. Much might be

gained from examining these competing areas of activity, as I do in what follows from the different directions of Britain and the Anglophone Caribbean.

Envisioning an American Locus for Africa:
An Emergent Provincialism in Curating Art and Artists of the Diaspora

What meanings should we draw from a London exhibition in 2005 that declared in its accompanying catalog that art and visual culture can help in "the rediscovery of Africa as black America's forgotten cultural locus"?[6] This was the leading premise for a major survey of the Black Arts Movement in the 1960s and 1970s, entitled Back to Black: Art, Cinema and the Racial Imaginary, staged at the publicly owned Whitechapel Gallery. Works by forty-seven artists, filmmakers, and photographers interacted over two gallery floors, filling the Whitechapel with a rich mixture of film and video, sculpture, print, text and image, photography, and painting. The ambition of its organizers—the freelance curators David A. Bailey of Britain and Petrine Archer-Straw of Britain and Jamaica, along with the Duke University–based art historian Richard Powell—was to elevate the African diaspora as a shared community of art and visual production implicating three national locations: the United States, Britain, and Jamaica.

A didactic sequence of themes was chosen for grouping the works: "Premonitions," "The World Is a Ghetto," "Tress/Passing," "Exploitation/Blaxploitation," "One Love," "By Any Means . . . ," and "Lost in Music/Through Space and Time." The largely black American experiences indicated by these headings, a narrative of black social protest and political struggles and victories, were corroborated best in artworks, film, and ephemera from North America. Less in evidence were categories and groupings with a more local relevance to the art from Jamaica and Britain. This was despite the international makeup of the exhibition's curatorial team, its London venue, and the several Atlantic locations from which its artworks were drawn. If indeed Africa was the site of black America's "forgotten cultural locus," as the show's curators argued, then Back to Black gave the overall impression that Jamaica and Britain were being assigned their cultural locus in black America.

The press responses to Back to Black in the United Kingdom were rather mixed. An entirely positive response came from the writer Sukhdev Sandhu in the art magazine *Modern Painters*. For Sandhu, the exhibition demonstrated that British and Caribbean artists of the 1960s to the 1970s were centrally "formative to the black Atlantic experience."[7] In contrast, another critic and photographer writing in the *New Statesman* confessed that he found the exhibition "deadly dull" and ridden with "cliché."[8] The main reason for his dismissal was that much of the North American art shown was already well known through popular reproductions: many of these works were by the best-known personalities of the North American black arts and music scene, and the exhibition featured them heavily in its publicity, in its main room, through a montage of album covers and video shorts, and in a compilation CD on sale in the gallery foyer. The prominence of these figures and works created a conspicuous disparity in emphasis. With much more established symbolic capital in the mainstream representational field, the North American material overshadowed the Jamaican or British works and asserted a far greater congruence with the exhibition's overall "black art" theme.

If displaying the North American images in the same exhibition space as works from the Caribbean did not achieve the outcome of a transfer of value or capital across the pieces, the same held true of the relation among visual works emphasizing elements of Rastafarian iconography and an accompanying verse from Bob Marley's "Redemption Song," enlarged on a gallery wall. Marley's text only thinly informed viewers of the complex biblical and Yoruba strands in works by the artist Osmond Watson, for example, in his three bas-reliefs in wood: *Madonna of Stony Gut* (1971), *Revival Kingdom* (1969), with its very subtly colored patina, and *Oguon, God of War and Metal* (1976), complete with metal inserts. The iconography of Marley's song also presented the difficulties of associating the exhibition's pieces with a visual record of Rastafarianism shaped much more by mass production and glib promotion. Additionally, if these works have yet to reach the wider attention of international art audiences, that desire was very much in competition with the more common associations viewers were likely to draw between the Jamaican art in the exhibition and tourism. Contributions such as Christopher Gonzales's messianic self-portrait, with subreferences to the tropes of Zion in his later wood busts, and Mallica "Kapo" Reynolds's paintings are the sort of items that visitors would easily find imitations of in Jamaica's Montego Bay, Ocho Rios, and various other entry points to the island from Caribbean cruise ships. The commercial status of these contexts—iconic North American black art, the market ubiquity of Jamaican musicians such as Marley, and the lingering resonance between certain artworks and tourist curios—meant that the Jamaican objects were assembled on an uneven plane.

The treatment of the British images in Back to Black failed to differentiate between British and North American black histories. A catalog essay by Mora J. Beauchamp-Byrd on Vanley Burke, the photographer of everyday scenes in the inner city of England's West Midlands, explored Burke's contribution in the context of connotations of the ghetto. This ghettoization both literally and figuratively frustrated the aim of bringing Burke's images out of a forgotten corner of art history. Subsequently, Beauchamp-Byrd's concluding claim was vague: "Above all, Burke's images reveal, in their startling range of expressiveness, how self-construction, pride and a tremendous sense of place may flourish, far beyond the boundaries marking those realms known (and variously represented) as 'ghetto life.' "[9] Reading these images from afar with an assumption of their racial exclusivity, Burke's "histograph" images as he calls them—scuffed terraces, Old World and penned in—might look just like shots of a ghetto, but this analysis alone ignores how black people in Britain have shared their neighborhoods and poverty with those of many other ethnicities, such as in Burke's Victorian working-class streets that are home to the poor of all kinds, or in postindustrial slums indifferent to any readable racial geography.[10]

Back to Black, according to its logic, could not engage productively with the fact that not all stories about creativity and blackness begin and end in the United States. The Back to Black exhibition catalog made generalizations that, during the period of the 1960s and 1970s, "there was an implicit recognition among most peoples of African descent," and "messages of national liberation, black power, black beauty and black pride became important all over the world during the period covered by this exhibition."[11] But the relationships of "equivalence" between North American, British, and Jamaican artists of various diasporas are more complex than this portrait allows. Back to Black did not attempt to show blackness when it has been renegotiated to meet local concerns, or when racial self-essentialism encounters serious strategic limits.[12] Since Britain's black art moment of the 1980s, market forces and public patronage have demanded representations of blackness that emphasize a recognizable version of cultural difference and diversity, one that would reify race in the art gallery and fracture the historical bonds of solidarity among British artists of many ethnicities.

As such, Back to Black broke from the curatorial custom of examining the degree of a given artist's identification with blackness. Equally, it avoided asking why certain artists have historically chosen not to identify themselves with such terms of difference. In so doing, it left aside conventions of documentation and display that would elucidate a distinction between contexts of visual meaning in the past and those of the present. Drawing on a cultural politics in which a concept of race is present but abstract, it elided the deep differences between issues faced by African American communities and those of minorities and imagined communities elsewhere. Rather than attempting to explore why these national histories are, perhaps predictably, mismatched, Back to Black elided discontinuities of experience and overemphasized the centrality of North American blackness for British and Caribbean art histories. If the exhibition became misleading on the historical value of its art, it weighed that loss against the gains of making a display of this scope accessible for the first time in Britain. Indirectly, Back to Black demonstrated that the most vigorous and best-resourced treatments of art of the African diaspora are those that bear the deep imprint of conditions and struggles over race and racism in the United States. The occasion placed that national setting at the forefront of the ways in which the remaining regions of the African diaspora are contemplating their art history and the discourses of race and blackness they are compelled to negotiate.

The Back to Black story of U.S. influences serves to place the Caribbean and Britain at an outer circle of black cultural identification. In this visual economy of blackness, a diffusionist model of black history passes unquestioned: a vision of black culture as emanating from a single place to take seed internationally, like a migration (or even a diaspora) of diaspora consciousness. This implies that certain regions of the African diaspora lag behind an ostensible vanguard of black cultural heritage epitomized at a North American epicenter. Its influence works along the same lines as the "modern blackness" or racialized vision of citizenship that Deborah Thomas has suggested took hold in Jamaica's public sphere during the late 1990s through youth culture and African American popular culture.[13] As a spatial-temporal scheme, this diffusionism is hegemonic, presenting art history and cultural modernity through a myth of a modernizing, progressive transition. If we are to take seriously what Dipesh Chakrabarty has suggested about historians of world history, that an underlying supposition "makes it possible to identify certain elements in the present as 'anachronistic,'" then curatorial spaces can also be complicit in ordering the African diaspora into reputedly "leading" metropolitan centers and belatedly "backward" and "secondary" peripheries.[14] Implicit in any such art display is the suggestion that those descendents of Africa who are not living within the shores of the United States should consider the advantages of adopting its modes of representation.

Tracing the Dynamic Geographies of Diaspora: The Lives and Works of Entwined Transnationalisms

Certain alternative curatorial approaches to understanding the works and artists of the African diaspora appear better able to describe key aspects of this multivalent form of creative experience. They purposefully steer away from vocabularies and terms of evaluation drawn from United States–based realities and the portraits resulting from such hegemonic approaches. By emphasizing those artistic subjects and artworks that physically connect or entwine Britain and the Caribbean, these alternatives radically expand the art historical record by transgressing its traditional attachments to nation and place.

In 1998, the very same Whitechapel Gallery of the Back to Black exhibition held a major retrospective of the career of the artist Aubrey Williams (born 1926), who made his first visit to Britain from British Guiana, now Guyana, in 1952. During the 1950s and 1960s Williams was dogged by the parochialism of London viewers who were unwilling to embrace his art without circumscribing or predetermining its significance, a phenomenon he struggled to overcome.[15] Williams's art was also included in the Back to Black exhibition, due to his ostensible place in the black diaspora. In 1998 that paradigm of belonging was treated very differently; in a retrospective of the artist that constructed him as embodying the very condition of transnationalism, the show not only undermined the older, parochial attitudes of Williams's London audiences but also contradicted the values of the new provincialism by refusing to place concerns with diaspora at the center of its historical analysis. The exhibition Aubrey Williams comprised a wide range of his works, including images of tropical flora and fauna and his three great series of abstract and figurative paintings: a body of canvases from 1969 to 1981 focusing on the chamber and orchestral music of Dmitry Shostakovich; his *Olmec-Maya* series (1981–85) reflecting on South American mythologies and the petroglyphs of Carib, Warrau, and Arawak peoples that he knew from the Guianas; and his *Cosmos* series from 1985.

Displaying the breadth of his practice, and supported by extensive biographical research, the Williams exhibition made it easier to see that Britain and Guyana have always had a peripheral status in the history of North American black art, as well as a different relation to blackness. The exhibition was a reminder of how Williams—like so many of his peers who had sojourned or settled in Britain to pursue their artistic futures—persisted in distinguishing himself from any overt or single racial identification. If the artist declared his entire career to have been an attempt to disentangle himself from a "European connection" ("All my life I have been trying to get rid of it"), he would also emphasize his mixed European, African, and Amerindian heritage, while the sophistication of his works themselves confounded a reading of any obvious racial identity.[16]

Another alternative to United States–based understandings of art and blackness can be found in the work of the Small Axe Collective. Founding members include the writer Annie Paul and the artist Christopher Cozier, both based in the Anglophone Caribbean, and the Jamaican-born political anthropologist David Scott. Positing a "Caribbean platform for criticism," a leading interest of the collective is to explore the sphere of visual creativity to disrupt a rendering of the Caribbean as a provincial zone. Its journal and curated online space have sought to promote an ongoing "conversation" about the region's postcolonial future, looking beyond the limits of an anticolonial and diasporic political and cultural architecture.[17] The collective presents the grounds for a refusal to be conscripted to local and national terms of historical explanation found within the Caribbean and resists paradigms of modernity imposed from outside the region.[18]

In September 2006 the Small Axe Collective met with a public opportunity to examine ways in which art in Trinidad might be brought into dialogue with prevailing attitudes around ethnicity, locality, and historical memory. This opportunity came with the launch of Galvanize, a series of artists' projects and events that happened alongside the largely state-funded, Caribbean-wide exposition Carifesta. Galvanize was not part of or in receipt of any of the allocated public money for Carifesta, and instead made resourceful use of an existing media base, including daily television interviews during the program's opening weeks, a mutually annotating web of Internet sites designed and written by publishing professionals, and features in globally distributed art magazines.[19] Assuming the title Visibly Absent, Galvanize set out to provoke thought on the strategies of racial and ethnic pluralism that have shaped anticolonial nationalisms in the Caribbean and that persist through representations such as Carifesta, Trinidad's annual carnival celebrations, and the island's local infrastructure for the arts and education.

Figure 1. External view of *La Fantasie*, a site-specific installation by Marlon Griffith, Jaime Lee Loy, and Nikolai Noel, staged in Port of Spain, Trinidad, on January 25, 2008. Supported by the Prince Claus Fund for Culture and Development. Courtesy of the artists/curators and copyright Georgia Popplewell, 2008.

A more recent curatorial project, *La Fantasie*, staged in Trinidad during late January and February 2008, further distanced contemporary artists from the ideologies that emerged in the Caribbean during decolonization.[20] Set in the former middle-class suburb of Belmont in the capital Port of Spain, the project used a single-story structure with added facings as an installation site to suggest a modest imitation of the wooden "jalousies" of an elite colonial residence (figure 1). Filling its darkened, nightmarish interior with place-specific works that combined photography, painting, and sculpture, its group of artist-curators invited visitors to enter at their peril using a handheld fluorescent light. *La Fantasie* was installed at 41–43 Norfolk Street, directly opposite the local constituency office of the country's ruling political party, the People's National Movement. This detail sharpened its deliberate affront to the liberal-rationalist fantasy of national prosperity that enervated the independence era: the dream of becoming urban and middle class and of owning a "Fantasie" home of one's own. In addition to the "underlying engagements with domesticity, settlement, abuse, and violence" of *La Fantasie*, the installation elaborated on the theme of an earlier video sequence created by Christopher Cozier in which repeating images of social housing units are played against a radio broadcast of Trinidad and Tobago's anthem.[21] Together these references to the politics of dwelling serve to question the value of Trinidad's scripted national development:

a planned racial pluralism that attempts to determine how ethnic differences are mapped onto the national landscape.

The contrast in meaning between the images of *La Fantasie* and the photographed streets of Vanley Burke in which black and white British subjects coexist could not be more pronounced. Yet such crucial discrepancies between these contexts in the African diaspora would not be conspicuous under a provincializing gaze. Whether in Britain or in Caribbean locations such as Trinidad, each of these projects indicates how curators and artists remain unconvinced of the expediency of placing blackness at the center of attempts to establish the historical sovereignty of art making and display, thereby differing from United States–based interventions in mainstream art history with their insistence on the theme of race. Theirs is a contribution to a more intersectional idea of art history that is missing from accounts of difference as either racial, or social, or gendered, and so on.[22] They ask what new questions emerge when the commas between these constructions are erased, making for a closer sense of how urgently visual encounters demand the comprehension of social relations and historical structures of power as permutated by multiple, conjunctive, and layered identities. In a related effort to go through and beyond the national, these initiatives have continued to explore collaborations that transcend the balkanized political geography of the African diaspora. Above all, they undertake to free art making and display from discourses of essential cultural or racial uniqueness, from the racialized vision of citizenship represented by the "modern blackness" that Thomas has observed. They trace out alternative transnational geographies that, from a provincializing perspective, have passed unrecognized.

Identifying such countercurrents begins to undermine the universalizing trend in curatorial representation in which certain nationally based conceptions of race, culture, and ethnicity are made to appear like a global rule. The repercussions of such universalism are being felt across the transatlantic African diaspora and deserve to be made transparent. Above all, it is the continuing reluctance of diaspora communities to misrecognize themselves in any "outside" image that animates negotiations with the new provincialism and that is most likely to shape their future within radical curatorial practice.

Notes

1. Mimi Sheller, *Consuming the Caribbean: From Arawaks to Zombies* (London: Routledge, 2004).
2. See, for example, Heike Raphael-Hernández, ed., *Blackening Europe: The African American Presence* (London: Routledge, 2004), 1–12.
3. Paul Gilroy, foreword to Raphael-Hernández, *Blackening Europe*, xvi. Gilroy's contribution to this volume is all the more fascinating for its cogent critique of the overall approach of its editor.
4. See Gina Dent, ed., *Black Popular Culture: A Project by Michele Wallace* (Seattle: Bay, 1992); Gen Doy, *Black Visual Culture: Modernity and Postmodernity* (London: I. B. Tauris,

2000); Michael Harris, *Colored Pictures: Race and Visual Representation* (Chapel Hill: University of North Carolina Press, 2003); Phoebe Farris-Dufrene, ed., *Voices of Color: Art and Society in the Americas* (Atlantic Highlands, NJ: Humanities Press, 1997); bell hooks, *Art on My Mind: Visual Politics* (New York: New Press, 1995).

5. Aihwa Ong, *Flexible Citizenship: The Cultural Logics of Transnationality* (Durham, NC: Duke University Press, 1999), 16.

6. Petrine Archer-Straw, David A. Bailey, and Richard Powell, eds., *Back to Black: Art, Cinema, and the Racial Imaginary* (London: Whitechapel Gallery, 2005).

7. Sukhdev Sandhu, "Say It Loud: Going Back to Black," *Modern Painters*, July–August 2005, 70–73.

8. Larry Herman, "Deadly Dull," *New Statesman*, July 4, 2005, 42–44 .

9. Mora J. Beauchamp-Byrd, "Everyday People: Vanley Burke and the Ghetto as Genre," in Archer-Straw, Bailey, and Powell, *Back to Black*, 182.

10. Mark Sealy, *Vanley Burke: A Retrospective* (London: Lawrence and Wishart, 1993).

11. Archer-Straw, Bailey, and Powell, *Back to Black*, 18; Paul Gilroy, "'No, I Do Not Have the Right to Be a Negro': Black Vernacular Visual Culture and the Poetry of the Future," in Archer-Straw, Bailey, and Powell, *Back to Black*, 168.

12. The term *black art* has a particular British history that the exhibition also ignored. As early as 1978, the presence of Pakistan-born Rasheed Araeen (a Black Panther, pamphleteer, artist-activist, and the author of *A Black Manifesto* [1978]) set in motion two decades of activity among other South Asian "black" artists for whom the U.S. Black Arts Movement offered blueprints for resistance on British soil. This period showed how the meaning of black art can be extended to include works by individuals both of the South Asian and the African diasporas. See Rasheed Araeen, "Preliminary Notes for a Black Manifesto," *Black Phoenix* 1 (1978): 3–12, reprinted in Rasheed Araeen, ed., *Making Myself Visible* (London: Kala, 1984), 73–97.

13. Deborah A. Thomas, *Modern Blackness: Nationalism, Globalization, and the Politics of Culture in Jamaica* (Durham, NC: Duke University Press, 2004).

14. Dipesh Chakrabarty, *Provincializing Europe: Postcolonial Thought and Historical Difference* (Princeton, NJ: Princeton University Press, 2000), 12. That spatial conceptions of "outsiderness" and the exotic in anthropological thought have been tied to temporal conceptions is examined at length by Johannes Fabian, who suggests that "the temporal discourse of anthropology as it was formed decisively under the paradigm of evolutionism rested on a conception of Time that was not only secularized and naturalized but also thoroughly spatialized. Ever since . . . anthropology's efforts to construct relations with its Other by means of temporal devices implied affirmation of difference as *distance*." Johannes Fabian, *Time and the Other: How Anthropology Makes Its Object* (New York: Columbia University Press, 1983), 16.

15. See Anne Walmsley, ed., *Guyana Dreaming: The Art of Aubrey Williams* (Coventry: Dangaroo, 1990); Anne Walmsley, *The Caribbean Artists Movement: 1966–1972* (London: New Beacon, 1992); Andrew Dempsey, Gilane Tawadros, and Maridowa Williams, eds., *Aubrey Williams* (London: Institute of International Visual Arts and the Whitechapel Gallery, 1998); see also Rasheed Araeen, "When the Naughty Children of Empire Come Home to Roost," *Third Text* 20 (2006): 233–39.

16. Williams qtd. in Walmsley, *Guyana Dreaming*, 61.

17. See the collective's Web site at www.smallaxe.net.

18. An account of the wider political history of this relationship with reference to modernity

is given in David Scott, *Conscripts of Modernity: The Tragedy of Colonial Enlightenment* (Durham, NC: Duke University Press, 2004).

19. The Galvanize project used a detailed and creative Web site presented in the format of a rolling diary of events and documentation (see projectgalvanize.blogspot.com). This was cross-referenced at the locally authored site of Caribbean Contemporary Art, Art Papers (artpapers.blogspot.com/), and in the program of film screenings (studiofilmclub.blogspot.com/), as well as on numerous other sites globally. Philip Sander, "Talking It Through," *Caribbean Beat* 83 (2007): 34–36; Courtney Martin, "Galvanize, Port of Spain, Trinidad," *Flash Art* 251 (2006): 46.

20. The artists who participated in the project were Jaime Lee Loy, Marlon Griffith, and Nikolai Noel, who together form the Collaborative Frog (see thecollaborativefrog.blogspot.com/2008/02/la-fantasie.html); see also Nicholas Laughlin, "La Fantasie," *Caribbean Review of Books* 15 (2008): 26–27.

21. The *La Fantasie* description can be found at thecollaborativefrog.blogspot.com/2008/02/la-fantasie.html. The video sequence reappears in the documentary by Richard Fung, *Uncomfortable: The Art of Christopher Cozier* (2005); see also Richard Fung, "Uncomfortable: The Art of Christopher Cozier," *Public* 31 (2005): 16; and www.digipopo.org/content/uncomfortable-the-art-of-christopher-cozier (accessed April 21, 2008). Aspects of the video are taken up in later work by the Trinidad artist Dean Arlen, and it is tempting to read Cozier's description of these houses as a comment on his own initial use of the motif. As he writes: "Ranks of little generic house shapes symbolize government-provided housing developments and imply the discomfort of the economically displaced, who also face new, unfamiliar social relations and environments." Christopher Cozier, "Boom Generation," *Caribbean Review of Books* 11 (2007): 21.

22. They share the approach of a special issue of *Signs*, "New Feminist Theories of Visual Culture," coedited by Jennifer Doyle and Amelia Jones, which insists on "the intersectionality of gendered experience as inherently, simultaneously, and irrevocably raced, classed, sexed, and so on." Doyle and Jones, "Introduction: New Feminist Theories of Visual Culture," *Signs* 31 (2006): 608. A related contribution made in the field of literary studies is Houston A. Baker Jr., ed., "Erasing the Commas: RaceGenderClassSexualityRegion," special issue, *American Literature* 77 (2005).

The African Diaspora Today:
Flows and Motions

Anthony Bogues

Wₑ live in a world of interconnections, of congeries that challenge both space and time. It is not that the center cannot hold, but rather that new centers are being formed. We live in a postapartheid, postcolonial (juridically), and post–civil rights moment as well, in which one main feature of our present is the wager of power that the planet will be flattened through the dominance of Western liberal civilization. In this moment, when white racial dominance seeks to reinscribe power by deploying itself as color-blind; when Africa's economic independence cannot simply be found by "seeking the political kingdom"; when the dream of Caribbean independence has floundered—how can one think conceptually and politically about this extraordinary category that we have historically called the African diaspora?

With reference to the peoples of African descent, Brent Hayes Edwards has credited George Shepperson's 1965 essay, "The African Abroad or the African Diaspora," with introducing the term *African diaspora* to the study of black cultural politics and history.[1] The African diaspora was the creation of the Atlantic slave trade. The forceful movement of millions of Africans into what became known as the New World transformed "African captives into Atlantic commodities," as Stephanie Smallwood reminds us. This transformation then effected another in which the African enslaved person was forcefully placed in regimes of racial slavery in the Atlantic world. The journey to the New World constructed the grounds for a third transformation, one in which the displacement of enslaved Africans from their original community turned into "disappearance . . . beyond both the physical and meta-

Radical History Review
Issue 103 (Winter 2009)   DOI 10.1215/01636545-2008-042
© 2009 by MARHO: The Radical Historians' Organization, Inc.

physical reach of kin. Would the exiles be able to return home . . . would their deaths take place in isolation? Would their spirits wander aimlessly, unable to find their way home to the realm of the ancestors?"[2] Due to these three sets of transformations, the search for origins and home would become central to black diasporic cultural practices and to black social and political ideas. The forced movement across the Atlantic created another history as well, one in which ideas about redemption and exodus into unknown lands became the meaningful imaginary landscape on which lives were lived and through which meanings sought, as black slave labor laid the material foundations for the modern world.

In these histories of the search for home and the redemptive power of exodus, movement is a singular feature and the image of the ship an important trope and signifier.[3] Newspapers, ships, and migratory moves made possible the blossoming of early twentieth-century radical political ideas about anticolonial struggles and black liberation. Throughout the colonial world and inside sites of racial domination there emerged a set of ideas about black liberation and anticolonial freedom that ranged from different forms of black religious nationalism to ideologies of black self-help, conceptions of black nationalism, notions of African nationalism, political action, and discourses that mixed Marxism and ideas of black liberation, pan-Africanism, and forms of black internationalism. When many of these ideas took root in a colony or at sites where racial domination was powerful, often they were influenced by ideas and practices that emerged from the activities of black radicals who had for whatever reason moved to major cities. From London, New York, Paris, Cape Town, São Paulo, and Moscow emerged a group of women and men who—sometimes independently, at other times in collaboration and then in competition—developed a set of political ideas about what would constitute black freedom. The complex character of this freedom occurred to some extent in dialogue with other radical ideas of the twentieth century, but it also had its own internal features in which a search for origins morphed into transnational links, and sometimes into diasporic collectives that promulgated world revolution led by black workers and colonial subjects; or into forms of religious black nationalisms in which the symbolic order of the West was overturned. In many of these movements and ideas, home was not a place of nostalgia but a horizon for new possibilities.[4] There was in twentieth-century radical black diasporic politics therefore both a looking back and a looking forward.

So what of the African diaspora today—how is its movement constituted, and what does that mean for contemporary radical politics? Are African diasporic communities now organized outside the origin points of geography in ways that belie investment not in homelands but rather in the desire to reinvent and reimage home? A reimaging that while drawing on some of the older ideas and politics of the African diaspora is different because the struggle for rights, for freedom, is not now connected to colonial geography but to the new global circuits of migratory labor? While space does not permit a full elaboration of these issues, I want to reflect on two things. The new, that is, how global circuits of labor may transform our think-ing about the African diaspora, and the old transformed, that is, how some of the configurations constituted by early diasporic histories today map themselves into new spaces.

In mapping a genealogy of Western cities Saskia Sassen makes the point that "today's global cities [are] the strategic sites for a whole new type of political actors and projects."[5] The new political actors in many of these cities are an African diasporic population. In London, Paris, Madrid, Rome, and many other cities the African diasporic population constitutes a central element of global labor whose struggles around questions of rights and citizenship have cracked open the con-ventional domains of liberal politics. This is not just a politics about immigration and race; rather it is about how the consequences of a historic wrong play out in today's world.

In the 1970s in the United Kingdom, one of the slogans proclaimed by the black movement was "We are here because you were there." This was an obvious ref-erence to the colonial relationship between Britain and the colonies. In part this slo-gan represented a historic shift in diasporic politics. Whereas black diasporic groups in England during the colonial period organized themselves around the ideas of political independence for the Caribbean and African colonies, today the struggles of the black population are about claims for rights *in* Britain. Of course, one cannot separate these claims from the heritage of colonialism, its racial order, and the shad-ows it cast over claims of rights and citizenship. But the main point is that the center of gravity of these claims is now within the former "mother" country. In France the situation is the same, and, as Étienne Balibar suggests, the lives of so-called immi-grants represent "a condition characteristic of the condition of subjects in opposition to that of citizens."[6] To put this another way, what is at work here are the ways in which colonial technologies of rule that were developed to create the category of the "native" are now deployed to construct African diasporan population subjects in global cities. Both the logic of capital and the rationalities of ruling combine to secure a ground where the African diasporic populations in these cities can be clas-sified by power as noncitizens and therefore treated without reference to rights.

In the United States in the so-called post–civil rights period, there are many African diasporas marked by specific nationalities and nation-states. Migratory pat-terns pushed by economic circumstances create a Caribbean diaspora that moves back and forth, while interaction with African Americans in the United States fur-ther complicates the notion of an African diaspora. Since the 1990s, the number of Africans moving to the United States has doubled, and within Africa, internal migratory movements among African peoples are increasingly becoming a central aspect of contemporary continental African life.[7] In Latin America, where there are by some estimates over 150 million people of African descent, the struggle for rights and against social exclusions continues in spite of legislation in many countries that supports multicultural citizenship. All these movements construct grounds for a new set of rights claims. In making these claims, however, these populations use languages that draw on the cultural politics of blackness created by the African diasporas of the past. Thus in many of these sites we find, for example, the influences of Jamaican Rastafarianism, African American music, and efforts to draw on the symbolic imaginary of black iconic figures of the 1960s as a new mapping and admixture of African diasporic cultural politics is created.

In relation to twentieth-century black radical diasporic thought, the African American intellectual Geri Augusto uses the phrase the "motion of the notion" to describe how ideas travel across borders, land, and then get readapted to local conditions, simultaneously creating forms of transnationalism. There were many such streams of black transnationalism, and one I wish to foreground here did not operate around the conception of individual nation-states but routed itself through a series of challenges to the global order. This transnationalism was an internationalism that expressed itself in the newspaper and the political practices of the International African Service Bureau (IASB), founded in London by George Padmore and C. L. R. James in 1937.[8] It can also be found in the pages of W. E. B. Du Bois's *Black Reconstruction*.[9] At the core of this internationalism was the idea that rights were not reposed in the artifices of citizenship but rather in the fact that there was a sociality to being human. This view elaborated itself again in the writings of Frantz Fanon in the early 1960s.[10]

Stuart Hall observed that one problem in thinking about diaspora is that we tend to "focus on its continuity and the return to its place of origins and not always and at the same time on its scattering, its further going out, its dissemination."[11] The historic black "experience" always recognized the need to make the world anew. Our present has not changed that recognition. What has changed are the conditions in which we must remake the world.

Notes

1. Brent Hayes Edwards, "The Uses of Diaspora," *Social Text*, no. 66 (2001): 51.
2. Stephanie Smallwood, *Saltwater Slavery: A Middle Passage from Africa to American Diaspora* (Cambridge, MA: Harvard University Press, 2007), 60.
3. See Paul Gilroy's *The Black Atlantic: Modernity and Double Consciousness* (London: Verso, 1993).
4. For a mapping of the ideas and movements of the African diaspora, see Édouard Glissant, *Caribbean Discourse: Selected Essays*, trans. J. Michael Dash (Charlottesville: University Press of Virginia, 1996), 258–59.
5. Saskia Sassen, *Territory, Authority, Rights: From Medieval to Global Assemblages* (Princeton, NJ: Princeton University Press, 2006), 281.
6. Étienne Balibar, *We, the People of Europe? Reflections on Transnational Citizenship*, trans. James Swenson (Princeton, NJ: Princeton University Press, 2004), 41.
7. For a discussion of African migration, see Manta Tienda et al., *African Migration and Urbanization: A Comparative Perspective* (Johannesburg: Wits University Press, 2007).

8. For a discussion of the political ideas of the IASB, see Anthony Bogues, "The Notion and Rhythm of Freedom: The Anti-colonial Internationalism of the International African Service Bureau," in *Twentieth-Century Internationalisms*, ed. Karin Fisher and Susan Zimmermann (Budapest: Promedia, 2008), 129–46.

9. W. E. B. Du Bois, *Black Reconstruction in America, 1860–1880* (1935; New York: Atheneum, 1969).

10. See the last chapter of Frantz Fanon's *Wretched of the Earth* (New York: Grove, 1963). In Providence, Rhode Island, in March 2008, there was a demonstration to support immigrant rights. One of the posters for the demonstration proclaimed that "no person is a non-citizen." The implicit argument here is that rights are rights and should not be conferred or taken away by power. It is an important argument since it suggests that we need to think about rights differently to collapse the distinctions between being a subject and a citizen. I would argue that this has been a central thread in black radical political thought.

11. Stuart Hall, "Epilogue: Through the Prism of an Intellectual Life," in *Culture, Politics, Race, and Diaspora: The Thought of Stuart Hall*, ed. Brian Meeks (Kingston, Jamaica: Randle, 2007), 284.

Blacks in European History

Tyler Stovall

Bernth Lindfors, ed., *Ira Aldridge: The African Roscius*. Rochester: University of Rochester Press, 2007.

Jacqueline Nassy Brown, *Dropping Anchor, Setting Sail: Geographies of Race in Black Liverpool*. Princeton, NJ: Princeton University Press, 2005.

Dominic Thomas, *Black France: Colonialism, Immigration, and Transnationalism*. Bloomington: Indiana University Press, 2007.

James A. Winders, *Paris Africain: Rhythms of the African Diaspora*. New York: Palgrave Macmillan, 2006.

Tina M. Campt, *Other Germans: Black Germans and the Politics of Race, Gender, and Memory in the Third Reich*. Ann Arbor: University of Michigan Press, 2004.

Heide Fehrenbach, *Race after Hitler: Black Occupation Children in Postwar Germany and America*. Princeton, NJ: Princeton University Press, 2005.

Extravagantly wide sidewalks with splendid trees marching along the curbs; beautifully laid out boulevards, avenues, and streets with fascinating names; lovely quiet shabby sections reeking with historical associations. . . . In such a setting, who would think of Negroes?
— Eslanda Goode Robeson, "Black Paris"

Radical History Review
Issue 103 (Winter 2009) DOI 10.1215/01636545-2008-043
© 2009 by MARHO: The Radical Historians' Organization, Inc.

Who indeed? In this 1936 description of Paris Eslanda Goode Robeson posed a challenge that historians have only recently begun to consider. Issues of blackness, and of racial difference in general, have played a small role in the historiography of Europe. For much of the historical literature, blacks existed in Africa or in the Americas: not for nothing have many undergraduates referred to European history as the study of dead white males. The most obvious reason for this tendency, of course, has been the small number of peoples of African descent on European soil. Yet as Robeson's quote suggests, the idea that blacks are foreign to Europe is rooted in racialized notions of civilization itself. If Europe stood for enlightenment and progress, then how could a people so often associated with barbarism be a part of it? At the same time, if the construction or reconstruction of an independent black consciousness meant rejecting European hegemony, then exploring the links between blackness and Europe became theoretically and politically problematic.

The past few years have witnessed renewed attention to the role of blacks in European history, challenging tendencies to construct Europe and blacks as opposites. A number of conferences, in both Europe and the United States, have taken place on the subject, and an institute for the study of black Europe, the Black European Studies Program (BEST), now exists at the Johannes Gutenberg University in Mainz, Germany. This surge of interest in black Europe reflects a significant change in scholars' approach to the study both of European history and of the black experience. The rise of diasporic conceptions of blackness, arguably the dominant intellectual trend among African American studies departments today, has shifted attention away from the black experience in the United States toward a more cosmopolitan vision of the field. Initially focusing on relations between Africa and the Americas, black diaspora studies has created a space for new investigations of the presence of peoples of African descent in Europe as well by embracing the diversity of blackness in all its forms. In addition, the historiography of Europe now gives much greater emphasis to the impact of colonialism and racial difference on European societies. In my own field, French history, roughly half of the PhD students in American universities today are pursuing colonial topics for their dissertation research. New interest in immigration, postcolonialism, and transnationalism have combined to energize interest in the histories and experiences of Europe's black minorities.

The six books reviewed in this essay all address the condition of blacks in European societies, both yesterday and today. One should note that, in spite of this field's significant roots in transnational approaches to history, all are based in specific national experiences, underscoring both the strengths and limits of diasporic analysis. At the same time they all share certain basic themes that speak to a common black European experience and that differentiate it from that of other parts of what Paul Gilroy has termed the Black Atlantic. All deal with societies that had no tradition of African slavery on their own national territory (although of course it often existed in their colonies). All analyze black populations not only much smaller than those found in the Americas but also frequently lacking any sense of community. Perhaps most noticeably, many if not all discuss people defined as black who are of mixed-race heritage and who sometimes did not even know their black fathers or any other black relatives. Perhaps more than other histories of the African diaspora, the study of black Europe pushes the limits of how we define blackness in general. Finally, in many of these texts one can discern a powerful commitment to the notion that blacks have a history in Europe, a rejection of the view of them as outsiders. Even though most of these studies privilege the period since 1945, when large black populations arose in many parts of Europe, they do frequently address the legacies of those who had come before. As a result, even an anthropologist like Jacqueline Nassy Brown, who clearly has her own issues with history writing, found herself pressured time and time again by her respondents to engage with the historical record. Clearly, for many black Europeans themselves, writing their history is a political act that challenges exclusion and bigotry in the name of a more cosmopolitan idea of Europe.

Of the three nations under consideration here, Britain's black experience is certainly the most familiar. Not only does Britain possess the largest population of African descent in Europe, thanks to its leading role in colonizing Africa and the Caribbean, but black British writers like Stuart Hall, Gilroy, and Hazel Carby have provided the intellectual leadership for African diaspora studies. The two books that deal with Britain, Bernth Lindfors's *Ira Aldridge* and Brown's *Dropping Anchor, Setting Sail*, approach what it means to be black and British in strikingly different ways. Lindfors's edited volume gives a multifaceted view of Ira Aldridge, an actor of African American origin who became one of the leading stage performers in England and Europe during the nineteenth century. Like other studies of black Europe, this book considers the important roles played by black expatriates from the United States. Born in New York in 1807, Aldridge made his debut on the London stage in 1824 and then carved out a successful acting career, unprecedented for a black man in Europe or America, until his death in 1867. He became widely known as the African "Roscius," following a reference to the classical Roman actor Quintus Roscius Gallus used at the time to characterize leading members of the profession. Lindfors includes a wide variety of essays in the volume, both ones written at the time about Aldridge and recent studies of the great actor, so that the book constitutes a minihistoriography not just of Aldridge but also of black Britain and British society in general in the nineteenth century. In the main, the essays dating from the nineteenth century emphasize Aldridge's renown and his achievements not only as an actor but also as a fighter for racial tolerance. In contrast, the more recent essays use Aldridge as an example of performativity and race, and his career as a window into contemporary British ideas about racial difference.

A few main themes emerge from these essays. One is the marked tendency of Aldridge to invent and reinvent his own story, both onstage and off. Like another African American who would triumph on the stages of Europe a century later, Josephine Baker, Aldridge presented ambiguous accounts of his life story, alleging, for example, that he was the son of an African prince who had fled to the United States. Moreover, his portrayal of both tragic and comedic roles on stage, not to mention of both white and black characters and his frequent use of blackface makeup, created a body of work that challenged and unsettled normative ideas about blackness. Another issue central to Aldridge's career is the contrast between the acclaim he received throughout provincial Britain (and much of Europe) and his lack of success in London. This contrast complicates the classic narrative of the African American who flees racism at home to find an enthusiastic and color-blind reception overseas. Finally, the essays consider what Aldridge's career says about racial thinking in contemporary Britain. Some authors note how *Othello* functioned as a mirror for changing attitudes. This was a play that made English society uncomfortable as racial thinking became more pronounced there, so much so that it was often changed into a color-blind tragedy or even a farce. Yet it was during this period that Aldridge became the first black man to play the title role of Shakespeare's great tragedy, and it became one of the staples of his dramatic repertoire. The story of Aldridge thus exemplifies the complex interplay between the racial codes of a society and the ability of an individual to represent and sometimes subvert them.

In general, *Ira Aldridge* presents a complex and nuanced portrait of its subject, drawing on many different perspectives. Unfortunately Aldridge's own voice is missing from the story, and there is virtually no attention to other black actors, or blacks in general, in nineteenth-century Britain. Yet still the book succeeds in going beyond a simple praise of an extraordinary individual to analyze what his career reveals about the possibilities and limits open to black Britons in the Victorian era.

We get a very different view of black life in Britain from Brown's *Dropping Anchor, Setting Sail.* An ethnography of black life in the important port city of Liverpool during the 1990s, *Dropping Anchor, Setting Sail* wrestles with how to conceptualize black identity in late-twentieth-century Britain. Brown is very well versed in diasporic debates about blackness in international contexts and deftly critiques Gilroy's attack on the nation-state as the primary locus of black culture. Instead, she emphasizes the role of place as seminal to the creation of black consciousness in Liverpool. Because Liverpool was until recently such an important seaport, one that centuries earlier was heavily involved in Britain's slave trade, "local" life in the city is intrinsically global, thus enabling the scholar to theorize local life from a transnational perspective. At the same time, Brown demonstrates how the stress on locality is very much an English characteristic, one that serves to ground black Liverpool in national culture.

At the heart of Brown's analysis lie the so-called LBBs, or Liverpool-born blacks. This term refers to place but also to more than place. LBBs are generally those blacks born in Liverpool to black fathers (usually sailors or port workers) and white mothers. The specificity of this identity is telling, for it does not include all peoples of African descent in Liverpool, and at the same time it embraces many whites (most notably the white mothers of black children). Such a community is both inclusive and exclusive at the same time: it rejects the concepts of "mixed-race" or "half-caste" in favor of identification as black, but at the same time it does not include people with different types of black identity. Brown points out tensions between the LBBs and peoples of Afro-Caribbean descent, two groups that despite commonalities seem to identify as separate constituencies, and notes how the LBBs' insistence that they are not immigrants but products of Britain can lead them to reject foreign-born blacks. As in *Ira Aldridge*, so, too, in *Dropping Anchor, Setting Sail* do African Americans play an important role in the history of blacks in Britain. Not only do many in Liverpool see black American culture as a template for blackness but locals remember both the African American servicemen stationed there during World War II and the many black Liverpool women who immigrated to the United States. As this latter point makes clear, differences of race and gender interact to produce ideas of blackness in Liverpool. Brown uses these gender distinctions to show how a certain diasporic romanticization of travel and displacement tends to leave out the women left behind. Finally, a central concern for many LBBs is mapping their own history and presence onto the identity of the city as a whole.

In general, Brown presents a portrait of a British black community shaped by notions of place yet also caught in a web of transnational relations, both past and present. It is a black community that is interracial and internally variegated, both inclusive and exclusive. *Dropping Anchor, Setting Sail* does not presume to give a complete account of blacks in Liverpool: it would be interesting to know why Brown chose to focus on the LBBs as opposed to other blacks in the city, and some sense of the relative size of these different black populations would prove very useful. In considering this text alongside Lindfors's, one comes away with a sense of black British history as transnational in scope, befitting the global reach of British power and empire in the modern period, very diverse in terms of black experiences, and usually pushed to the margins of national identity. As both Lindfors and Brown make clear, the challenge lies in creating new ideas about Englishness that would give space for the articulation of this history both within and beyond the national framework.

Similar considerations arise when one crosses the English Channel. France's history has involved many intersections with black experiences, yet many French strongly resist considering racial difference as part of the country's national narrative. On the one hand, the many contributions of France to the African diaspora range from the Haitian Revolution and literary theories like negritude and *créolité* to the revolutionary anticolonialism of Frantz Fanon. No nation has proven more attractive to African American expatriates than France, and these exiles became key exponents and symbols of the idea that this was a nation that knew no racial prejudice. On the other hand, the color-blind ideal, a central component of republican universalism, has not only made it difficult to measure the extent of racism in France but has also tended to render black and other minority populations invisible. France thus presents a paradox: a nation with strong black traditions whose reputed tolerance has often been held up as a mirror to American racism, yet at the same time one that has generally refused to recognize the existence of racial minorities as a part of what it means to be French.

The two books on France considered in this essay, Dominic Thomas's *Black France* and James Winders's *Paris Africain*, have much in common. Both deal with very recent history, essentially the last quarter of the twentieth century. Both analyze the intersections between race, blackness, and the creative arts, literature for Thomas and music for Winders. Both give priority to blacks from Africa, although they at times refer to the Caribbean diaspora in France. Finally, both take a transnational approach to the study of blacks in France, grounding their work in the broader contexts of French colonialism and the African diaspora. In *Black France*, the Francophone literary scholar Thomas approaches his subject as a classic example of local culture in a global context. Analyzing African literature written in French by writers residing in France, Africa, or both, Thomas deploys transnationalism to call into question ideas of "minority" cultures and indeed traditional ideas of French identity in general. Noting that in recent years many of France's top literary prizes have gone to Francophone writers, he argues that France and Africa are inextricably intertwined and that at the same time Paris in particular continues to fascinate and lure African intellectuals. *Black France* focuses on immigrant literature, but rather than portraying the assimilation of blacks into French culture, Thomas uses this work to give a globalized, diasporic account of contemporary French identity.

The heart of Thomas's study consists of analyses of specific novels written by African writers in France. Because he insists on the salience of colonial legacies in the postcolonial era, Thomas devotes one substantial chapter to novels written before African independence, arguing that black immigration to France was central to the colonial era. The bulk of the text, however, deals with postcolonial France and shows how African writers negotiated the intersections between France and Africa, in the process creating a new transnational culture. Thomas both provides fine capsule analyses of these novels and uses them to illustrate broader questions of black life in France. One chapter, for example, addresses the extremely sensitive question of female excision in African communities in France, showing how writers confronted the feminist, traditionalist, and other perspectives that shaped debates about this issue. Another deals with *la sape*, the neodandy fashion movement launched in Paris by young Congolese men that complicates normative images of African immigrants in France. Thomas's focus on literature leaves unanswered some questions that might interest historians, such as the overall profile of African communities in France and their relationship to other blacks and to other immigrants. Yet this is not the concern of the literary scholar, and *Black France* skillfully shows how black culture is transforming a central aspect of French identity.

Winders looks at the impact of African immigrants on another type of culture, popular music. *Paris Africain* gives the first systematic history in English of the phenomenon known as world beat or Afropop. During the 1980s, Paris in particular became the center of a new style of African music, one oriented toward global markets and drawing on traditional African, African American, and other "ethnic" styles. Musicians like Salif Keïta, Alpha Blondy, and Touré Kunda made the French capital an international pop music center briefly rivaling London and Los Angeles. Both increased African immigration to France, and changes like the deregulation of French radio in the early 1980s (the birth of the famous *radios libres*) drove the new African music scene in France. As Winders notes, although African music has remained popular in Paris, the glory days of the 1980s have faded, in part due to the increased commercialization of the global music industry. In response, world beat music has become more truly transnational, as musicians travel between Dakar, Paris, New York, and other music centers.

Winders focuses on the relationship between African music and African immigration. *Paris Africain* sees the rise of substantial African immigration to Paris in the 1970s and 1980s as key to the origins of Afropop and argues that after 1990 a harsher climate for immigrants limited the attraction of France for Africans in general, musicians or not. Yet his story is not so simple, for he also considers the paradox between the French love for African music and their resistance to the presence of Africans in France. Winders gives an overview of some of the main conflicts over immigration in France recently, including the movements for the rights of undocumented aliens, the expulsion of African asylum seekers from Parisian churches, and the struggles over the wearing of the veil by Muslim women. More attention to the conditions of African life in Paris would have made this a richer book, as would a more in-depth study of those who listen to this music, both in France and abroad. Ultimately, like Thomas, Winders portrays African culture in France as both marginal and central to contemporary French identity.

The last two books reviewed in this essay address the history of blacks in Germany. To a greater extent than in Britain or France, blacks have historically been a tiny minority in Germany, which played no role in the slave trade or the colonization of the Caribbean and a relatively minor one in imperial rule over Africa. To a greater extent than elsewhere, many blacks in Germany have been of mixed-race heritage, often raised by single white mothers who only rarely lived in black communities. The influence of black Americans—as fathers, members of foreign occupation armies, and symbols of blackness in general—has been especially pronounced. Finally, in

few other European nations has the politics of race been so central to national identity, thanks to the Nazi era and the Holocaust. Germany thus is a nation where race
and blackness have had separate (if not entirely distinct) histories.

Tina Campt's *Other Germans* and Heide Fehrenbach's *Race after Hitler*
discuss different aspects of Afro-German history in the twentieth century. Interestingly, both texts, and much of the historiography of black Germany in general,
deal heavily with childhood and memories of childhood, a theme absent from the
other works reviewed here. One knotty methodological question that emerges is
how to analyze the history of childhood memories when the process of becoming
an adult in part consists precisely of forgetting how to view the world and one's own
life through the eyes of a child. Campt confronts this issue in her study of black
Germans in the Third Reich. In *Other Germans*, she looks at the question of race
in Nazi Germany by considering the experiences of blacks rather than Jews, arguing
that this provides new insights into the history of racial thinking in general. Campt
shows how Germany's colonial experience in Africa created laws and practices concerning race relations and how the Nazi regime adopted and deepened them. She
highlights the tragic history of the so-called Rhineland bastards, those children of
German women and French colonial soldiers born after World War I. Roughly half
of them were sterilized by the Nazi regime, yet the Nazis never tried to exterminate
them systematically, in contrast to the Jews. Campt shows that the racism of the
Third Reich was not uniform, but varied according to the communities targeted and
their specific histories in Germany.

The heart of *Other Germans* is its use of oral history, analyzing the testimonies of two Afro-Germans, Hans Hauck and Fasia Jensen. This is the most innova-
tive part of the book, and at the same time the most problematic. Campt addresses
the problem of writing a historical study based on the memories of only two individuals, yet she does not convincingly answer the objections that most historians
would raise. She treats and analyzes the testimonies as memory texts and does a
good job of exploring their silences as well as their statements. However, the reader
still comes away feeling that she or he knows relatively little about these individuals
and about how they conceive of their lives as a whole. As a result, *Other Germans*
provides neither the systematic sweep of conventional histories nor the deep personal analysis of the best biographies. In an epilogue Campt explores how the Afro-
German experience reshapes our ideas about the African diaspora in general and
considers within that context the relationship between Afro-Germans and African
Americans. Of all the books considered in this essay, Campt's poses these questions
most directly, and they certainly deserve much more analysis.

In *Race after Hitler*, Fehrenbach focuses on the decade or so after World War
II and the fate of mixed-race children born to German mothers and African American fathers, soldiers in the American occupation forces in West Germany. She takes
an explicitly transnational and comparative approach, considering the responses of

both Germans and Americans to these children. Like Campt, Fehrenbach explores the relationship between Nazi anti-Semitism and views of blacks. She notes that because the defeat of the Nazi state effectively outlawed anti-Jewish sentiments, racialized discourses shifted to blackness. Moreover, the discriminatory practices of the American armed forces in Germany in effect taught the Germans that racism and democracy could go together, while at the same time reinforcing already existing negative views of blacks.

Race after Hitler deftly explores the nuances of racial thinking and practices in West Germany after the war, showing how Germans could both see Afro-German children as a problem and as not really German while still giving African American soldiers much more respect than they were used to receiving at home. She notes, for example, that many of these children were raised by single mothers because American authorities resisted both allowing African American soldiers to marry German women and the attempts of blacks to adopt these children and bring them to the United States. At the same time, Fehrenbach describes the West German obsession with the roughly three thousand German children of black American GIs, often resulting in tolerance of the (ostensibly inferior) Other, rather than full-fledged integration into mainstream German life. As a result, blackness assumed a new centrality in German racial thinking. Unlike Campt, Fehrenbach devotes little attention to oral history, so one misses the voices of these children and of their parents, both American and German, in this text. Nonetheless, *Race after Hitler* is an important addition to the history of Afro-Germans, and to the transnational history of race in general.

In conclusion, these six works, and others like them, give us new and sometimes startlingly different takes on the nature of both European and black identities. They have expanded the boundaries of both black studies and European history and, more important, have forced them into dialogue with each other. More than anything else, this is both the challenge and the promise of histories of black Europe.

Centering Africa in African American Diasporic Travels and Activism

Dayo F. Gore

James T. Campbell, *Middle Passages: African American Journeys to Africa, 1787–2005*. New York: Penguin, 2006.

Kevin K. Gaines, *American Africans in Ghana: Black Expatriates and the Civil Rights Era*. Chapel Hill: University of North Carolina Press, 2006.

Marie Tyler-McGraw, *An African Republic: Black and White Virginians in the Making of Liberia*. Chapel Hill: University of North Carolina Press, 2007.

Long-standing calls to internationalize U.S. history have produced a new wave of scholarship that examines the African continent as a central site of engagement for African American activists and U.S. foreign policy.[1] These new studies have forced scholars to address the hegemonic image of Africa as the monolithic and under-developed "dark continent" defined by the lasting legacies of colonialism and the continued realities of neocolonialism. Moreover, as scholars rethink the meanings and methods of diasporic studies, questions about definition, terminology, and the historical specificity of local and global interactions have emerged as central points of inquiry.[2]

James T. Campbell's *Middle Passages: African American Journeys to Africa, 1787–2005*, Kevin K. Gaines's *American Africans in Ghana: Black Expatriates and*

Radical History Review
Issue 103 (Winter 2009)   DOI 10.1215/01636545-2008-044
© 2009 by MARHO: The Radical Historians' Organization, Inc.

the Civil Rights Era, and Marie Tyler-McGraw's *An African Republic: Black and White Virginians in the Making of Liberia* each reflect key aspects of this new scholarship. All three works train a historical lens on African Americans who traveled to a variety of African countries and uncover how such travels positioned the African continent as a crucial site in debates over African American citizenship, white supremacy, and transnational affiliations. In addition, these works address central questions shaping African diasporic studies as they each trace the shifting political and cultural meanings African Americans (and the Western world) have mapped onto Africans and the African continent.

The broadest and most ambitious of these three works is Campbell's *Middle Passages*. As the first publication in the Penguin History of American Life series, the work is geared toward a general audience. The study employs the brutal transatlantic voyage of over 12 million Africans from the continent to slavery in the Americas as its framing device and traces the legacy of this forced migration through the numerous return voyages taken by Africans and their descendants in the United States. *Middle Passages* opens with a prologue recounting Abuya Suleiman Diallo's 1730 transatlantic journey into slavery and his unlikely return voyage to London and eventually back "home" to the Bondou region of Africa. The remaining chapters track the varied experiences of African Americans who also made this transatlantic "return" voyage. Most of the chapters revisit well-known travel accounts including African American colonization of Liberia, the black nationalist inspired emigration efforts of Henry McNeal Turner and Martin Delany, William Sheppard's missionary work in King Leopold's Congo, and Ghana's magnetic pull for African American radicals during the 1950s. The book also includes less familiar stories such as the conflict between W. E. B. Du Bois and George Schuyler over U.S. support for Liberia during the 1920s and the more contemporary travel narratives of black journalists who covered crises in Africa during the 1990s, from the Ebola virus to Rwanda.

Campbell's engaging narrative and writing style fits well with this sweeping history. He succeeds in drawing the reader into each of these journeys while still addressing overarching themes. Moreover, Campbell demonstrates an impressive scholarly breadth and provides an important historical account of shifting transnational relationships. The book's historical narrative addresses the impact of white supremacy and imperialism while also making visible African Americans' and Africans' agency and engagement with these forces. This becomes clear in the opening pages of Abuya's story, which documents the complexities of African participation in the slave trade without discounting the ways Europe's "opening of transatlantic trade radically transformed the institution's scale and character" (9).

While Campbell's work is clearly grounded in exploring how "the perplexities of black life in America would play out on the terrain of Africa" (370), he is also invested in African history and in making visible the "neglected African perspective" (428). This reflects one of the greatest strengths of *Middle Passages* as it emphasizes the diversity of Africans on the continent and gives meaning to the range of ethnic affiliations and political diversity that African Americans encountered in Africa. Moreover, challenging perceived common knowledge, *Middle Passages* provides crucial correctives to many of the myths and misconceptions that persist about Africa and black diasporic relations.

One of the drawbacks of this powerful synthesis of African American travel is that it marginalizes the voices of black women travelers. Campbell briefly addresses the goal of "uplifting African women" that informed the missionary work of the black women who joined William Sheppard in the Congo and provides some coverage of the journalist Era Thompson's travel writings. Yet he only mentions Eslanda Robeson's extensive travels in Africa as an aside and gives limited attention to the vibrant community of African American women in Ghana. For the most part, we learn little about how African American women negotiated a range of diasporic encounters or about the ways long-standing and explosive debates over African American womanhood and sexuality played out on the African continent.

Gaines's monograph *American Africans in Ghana* stands as one of the defining studies of African American expatriate life in Ghana. Gaines's work examines the brief ten-year span that marked Kwame Nkrumah's rise to international prominence as the first black leader of Ghana and as a leading advocate of pan-African solidarity. Tracing the multiple alliances that tied black activists on three continents to Ghana's anticolonial struggle and to Nkrumah's nation-building efforts, Gaines details the political vision, ideological debates, and global politics that drove black transnational solidarities during the post–World War II years.

Nkrumah's multivoiced calls for pan-African solidarity proved attractive to a diverse range of activists from the staunch pan-African anticommunist George Padmore and the newly minted Communist Party supporter Shirley Graham Du Bois to black power advocates like Malcolm X and a liberal-leaning (but clearly left-affiliated) Pauli Murray. In tracing the community of black activists who found hope and inspiration in Ghana, the study examines the experiences of major figures including Padmore, Martin Luther King Jr., W. E. B. Du Bois, Richard Wright, and Malcolm X as well as some lesser-known activists such as Julian Mayfield and Bill Sutherland.

Highlighting the influences of mass migration, industrialization, communist internationalism, and Third World anticolonial struggles, Gaines uncovers the shared history of travel, exchange, and resistance that helped tie black activists and intellectuals in the Caribbean, the United States, and Europe to Africa's battle for independence. For Gaines, these solidarities can only be fully understood through the histories of political and social movements that connected black diasporic intellectuals and activists and the "specificity of political projects, lived experience and emancipatory hopes" that served as a basis for "a global culture of black modernity"(28–29).

By grounding his study of Ghana in this historical context, Gaines is able to trace the power and limitation of diasporic alliances and pan-African politics. He also demonstrates the ways in which Western imperialism, anticolonial resistance, and a bourgeoning U.S. civil rights movement helped frame the African continent, and Ghana in particular, as a central Cold War battleground. The impact of these contested forces and their influence on African Americans' efforts to redefine "the content and parameters" of black consciousness, African American citizenship, and U.S. foreign policy provide the core of Gaines's story. Including Wright's rejection of both African hybridity and Western imperialism, as well as the "Afros" black radical visions reshaped by exile and revolution, Gaines' study unveils the myriad ways African Americans connected the struggle for black liberation in the United States to the nation-building projects in Africa. However, he also reveals the role of heightened U.S. intervention and the pressures of nation building in intensifying the ideological, personal, and national division that existed in the pan-African community.

Despite its strengths, Gaines's study pays only sparing attention to black women's experiences. Although he includes a chapter on Murray as one of the most vocal supporters of American liberalism, the study provides little detailed discussion of African American women's diasporic politics. From an isolated Murray to a more engaged pan-African activist, Maida Springer Kemp, as well as the diverse group of women radicals who helped define the "Afros" expatriate community, Gaines produces black women activists as victims silenced by "gender tensions," "African customs," and the "community of men" who represented pan-Africanism (128, 265, 16). This emphasis on "male dominance" obscures the fact that many African American women, such as the labor radical Vicki Garvin, arrived on the continent with an already honed commitment to women's equality and found ways to negotiate the very real limits produced by sexist imaginings and practices. In so doing, the study misses an opportunity to examine the influence of gender politics on African American women's vision of pan-African solidarity and black radicalism.

Although investigating an earlier period of transatlantic travel, Tyler-McGraw's *An African Republic* also explores African Americans' participation in nation building on the African continent. This monograph examines the community of black and white Virginians who worked alongside the American Colonization Society (ACS) in settling Liberia during the 1800s. Founded in 1816 as a national organization, the ACS and its white male leadership coalesced around the belief "that domestic tranquility required resolution of the 'problem' of free African Americans" (2).

Most of *An African Republic* considers the ways in which ACS colonization efforts played out in the United States. Support for the project ebbed and flowed in response to shifting local and national politics and debates over black citizenship and emancipation. As debates over slavery developed into a divisive national issue, support for colonization increasingly could be seen either as a form of gradual emancipation or as proslavery, and the ACS faced criticism from both white southerners and northern abolitionists.

An African Republic also investigates these regional divides within "African American dialogue over the meanings of African Colonization for black identity and nationality" (26). While most free blacks remained largely distrustful of the ACS, black Virginians "who accounted for one-third of all emigrants between 1820 and 1860" (128), stood as leaders in conversations about the best path to full liberation and citizenship for African Americans. Tyler-McGraw outlines these debates as the United States moved from a new republic to a nation at war with itself. In church meetings, newspapers, and personal letters, African Americans spoke honestly and bitingly about the force of white supremacy in limiting black freedom and parsed the dangers, both personal and political, of shifting the struggle for black citizenship to an African republic.

Tyler-McGraw's consideration of the ways in which African colonization and the founding of Liberia served as a vehicle for debate among black and white Virginians about slavery, the boundaries of an American republic, and the path toward black equality and citizenship reflect some of the sharpest points in the book. Drawing on a rich knowledge of Virginian history, the author provides an informative analysis of local politics, national debates and key leadership that shaped Virginia's engagement with colonization. In a fuller way than the previous two studies, Tyler-McGraw incorporates women's voices into these discussions and highlights the contested conceptions of black womanhood, the black family, and sexuality on the colonization movement. Although these voices are mostly embedded in a discussion of white women reformers' support for "uplifting" the black family, Tyler-McGraw does a nice job of detailing the racialized gender and sexual politics that informed debates over colonization and traveled with Liberian emigrants across the Atlantic. From negotiating complicated relationships with the white women who supported their emigration and standing as "the very model of an industrious Victorian woman" to their travels as representatives of the African nation, black women, as Tyler-McGraw highlights, played varied roles in constructing Liberia as a viable republic (177).

In these moments, Tyler-McGraw convincingly demonstrates the ways in which Liberia operated "as a malleable symbol for Virginians" (173). Yet as she moves to recounting black Virginians' experiences on the African continent, the story loses much of its force and richness. Compressed into two chapters, this narrative explores the inner tensions and struggles of African American emigrants as Liberia moves from a fledgling experiment controlled by the white ACS leadership into an African (American) republic. Thus, unlike in Campbell's and Gaines's studies, here we learn little of the African perspective on the founding of Liberia, or of other freed black communities who also settled in the region.

Read together, Campbell's *Middle Passages*, Gaines's *American Africans in Ghana*, and Tyler-McGraw's *An African Republic* illuminate the multitude of ways in which African Americans and Africans engaged each other and sustained a range of cultural, historical, and political solidarities across the Atlantic. Although centered on African American encounters in Africa, these works remind us that diasporic routes flowed not only to and from the United States but also through North and South America, the Caribbean, and Europe. Such insights highlight several of the contributions African diasporic scholarship has made to internationalizing African American and U.S. history. These monographs also make visible some of the gaps within African diaspora studies. There remains a tendency within many studies to address gender through discussions of black masculinity and sexuality, but rarely to include a discussion of black women's experiences and transnational politics.[3] This absence of black women's voices reflects the need to incorporate gender and women's history more fully into the field.

Notes

1. Thomas Borstelmann, *The Cold War and the Color Line: American Race Relations in the Global Arena* (Cambridge, MA: Harvard University Press, 2002); Mary Dudziak, *Cold War Civil Rights: Race and the Image of American Democracy* (Princeton, NJ: Princeton University Press, 2000); and James H. Meriwether, *Proudly We Can Be Africans: Black Americans and Africa, 1935–1961* (Chapel Hill: University of North Carolina Press, 2002).

2. Brent Hayes Edwards, "The Uses of Diaspora," *Social Text*, no. 66 (2001): 45–73; Robin D. G. Kelley, "But a Local Phase of a World Problem: Black History Global Vision, 1883–1950," *Journal of American History* 86 (1999): 1045–77; and Tiffany Ruby Patterson and Robin D. G. Kelley, "Unfinished Migrations: Reflections on the African Diaspora and the Making of the Modern World," *African Studies Review* 43 (2000): 11–45.

3. Sandra Gunning, Tera W. Hunter, and Michele Mitchell, introduction to *Dialogues of Dispersal: Gender, Sexuality, and African Diasporas*, ed. Gunning, Hunter, and Mitchell (Malden, MS: Blackwell, 2004), 1–12.

"What's in a Name?" That Which We Call Brilliance by Any Other Name Would Read as Festus Claudius McKay

Laura A. Harris

Kotti Sree Ramesh and Kandula Nirupa Rani, *Claude McKay: The Literary Identity from Jamaica to Harlem and Beyond*. Jefferson, NC: McFarland, 2006.

Josh Gosciak, *The Shadowed Country: Claude McKay and the Romance of the Victorians*. New Brunswick, NJ: Rutgers University Press, 2006.

Lloyd D. McCarthy, *"In-dependence" from Bondage: Claude McKay and Michael Manley; Defying the Ideological Clash and Policy Gaps in African Diaspora Relations*. Trenton, NJ: Africa World Press, 2007.

Gary Edward Holcomb, *Claude McKay, Code Name Sasha: Queer Black Marxism and the Harlem Renaissance*. Gainesville: University Press of Florida, 2007.

Of all the poets I admire, major and minor, Byron, Shelley, Keats, Blake, Burns, Whitman, Heine, Baudelaire, Verlaine, and Rimbaud and the rest—it seemed to me when I read them—in their poetry I could feel their race, their class, their roots in the soil, growing into plants, spreading and forming the backgrounds against which they are silhouetted, I could not feel the reality of them without that. So likewise I could not realize myself writing without conviction.
—Claude McKay, *A Long Way from Home*

Radical History Review
Issue 103 (Winter 2009)   DOI 10.1215/01636545-2008-045
© 2009 by MARHO: The Radical Historians' Organization, Inc.

Canonically speaking, Festus Claudius McKay is popularly known as the New Negro Renaissance or Harlem Renaissance poet who wrote "If We Must Die" in 1919: the militant Shakespearean sonnet with no specific mention of blackness that yet sounded a clarion call to battle for twentieth-century blackness in its distinct invocation of mortal self-defense against lynching:

If we must die, let it not be like hogs
Hunted and penned in an inglorious spot.
. . . .
If we must die
O let us nobly die
. . . .
What though before us lies the open grave?
Like men we'll face the murderous, cowardly pack
Pressed to the wall, dying, but fighting back![1]

In the post–World War I context of a singularly North American yet globally enacted white supremacist attack on blackness — both formally through national and international expansion of Jim Crow legislation and informally through the increased lynching of and white labor mob attacks on blacks during the Red Summer of 1919 — "If We Must Die" sounded like a global black (trans)national anthem.

McKay described how the Red Summer influenced him in writing the poem and how the poem influenced his subsequent authorial reception as an agent of social change:

It was during those days that the sonnet, "If We Must Die" exploded out of me. And for it the Negro people unanimously hailed me as a poet. Indeed, that one grand outburst is their sole standard of appraising my poetry. It was the only poem I ever read to the members of my crew. . . . Even the fourth waiter — who was the giddiest and most irresponsible of the lot, with all his motives and gestures colored by a strangely acute form of satyriasis — even he actually cried. One, who was a believer in the Marcus Garvey Back-to-Africa Movement, suggested that I should go to Liberty Hall, the headquarters of the organization, and read the poem. As I was not uplifted with his enthusiasm for the Garvey Movement, yet did not like to say so, I told him truthfully that I had no ambition to harangue a crowd.[2]

Given the black reader's potentially class-based affiliation for formal verse or the more direct appeal of racial outrage, the poem's influential status across black communities occurred both because of and despite its traditional verse form coupled with its strident call for black self-defense "by any means necessary": "It was a combination that pleased both the high culture folks and the low-down folks as Langston Hughes might observe, an electric verse in which McKay so eloquently indicted white supremacy that his poetic voice cut across class, nationality, political affiliation, religion, and other differences of a majority of those (non) citizens of the African diaspora."[3]

Thus, in canonical terms, McKay's traditional poetic formality, his use of very strict rules, coupled with the non-Shakespearean tradition found in McKay's topic of justifiable racial agency, greatly influenced Harlem and other black diaspora poets in affirming that a black writer's racial themes were indeed suitable for poetic form. It is equally arguable that to characterize McKay as a Harlem Renaissance poet, as a formative influence within it, immediately begs the question of what, where, when, how, and who is the Harlem Renaissance, since McKay evidences what many might consider an antithetical aesthetics to that canonically formed period, an aesthetics not of black middle-class racial uplift within a capitalist system, but rather an aesthetics of Jamaican peasant-inspired and international working-class demand for social change and radical transformation, of black and socialist agitation against the Western capitalist status quo. Of course, as shown throughout the continually emerging field of Harlem Renaissance studies, the Harlem Renaissance was politically radical and not—and much more; and McKay was of the Harlem Renaissance and not—and much more. The four books under review here range from reconceptualizing the cultural and intellectual import of the African diaspora (Harlem being but one stop) via McKay to radically queering McKay and his political, historical, and aesthetic contexts.

McKay's formal militancy inaugurating the Harlem Renaissance is often contrasted with his earlier renown as a young peasant poet laureate through his excellent rendering in 1912 of island folklore and Jamaican dialect verse in two books: the first, *Songs of Jamaica*, was primarily a celebration of a rural Jamaican peasant life free of social bigotry, whereas the second, *Constab Ballads*, treated the intraracial class and color conflicts between darker- and lighter-skinned blacks within a white social order in urban Kingston. Then again, a few decades later, Winston Churchill, rumored to have been uninformed concerning the *black* Jamaican origins of its author, recited "If We Must Die" in a speech against the Nazis as a means to rally British troops fighting in World War II, generating quite a different national enthusiasm for it than that found in 1922 Moscow, where McKay recited his poem in honor of the Red Army. To Churchill, McKay and his poetry could represent an idealized patriot, one Churchill could ironically perceive of as *the* nation-state's heroic citizen. But beyond offering a brief moment of black schadenfreude at this British faux pas, what Churchill's alleged historical (mis)read further indicates is the many McKays that abound globally, concurrently, regeneratively—not reductively as formal contradictions, but rather as the many historical contexts, political intersections, radical epistemologies, transnational geographies, and intellectual transitions that McKay facilitated in representing or became represented as through his Black diasporic art and life. This includes the Jamaican dialect poet versus the formal English verse poet and the lived McKay whose identity ranged from communist internationalist to devout Roman Catholic convert. There is the black Jamaican Marxist McKay who published and worked primarily in white leftist journals during the Harlem Renaissance (like Max Eastman's *Liberator* out of Greenwich Village) since he neither admired much of the work of the Harlem Renaissance nor got along with many of its luminaries. McKay once infamously quipped that Alain Locke's 1925 *The New Negro* anthology was like a "remarkable chocolate soufflé of art and politics," while W. E. B. Du Bois famously claimed he needed to bathe after reading McKay's 1928 novel *Home to Harlem*.[4] Then there is the McKay who became a celebrated yet controversial communist icon in Russia or poverty-stricken sojourner in North Africa; or the McKay who took male lovers and traveled so relentlessly (in part as a result of criminal laws against homosexuality) across nations that he rarely lived in Harlem during its heyday. Thus, being a long way from home came to be the appropriately defining metaphor of his memoir and politics of writing.[5] That none of these lived McKays have been widely disseminated, discussed, or debated is indeed the connecting tissue in the critical analyses of the books reviewed here. All four argue for McKay's lyrical, diasporic, transnational, queer, and Marxist import, and his obvious centrality to global twentieth-century literary and political movements, both regardless of race, politics, and sexuality and specifically because of race, politics, and sexuality—and much more.

Two of the books, Gary Edward Holcomb's *Claude McKay, Code Name Sasha* and Kotti Sree Ramesh and Kandula Nirupa Rani's *Claude McKay: The Literary Identity from Jamaica to Harlem and Beyond*, are more apparently a direct result of the intellectual barbarians who crashed the gates of the ivory tower in the last quarter of the twentieth century to proclaim the much-needed analytical centrality of race, gender, class (Marxism), diaspora, and sexuality studies in the master narrative of academic knowledges. While Lloyd D. McCarthy's *"In-dependence" from Bondage: Claude McKay and Michael Manley; Defying the Ideological Clash and Policy Gaps in African Diaspora Relations* and Josh Gosciak's *The Shadowed Country: Claude McKay and the Romance of the Victorians* may seem less directly influenced by contemporary theoretical studies, these two texts do provide more McKay multiplicities and sites of complexity in correlation with African diaspora and postmodern criticism, enriching our sense of McKay's significance politically and aesthetically. Both argue for distinctly different yet highly original, complex McKays: in McCarthy's study a McKay whose political import is better understood in comparison with a socialist prime minister of Jamaica (Michael N. Manley) whose politics and ideological perspective shared the same legacies as McKay's art and writing critizing northern elitism and forwarding a proletarian advocacy for the African diaspora and the global south; and in Gosciak's assiduous analysis another

McKay who as a hybrid, diasporic Victorian writer maintained his commitment to English lyricism throughout his multiple and conflicting political and literary personas, thus innovating lyric poetry's formal potential and content.

Somewhat similar to McCarthy and distinct from Gosciak, Ramesh and Rani are reconceptualizing the parameters of modernity and of the African diaspora. They foreground the personal and political complexities and ambivalences of McKay's biography in relationship to his literary productions while resisting a facile reliance on either. Their study strongly positions McKay within relevant discourses on the significances of blackness as a global discourse and offers a theoretical inquiry into the ambiguities invoked whenever McKay is classified as a writer and social subject. Their analyses do seek to reclaim McKay in great part due to the import of his straddling two major black diaspora literary movements, the Harlem Renaissance and Negritude, even when the authors understand that both those movements are far more layered and diverse than their constrained historical space and canonical times would allow. In establishing McKay as a "paradigmatic Black West Indian colonial writer in exile" (2), these scholars offer an important theoretical practice in their sustained interrogation, even when they use Western critical theory alongside McKay's own radically lived and literary analyses of the same. Rameesh and Rani write: "Western critical methods and literary tradition as measures of evaluation in the context of West Indian literature is likely to be a major obstacle in the critic's endeavor to interpret. . . . [Their methods] are likely to fall short of their analytical promises, if adapted, uninterrogated" (27). In their theoretical negotiation of these critical divides Rameesh and Rani offer a rich, inviting, and politically assertive reading of McKay's cultural and political contributions as an exile writer.

Holcomb's theoretical interventions are original and quite comprehensive (if somewhat jargoned) analyses of what he names as McKay's "queer black marxism." Holcomb forwards his argument through a historical contextualizing and the close readings of three of McKay's most important works, *Home to Harlem*, *Banjo*, and the unpublished "Romance in Marseille," as well as of McKay's memoir, *A Long Way from Home*. And perhaps most intriguingly, Holcomb also includes a critical discussion of an extensive FBI file on McKay, from which he culls McKay's alter ego name of "Sasha." Holcomb's interventions stand specifically at the intersections and cross-pollinations of political, racial, and sexual dissidences, and he describes his project as distinct from other recuperations: "The radical recovery work on McKay, whether oriented in black transnational diaspora or leftism internationalist studies, has not shown sufficient interest in the question of how his bisexuality bisected his Marxist engagement. . . . inquiries into his divergent sexuality have tended to overlook the evidence of his proletarian radicalism, preferring to isolate sexually indicative passages of his writing in order to verify his gay identity" (5). Instead Holcomb pursues a line of inquiry that accounts for McKay's "diaspora cruising" (5) politically, racially, and sexually; and that seeks to "open the black diaspora author's con-fidential interior space" to suggest other ways of reading "problematic black Atlantic texts, while recognizing that all diaspora texts may challenge received critical and ideological apparatuses" (20). While Holcomb's theoretical sophistication and wide-ranging material and analyses place his book at the forefront of recent McKay stud-ies, his attempt to reveal McKay's "interiority" presents problems throughout his analyses. This impulse disturbs the close readings and deft political contextualizing with confusion as to what and whose interiority the critic imagines he can, will, or does reveal. This holds even truer when referencing blackness and queerness, two theoretical sites that have arguably been central to dismantling the problematic contours of any racial or sexual "interiority" through which originating truths and subjective authenticities can be revealed or classified.

These four recent books have two apparent commonalities. First, all four are a productive result of latter twentieth-century developments in academic disciplines, such as the rise of intellectual fields of expertise intersecting with social liberation movements and theoretical changes such as challenges to universal canonical cat-egories. They thus dismantle status quo cultural valorizing in a range of critical worldviews, but primarily in the terrain of social and aesthetic histories and of black diasporic queer analyses situated within the context of an intellectual postmodern global Marxist geopolitics. The second commonality is that all four books succeed at resurrecting McKay out of the ashes of a reductive past, which pigeonholed him as a New Negro writer during the Harlem Renaissance. All four authors seek to account for McKay's hybridity that we can now better represent via the prismatic lens of postcanonical theoretical interrogations and rents in the fabric of linear, enclosed narratives of authors and literatures. Yet all four also fail to observe, reflect, and theorize on how McKay's Lazarus-like twenty-first-century resurrection impacts the histories, politics, and contexts out of and within which our contemporary theoreti-cal perspectives arise and circulate.

If all four books theoretically work from the premise that disciplinary and theoretical insights of the past few decades have allowed us to see the multiple historical relevances and artistic brilliances of McKay, then the question becomes not solely what new literary and cultural analyses or changing historical perspec-tives can reveal about the flattened script of a past McKay but also what the many competing textures of a currently theoretically desirable McKay reveal or transform about such new theories. If contemporary criticism releases previously unrealized McKays, then how do these McKays not only influence but now realize these theo-ries? It is perhaps an overly demanding question, one that asks too much of any one book or argument caught in its own historical swirl, but it is a particularly relevant philosophical query, as McKay's influence is found in good part in his capacity to self-criticize, reflect, and transform throughout his life and writing span: the politics of his aesthetics were as much about critiquing and changing the world at large as his social and artistic convictions resonated with a humble attempt to live in and learn from that world. Thus might theory be poised to unresolve and recomplicate how and why McKay's talent for contradictions and change, those radical unfixed elements of his activist life and art, are now desirable subject/object and confirmation of present-tense intellectual radicalism(s). In short, theorists might practice asking, why does McKay now neatly tuck into a posttheoretical production, and thus not only how is McKay an early-twentieth-century progenitor of such theories but what are the complexities of this historical dialogue? Or at the very least, perhaps the academician's theoretical tucking in needs to be far less neat, if not far more messy.

If only Claude McKay had known that while living in poverty and poor health in locales as disparate as Morocco and Chicago, in personas as different as a black queer transnational and a Roman Catholic apostle, from where and which he sometimes wrote woeful letters to friends detailing his sense of literary and social failures (while requesting any financial support they might provide), by the first decade of the twenty-first century there would be four books recommending his life and work as a combination of biographical, literary, and cultural analyses at the theoretical interstices and material boundaries of black (trans)nationalisms, social histories, aesthetic theories, global politics, and sexual dissidences. And if he had had premonition of this, that he and his writing would come to provide these contemporary theoretical perspectives with a subject, form, and content ranging from black Marxist queer to African diasporic agitator to global statesman to Victorian poet of hybrid individualism, might he have been comforted or confused? It is hard to know how McKay might have responded to such news, but what may have consoled McKay in a desolate author's hour is that all four books offer intense intellectual pleasures, insightful knowledges, challenging theories, and variously emphasized lived McKays. All four books are recommended for readers and scholars of McKay, as long as they also read *A Long Way from Home* and a good portion of the rest of McKay's oeuvre to appreciate the McKay each critical analysis offers. McKay himself most likely would demand this of us as a way to navigate our own intellectual relationship to and desired personification of Festus Claudius McKay, since often it is the author's own words that offer the best analysis of his post–twentieth century relevance and brilliance.

Notes

1. Claude McKay, "If We Must Die," in *Norton Anthology of African American Literature*, 2nd ed., ed. Henry Louis Gates Jr. and Nellie Y. McKay (New York: Norton, 2004), 984. In William J. Maxwell, ed., *Complete Poems: Claude McKay* (Urbana: University of Illinois Press, 2004), a slightly different version of the poem is reprinted, and Maxwell locates "if we must die" as a line from Shakespeare's play *Measure for Measure* (1604), 332–33.

2. Claude McKay, *A Long Way from Home* (1937; New Brunswick, NJ: Rutgers University Press, 2007), 30.

3. David Levering Lewis, *When Harlem Was in Vogue* (New York: Penguin, 1997); Steve Watson, *The Harlem Renaissance: Hub of African-American Culture, 1920–1930* (New York: Pantheon, 1996).

4. McKay, *Long Way from Home*, 247; Lewis, *When Harlem Was in Vogue*, 225.

5. Gene Andrew Jarrett, introduction to McKay, *Long Way from Home*, 33.

Anne-Marie Angelo is a PhD candidate in history at Duke University. Her dissertation examines the transnational formations of the British Black Panther Movement, the Mizrahi Panthers of Israel, and the U.S. Black Panther Party. Her writing has appeared in *Transforming Anthropology* and she currently holds a Foreign Language and Area Studies Fellowship in Arabic.

Erica Ball is an assistant professor in the American studies department at California State University, Fullerton, and a member of the *Radical History Review* collective. She is currently working on a book manuscript tentatively titled "Mothers and Fathers of the Race: The Cultural Origins of the Black Middle Class, 1820–1860."

Anthony Bogues is the Harmon Family Professor and a professor of Africana studies at Brown University, where he is also the current chair of the Africana studies department. He is an honorary professor at the Center for African Studies, University of Cape Town, an associate director of the Center for Caribbean Thought, University of the West Indies, an associate editor of the journal *Small Axe*, and a member of the editorial collective of the journal *Boundary 2*.

Lisa Brock is the chairperson of the Department of Liberal Education at Columbia College in Chicago. Her articles on Africa and the African diaspora have appeared in such journals as *Cuban Studies*, *Contributions in Black Studies*, *Souls*, *Peace Review*, and *Temas: Cultura, ideologa, sociedad*. She coedited *Between Race and Empire: African-Americans and Cubans before the Cuban Revolution* (1998) with Digna Castañeda.

Sara Busdiecker holds a PhD in anthropology from the University of Michigan. She is currently an assistant professor in the department of anthropology and in the program of Africana studies at Texas A&M University.

Prudence D. Cumberbatch is an assistant professor in the Department of Africana Studies at Brooklyn College, where she teaches courses in African American and black diasporic history. She is currently completing a book-length study of black women's activism in Baltimore, Maryland.

Jacqueline Francis teaches art history at the California College of the Arts. She has published in *American Art*, *Callaloo*, *Mississippi Quarterly*, *Nka*, and *Third Text*. Her book *Race-ing Modernism: Malvin Gray Johnson, Yasuo Kuniyoshi, Max Weber and "Racial Art" in Interwar America*, is forthcoming from the University of Washington Press.

Anita González is an associate professor at the State University of New York, New Paltz, and the author of *Jarocho's Soul: Cultural Identity and Afro-Mexican Dance* (2004) and the forthcoming *Afro-Mexico: Dancing between Myth and Reality*. She has published essays in *Modern Drama*, the *Journal of Dramatic Theory and Criticism*, the *Community and Performance Reader* (2007), and in the *Dance Research Journal*.

Dayo F. Gore is an assistant professor in the women's studies program at the University of Massachusetts, Amherst. Her areas of interest include African American history and the African diaspora, twentieth-century U.S. political and cultural activism, and women and gender in U.S. history. She is currently completing a manuscript titled "The Work of Radicals: Black Women's Political Thought and Activism in the 1950s." She is also the coeditor (with Jeanne Theoharis and Komozi Woodard) of the forthcoming anthology *"Want to Start a Revolution?" Women and the Black Freedom Struggle, 1940–1980*.

Laura A. Harris is an associate professor of English and black studies at Pitzer College. She publishes in the areas of literary criticism, feminist and queer studies, black studies, African diaspora studies, and fiction and poetry. Her publications have appeared in venues such as the *Journal of Lesbian Studies* and the *African American Review*. Her last book, *Notes from a Welfare Queen in the Ivory Tower: Poetry, Fiction, Letters, and Essays* (2002), was an American Library Association 2002 Stonewall Book Award nominee.

Christopher J. Lee is an assistant professor of African history at the University of North Carolina at Chapel Hill. His articles have appeared in *Radical History Review* as well as the *Journal of African History*, *Politique Africaine*, *Transition*, and the *South African Historical Journal*.

Conor McGrady studied at the University of Northumbria, Newcastle, UK, before receiving his MFA in 1998 from the School of the Art Institute of Chicago. Most recently, his work has been exhibited in the one-person exhibitions New Arcadia at M.Y. Art Prospects in New York; Purity at Thomas Robertello Gallery in Chicago; and Social Security at the Customs House, South Shields, UK. In 2002 he was selected to participate in the Whitney Biennial at the Whitney Museum of American Art in New York. He is a member of the Culture and Conflict Group and currently lives and works in New York.

Kevin Mumford teaches in the Department of History and in the African American Studies Program at the University of Iowa. He is the author of *Interzones: Black/White Sex Districts in Chicago and New York in the Early Twentieth Century* (1997) and of *Newark: A History of Race, Rights, and Riots in America* (2007), and he is currently at work on a book about black gay history from the 1960s to the 1980s.

Melina Pappademos is an assistant professor of history and African American studies at the University of Connecticut, Storrs. She is a member of the *Radical History Review* collective and is completing a book manuscript on racial consciousness and political mobilization among African-descended Cubans in the republican period, which is tentatively titled "Negotiating Race: Black Cuban Activism and the Republican State, 1899 to 1940."

Rochelle Rowe is a doctoral candidate and an Arts and Humanities Research Council doctoral award holder in the Department of History, University of Essex. Her doctoral research is concerned with the changing representations of Caribbean femininity in the mid-twentieth century. She has conducted field research in the Caribbean.

Theresa Runstedtler is an assistant professor in American studies at the State University of New York at Buffalo, specializing in the intersections of race, gender, and resistance in popular culture. She is currently revising a book project titled "Journeyman: Race, Boxing, and the Transnational World of Jack Johnson."

Michelle Stephens is an associate professor of English at Colgate University and the author of *Black Empire: The Masculine Global Imaginary of Caribbean Intellectuals in the United States, 1914 to 1962* (2005). She is a member of the *Radical History Review* editorial collective and is currently working on a manuscript titled "Black Acts: Race, Masculinity, and Performance in the New World," which examines the relationships among masculinity, race, and sexuality in intercultural performance.

Tyler Stovall is a professor of French history at the University of California, Berkeley. He has written numerous books on the subject, including *Paris Noir: African Americans in the City of Light* (1996). He has also coedited (with Sue Peabody) *The Color of Liberty: Histories of Race in France* (2003).

Deborah A. Thomas is an associate professor in the department of anthropology at the University of Pennsylvania. She is the author of *Modern Blackness: Nationalism, Globalization, and the Politics of Culture in Jamaica* (2004) and the coeditor of the volume *Globalization and Race: Transformations in the Cultural Production of Blackness* (2006). She is also the coeditor of the journal *Transforming Anthropology*.

Cristóbal Valencia Ramírez is a Chicano PhD candidate in sociocultural anthropology at the University of Illinois. His primary interests include the roles race-based and poor-class grassroots political participation play in processes of state formation and in establishing democracy in Latin America and the United States. His dissertation research focuses on Chávez supporters living in Caracas barrios.

Leon Wainwright is a lecturer in the history of art and design at Manchester Metropolitan University, a visiting scholar at University of California, Berkeley, and a member of the editorial board of the journal *Third Text*. His forthcoming monograph addresses modern and contemporary art and artists in Britain and the Caribbean.

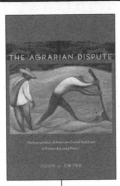

Colonial Latin American Historical Review (*CLAHR*)

Featuring the *COLONIAL ERA*
IN LUSO-HISPANO AMERICA

MANUSCRIPT SUBMISSIONS INVITED
Original essays based on archival sources, max. 25-30 pp. + footnotes
3 copies + disk, Microsoft Word preferred
or PC compatible, English or Spanish

- -

Subscription Form:

Name: _____

Address: _____

Telephone: _____

E-mail: _____

❏ Individual $35   ❏ Institution $40   ❏ Student $30   ❏ Single Issue $9
(Add $5.00 for areas outside of the United States, Mexico, and Canada)

❏ Check or money order payable to: *Colonial Latin American Historical Review*
❏ VISA ❏ MasterCard Acct.# _____ Exp. Date _____

Cardholder's Signature _____

Please send this form with the appropriate payment to Dr. Joseph P. Sánchez, Editor:

Mailing Address:
Spanish Colonial Research Center, NPS
MSC05 3020
1 University of New Mexico
Albuquerque NM 87131-0001 USA

Location/Ship To:
Spanish Colonial Research Center, NPS
Zimmerman Library
1 University of New Mexico
Albuquerque NM 87131-0001 USA

Telephone (505)277-1370 / Fax (505)277-4603
E-mail clahr@unm.edu / Home Page http://www.unm.edu/~clahr